Scousers

THE PEOPLE. THE PRIDE. THE PASSION.

"Scousers" is published by :

Trinity Mirror NW²

Trinity Mirror North West & North Wales
PO Box 48
Old Hall Street,
Liverpool L69 3EB

Trinity Mirror Sport Media Executive Editor:
Ken Rogers
Design / production:
Daisy Dutton, Jonathan Low, Emma Smart

Contributors:
Dawn Collinson, Peter Grant, Tony Hall, Alan Jewell, Catherine Jones, Tony Martin,
Chris McLoughlin, Barrie Mills, David Prentice, Ken Pye, Cheryl Rawlinson, Joe Riley,
Stephen Shakeshaft, Paddy Shennan, Natasha Young
and
Eddie Barford and the Daily Post & Echo photographic team
Daily Post & Echo Library Services
The Spirit of Liverpool team

Thanks to:
The wonderful city of Liverpool and its people

© Pictures and text, unless otherwise stated:
Trinity Mirror / Liverpool Daily Post & Echo.

Sir Leslie Patrick Abercrombie (1879-1957), town planner; Derek Acorah (1950-), psychic; Alan A'Court (1934-), footballer; Thomas Agnew, philanthropist; James Aiken, merchant and shipowner; Edward Alanson (1747-1823), surgeon; John Aldridge (1958-), footballer; Jean Alexander (1926-), actress; Lord Alton (1951-), politician; Chris Amoo (1952-), musician; Eddie Amoo (1950-), musician; Michael Angelis (1952-), actor; Avril Angers (1918-2005), comedienne and actress; Richard Ansdell (1815-85), artist; William Armstrong (1882-1957), theatre director; Alan Ashcroft, rugby union; Arthur Askey (1900-82), comedian; Robin Askwith (1950-), actor; Neil Aspinall (1942-), music executive; Robert Atherton (1861-1930), poet; Charles Atkinson sr (died 1997), boxing coach; Charles Atkinson jr (1941-), boxing coach; George Audsley (1838-1925), architect; Ethel Austin (1900-89), retailer; Bob Azurdia (1936-96), radio presenter; Tommy Bache, boxer; John Bailey, footballer; Dame Beryl Bainbridge (1932-); Benjamin Howard Baker (1892-1987), footballer and athlete; Tom Baker (1934-), actor; Herbert Stewart Bale (1859-1929), printer; Alexander Balfour (1824-86), shipping merchant; Jackie Balmer, footballer; Walter Balmer (1877-1937), footballer; Mary 'Ma' Bamber (1874-1938), politician and women's activist; Peter Banasko (1916-93), boxer; Paul Barber (1952-), actor; Clive Barker, writer; Charles Glover Barkla (1877-1944), physicist; Francis James Barraud (1856-1924), artist; Carl Bartels (1866-1955), sculptor; James Barton (1968-), promoter; Hogan 'Kid' Bassey (1932-98), boxer; Sir Thomas Beecham (1879-1961), conductor; Tom Bell (1933-2006), actor; Mitch Benn (1970-), comedian; Thomas Bentley (1730-80), retailer; Pete Best (1941-), musician; Brian Bevan (1924-91), rugby union player; John Bibby (1775-1840), ship owner; Sarah Biffin (1784-1850), painter; Augustine Birrell (1850-1933), author and politician; William Blair-Bell (1871-1936), physician; Alan Bleasdale (1946-), writer; Cilla Black (1943-), singer; Nigel Blackwell (1965-), musician; Chris Boardman (1968-), cyclist; Stan Boardman (1940-), comedian; Jean Boht (1936-), actress; Charles Booth (1840-1916), philanthropist; Cherie Booth QC (1954-), lawyer; Henry Booth (1788-1869), railway inventor; Tony Booth (1931-), actor; Frank Cottrell Boyce (1961-), writer; Russell Boulter (1963-), actor; Eddie Braben (1923-), writer; Bessie Braddock (1899-1970), politician; John 'Jack' Braddock (1893-1963), politician; Ike Bradley (1883-1951), boxer; Les Braid (1937-2005), musician; Peter Briggs (1965-), screenwriter; Ronald Brittain (1899-1981), soldier; John Brodie (1858-1934), city engineer; Tom Bromilow (1894-1959), footballer; Ian Broudie (1958-), musician; Faith Brown (1944-), comedienne; Dora Bryan OBE (1924-), actress; David Burke (1934-), actor; David Burke (1975-), boxer; Pete Burns (1959-), musician; Kenneth Burrell (1893-1956), photographer; Malandra Burrows (1965-), actress and singer; Molly Bushell (1746-1818), sweet-maker; Billy Butler, broadcaster; Thomas Cairns, swimmer; Ramsey Campbell (1946-), author; Ian Callaghan (1942-), footballer; Mike Carey (1959-), writer; Jamie Carragher, footballer; Jimmy Case, footballer; Sir Philip Carter, football chairman; Kim Cattrall (1956-), actress; Sir James Chadwick (1891-1974), scientist; Guy Chambers (1963-), musician and songwriter; Harry Chambers (1896-1949), footballer; Keith V Chapman (1957-), writer; Craig Charles (1964-), actor and comedian; Noel Chavasse (1884-1917), soldier; Sam Chedgzoy (1890-1967), footballer; Keith Chegwin (1957-), presenter; Melanie Chisholm (1974-), singer; Jim Clarke (1886-1946), swimmer; Margi Clarke (1954-), actress; Sarah Clayton (1712–1779), property developer; Anne Clough (1820-92), suffragette and educationalist; Andrew Collinge, hairdresser; Lewis Collins (1946-), actor; John Conteh (1951-), boxer; Johnny Cooke (1934-), boxer; Kenneth Cope (1934-), actor; Elvis Costello (1954-), musician; Alex Cox (1954-), director and actor; Peter Coyle (1962-), musician; Daniel Craig (1968-), actor; Tony Crane, musician; Walter Crane (1845-1915), artist; Kenneth Cranston (1917-2007), cricketer; Peter Craven (1934-63), speedway rider; Charles Crichton (1910-99), film director; Jessie Reid Crosbie (1876-1962), educationalist; Will Cuff (1869-1949), football administrator; Jon Culshaw (1968-), impressionist; Peter Culshaw (1973-), boxer; Steve Cummings (1981-), cyclist; Joe Curran (1915-84), boxer; Edwina Currie (1946-), politician; Daisy Curwen, swimmer; Doug Dailey, cyclist; Gary Daly (1962-), singer; Pauline Daniels (1955-), actress and comedienne; William Daniels (1813-80), painter; Terry Darracott, footballer; George Davies (1941-), fashion retailer; Robbie Davies (1950-), boxer; Terence Davies (1945-), film director; Matt Dawson (1972-), rugby union footballer; John Deakin (1912-72), photographer; William Ralph 'Dixie' Dean (1907-80), footballer; Carol Decker (1957-), singer; Les Dennis (1954-), actor and comedian; Matthew Dobson (1732-84), physician; Lottie Dod (1871-1960), tennis champion, golfer and archer; Ken Dodd (1927-), comedian; Professor Ray Donnelly, health campaigner; Arthur Dooley (1929-94), sculptor; Brian Dooley (1971-), writer; Aynsley Dunbar (1946-), drummer; Dr William Duncan (1805-63), health campaigner; Jimmy Dunne (1941-), boxer; Frankie Durr (1926-present), jockey; Pat Dwyer (1946-), boxer; Ernest Edwards, sports journalist; Annette Ekblom (1959-), actress; Alf Ellaby born 1902), rugby league footballer; Billy Ellaway, boxer; Ralph Ellis (1942-), musician; Jennifer Ellison (1983-), actress; Louis Emerick (1953-), actor; Ray Ennis (1942-), musician; Brian Epstein (1934-67), Beatles manager; Greg Evans (1952-), boxer; Tom Evans (1947-83), musician; Kenny Everett (1944-95), comedian; Alicya Eyo (1975-), actress; Joe Fagan (1921-2001), football manager; Willie Fagan (1917-1992), footballer; David Fairclough (1957-), footballer; Peter Fallon, boxer; Mark Farrell, tennis player; Peter Farrell (1922-2001), footballer; Frank Field (1942-), politician; Sir Samuel Luke Fildes (1843-1927), artist; Tim Firth (1964-), writer; Neil Fitzmaurice (1970-), actor and writer; Paul Fletcher (1958-), boxer; Katie Flynn (1936-), writer; Chris 'Ginger' Foran (1913-55), boxer; Gus Foran (1919-91), boxer; Helen Forrester (1919-), writer; Robbie Fowler (1975-) footballer; Frederic Franklin (1914-), ballet dancer; Eric Fraser (1932-2000), rugby league footballer; Ian Fraser VC (1920-), war hero; Jenny Frost (1978-), singer; Joey Frost (1960), boxer; June Furlong, artists model; Billy Fury (1940-83), musician; Tom Georgeson (1941-), actor; Steven Gerrard, footballer; Sugar Gibiliru (1966-), boxer; George Gilbody (1955-), boxer; Ray Gilbody (1960-), boxer; William Gladstone (1809-1898), politician; Ronny Goodlass, footballer; Léon Goossens CBE (1897-1988), musician; Sidonie Goossens (1899-2004), musician; Baron Goldsmith of Allerton (1950-), lawyer; John Gorman (1936-), musician; James Graham, RL player; John Gregson (1919-75), actor; Krishnan Guru-Murthy (1970-), journalist; Deryck Guyler (1914-99), actor; John Hamilton (1922-2006), politician; Natasha Hamilton (1982-), singer; Frank Hampson (1918-85), comic illustrator; Tommy Handley (1892-1949), comedian; Will Hanrahan, journalist; Alf Hanson (1912-93), footballer; Edward Chambré Hardman (1898-1988), photographer; Eric Hardy (1912-2002), naturalist; John Hargreaves (1944-), businessman; Alan Harper (1960-), footballer; Brian Harris (1935-), footballer; Jimmy Harris (1933-), footballer; George Harrison (1943-2001), musician and songwriter; James Harrison (1821-91), ship owner; Rex Harrison (1908-90), actor; Ian Hart (1964-), actor; Jesse Hartley (1780-1860), dock engineer; Colin Harvey (1944-), footballer; Jonathan Harvey (1968-), playwright; Billy Hatton (1941-), musician; Derek Hatton (1948-), politician; Austin Healey (1973-), rugby union footballer; Jack Heaton (born 1910), rugby union footballer; Paul Heaton (1962-), singer; Dame Rose Heilbron (1914-2005), lawyer; Felicia Hemans (1793-1835), poet; Professor Janet Hemingway (1957-), scientist; Adrian Henri (1932-2000), poet and artist; Tony Hibbett, footballer; Dave Hickson (1929-), footballer; Harold Hilton (1869-1942), golfer; Jim Hitchmough (died 1997), writer; Paul Hodkinson (1965-), boxer; Michael Holliday (1924-63), singer; Andy Holligan (1967-), boxer; Alfred Holt (1829-1911), ship owner; Johnny Holt (born 1865), footballer; Peter Hooton (1962-), musician; Frank Hope, boxer; Clive Hornby (1944-), actor; Frank Hornby (1863-1936), inventor; Jeremiah Horrocks (1619-41), astronomer; Stephen Hough (1961-), pianist; John Houlding, football chairman, LFC's founder father; Alf Howard, boxer; Roly Howard (1935-), football manager; Geoffrey Hughes (1944-), actor; Shirley Hughes (1927-), illustrator and author; TJ Hughes (1890-1933), retailer; Paul Humphreys (1960-), musician; Rita Hunter (1933-2001), opera singer; John Hyland (1962-), boxer and promoter; Andrew "Sandy" Irvine (1902-24), mountaineer; Jason Isaacs (1963-), actor; J Bruce Ismay (1862-1937), ship owner; Glenda Jackson (1936-), actress and politician; Brian Jacques (1939-), writer; Hilda James (born 1904) swimmer; Andrew Jameson (1965-), swimmer; Helen Jameson swimmer; George Jardine (1920-2002), artist; Albert Johnson, rugby league footballer; David Johnson, footballer; Holly Johnson (1960-), singer and artist; Sir Thomas Johnson (1664-1729), merchant; Sue Johnston (1943-), actress; Joan Jonker (1922-2006), writer and campaigner; Agnes Jones (1832-68), nursing pioneer; Hughie Jones, musician; Jack Jones (1913-), trade unionist; TE Jones (1930-), footballer; Tony Jordan, writer; Tony Jordan (1934-), badminton player; Ben Kay (1975-), rugby union footballer; Gillian Kearney (1972-), actress; Sir Lancelot Keay (1883-1974), city planner; Jeremy Kelly (1962-), musician; Jude Kelly (1954-), artistic director; Margaret Kelly (1912-2004), dancer; Margaret Kelly, swimmer; John Kemble (1757-1823), actor; Bill Kenwright (1945-), theatre impresario; Peter Kilfoyle (1946-), politician; Johnny King (1938-), football manager; Billy J Kramer (1943-), singer; Brian Labone (1940-2006), footballer; Charlie Landsborough (1942-), musician; Andrew Lancel (1970-), actor; Carla Lane (1937-), writer; Thomas Lang (1962-), singer; Lynda La Plante (1946-), actress and writer; James (Big Jim) Larkin (1876-1947), trade unionist; William Lassell (1799-1880), astronomer; Sam Leach, promoter; Sir Terry Leahy (1956-), retailer; Henry Boswell Lee, retailer; Maureen Lee (1942-), writer; Sammy Lee, footballer; Cynthia Lennon (1939-), artist and author; John Lennon (1940-80), musician; Julian Lennon (1963-), musician; Frederick Richards Leyland (1832-92), ship owner and art patron; Phil Liggett (1943-), journalist; Malcolm Lipkin (1932-), composer; Lord Liverpool (1770-1828), politician; David Lloyd, cyclist; Jim Lloyd (1939-), boxer; Jackie Lomax (1944-), musician; Janice Long (1955-), DJ; Leon Lopez (1979-), actor and singer; Eddie Lundon (1962-), musician; John Lynch, boxer; Mike Lyons, footballer; John McArdle (1949-), actor; Les McAteer (1945-), boxer; Pat McAteer (1932-), boxer; Dave McCabe (1981-), musician; John McCabe (1939-), composer; Peter McCann (1947-), boxer; Don 'Ginger' McCain (1930-), racehorse trainer; Mike McCartney (1944-), photographer; Sir Paul McCartney (1942-), musician; Andy McCluskey (1959-), musician and producer; Ian McCulloch (1959-), musician; Terry McDermott, footballer; John McDonnell (1951-), politician; Ray McFall (1927-), club owner; Joe McGann (1958-), actor; Mark McGann (1961-), actor; Paul McGann, (1959-), actor; Stephen McGann (1963-), actor;

WHAT IS A SCOUSER?

Scouse *skows*, (*colloq*) *n* a native or inhabitant of Liverpool (also **scous'er**); the northern English dialect spoken in and around Liverpool; (without *cap*) a stew or hash, often made with meat scraps. [Short for *lobscouse*, a vegetable stew, a sea dish.]

from Chambers Concise Dictionary

"Scousers are human magnets. They draw people to them, whether it's the accent or the humour. Every time I come home I start speaking 100 per cent Scouse. You can take a Scouser out of Liverpool but you'll never take the Scouse character out of anyone born here."

FAITH BROWN
COMEDIAN

"My view of Scousers is simple. If you confront them, they will confront you back. No danger about that. But if you hold out the hand of friendship, you will get friendship back ten times over.

I'm prouder than ever to call myself a Scouser."

TOMMY SMITH
FOOTBALLER

"You've heard the phrase House Proud, well, I am Scouse Proud it sums up my feelings towards our unique and envied culture. Even the dogs have a Scouse swagger. You can tell a Scouse dog a mile off – it just knows where it's going."

MICKEY FINN
COMEDIAN

"There's nothing better than a Scouse sunset. When I return home to my Toxteth roots I will sit and watch the sun go down. It's like Scousers themselves – different and special."

PAUL BARBER
ACTOR – STAR OF ONLY FOOLS AND HORSES & THE FULL MONTY

"I am proud to be a Scouser and I have a little pewter Liver Bird by my bed – a symbol of home and my roots."

TRICIA PENROSE
ACTRESS

"One of the highlights of my touring schedule has been playing in Australia to an organisation of ex-pats who miss their home town enormously. It's called Scousers Down Under. Doesn't that say it all? Pesky Scousers get everywhere."

GERRY MARSDEN
MUSICIAN

"There's a phrase of mine, apart from the other famous one, that says 'Sound as a pound.' Well that's what I think about being a Scouser. Full stop. We are dead sound, like. . . "

RICKY TOMLINSON
ACTOR

"I'm a Scouser from the Blue half of Merseyside, proud of my lifetime links with Everton.

One thing I notice is the way Scousers are attracted to people like the Geordies and the Glaswegians, working class cities like our own.

I have always found Scousers to be very positive people who enjoy life. We don't do things by halves."

COLIN HARVEY
FOOTBALLER

"When I was in Brookside I played Sinbad the window cleaner, an identifiable, loveable Scouser. It was great to see people across the country take to him. He embodied all the Scouse traits – humour and a natural ability to help people."

MICHAEL STARKE
ACTOR

FOREWORD

TELL anyone beyond our famous city boundaries that you are a Scouser and there is a very good chance they will look right through your real persona and see a shell-suited character with a penchant for leaving stolen cars standing on bricks.

There is a new slant on this logic. A group of high-flying Merseyside businessmen were recently at a glitzy function at the Grosvenor Hotel in London. The presenter bounced onto the stage and said:"Any Scousers in the house?" The hands went up.

"I see you're the European Capital of Culture in 2008. Does that mean all the stolen cars in Liverpool will now be standing on books?"

Now it's actually quite a funny line and not one we are going to get uptight about, especially as we are also the undisputed Capital of Comedy.

But there is a sterotypical reaction to the word "Scouser" that has been reinforced in recent times by the confrontational Harry Enfield characters with their drooping moustaches, curly wigs and "Calm Down, Calm Down' catchphrase.

This book is not about reinforcing the image, but rather taking the definition of Scousers onto a whole new level without trying to hide the fact that we have our fair share of scallies, drug dealers and car thieves in tandem with all the big cities like London, Manchester, Birmingham and the rest.

But Liverpool is an amazing city of contrasts above and beyond the fact that we are world renowned for the Beatles and our passion for football.

The ballet is as likely to sell out in Liverpool as much as a big game at Anfield. We have more listed Georgian buildings than any city outside London. We have a supremely successful Tate Gallery. We boast a sensational world heritage waterfront, a vibrant modern music and and comedy scene and an army of citizens who have a massive pride in the city of the "Scousers" where regeneration and optimism for the future merge with the history and heritage of the past.

We define what a "Scouser" is in this book, but look beyond the dictionary definition. Can you be a "Scouser" if you live beyond the acknowledged city boundaries? This book answers the question by paying tribute to many of the world famous "adopted Scousers" who we respect and admire.

In sparking the debate, someone said that you can only be a Scouser if you have a purple wheelie bin! If you understand this in-joke, you can almost certainly lay claim to being a genuine Scouser although there are many definitions.

Scousers are part of a unique tribe in the same way that Cockneys, Brummies and Geordies are tribal in their own way and proud of it.

Enjoy this book.

If you are not from Merseyside, it will hopefully give you a new slant on our famous home.

If you are a Scouser, stand proud that you come from such a fantastic river metropolis with an identity all of its own.

THE SPIRIT OF LIVERPOOL

THE Liverpool Echo, the voice of Merseyside since 1879, asked its respected and loyal readers to vote for the people who had made a massive impact on the city.

In association with the Alliance and Leicester Commercial Bank, the Echo set out to establish a shortlist of 100 names for its "Spirit of Liverpool" project.

A judging panel, headed by Echo arts editor Joe Riley, set about choosing those individuals and institutions – both past and present – who remain inextricably identified with the fortunes of Merseyside.

These giants who made such an impression on Merseyside life are featured throughout this book.

But what makes a Scouser? Liverpool prides itself in welcoming people from all over the UK - and all over the world.

There are people who were not born in Liverpool but have done so much for Merseyside that they have become honorary Scousers. Many of these individuals feature in the Spirit of Liverpool list.

Wherever you come from, one thing's for sure. Let Liverpool into your heart and you will be welcomed as one of the city's own.

TOM O'CONNOR

LIVERPOOL and all it stands for beats in the heart of every Scouser.

I know because I meet them all over the world on my travels.

A Scouser is a modest type of person yet someone who can beat anyone at anything when they put their minds to it. You walk in a room and you can tell another Scouser.

I would urge Liverpool comedians to stop bringing down the city. They have responsibility to stop the consistent negative labelling as thieves and vagabonds.

And its not just comics. Everyone has a duty to say: "Look, I am Scouser and we are what we are and mighty proud of it."

The Irish get jokes made about them but can take it. The jokes are often silly and ironic, after all Irish people are not stupid.

Scousers are always great listeners and, as a comedian, I know that Scouse audiences will give you ten minutes to win them over whereas in other parts of the country they will give you half that time.

Scousers are a patient lot.

That said if you're not that good, you will soon be off.

I am proud of my Scouse heritage and capital of culture status. I fly the banner everywhere.

I can make jokes about my city because I'm from Bootle, which is like Romania without gymnasts.

But, seriously, Scousers have a speed of thought that is unmatched.

We have a sharpness of wit and above all else we have put up with so much that we have immense tolerance – why don't people talk about that instead of the negative?

Tolerance, patience and humour – not bad things to have on our great city's CV.

STAN BOARDMAN

SCOUSER is a great name to be called.

I know because I am one ... it says so on my birth certificate.

I was born here and I grew up amid the war time blitz.

It is not in any way sentimental to say it but I am so proud of that legacy; that no matter where I go in the world where my job has taken me I am a Scouser.

I am so happy to shout about my true colours.

I did it in holiday camps and the tough clubs across the UK and I did it on telly and in the Palladium.

It's in my roots.

Just like people from the North East are Geordies. And Lononers are Cockneys they celebrate it and we should. We do. I do.

We are capital of music and capital of creativity and certainly capital of comedy.

When a Scouser is portrayed on television it is usually in the dock in some courtroom drama or something about stealing cars. Some scriptwriters who have never set foot here haven't a clue what it means.

Well, it's like a good bowl of Scouse which is a healthy mixture of meat and vegetables - it is full of richness. It's unique.

I have grown up in the city and even when I am playing some exotic place abroad I just can't wait to get home.

Home is where the heart is.

So if I see someone on telly knocking Scousers I always feel they are envious that they may not have an identity of their own.

Being a Scouser is an asset; It's a degree from the university of hard knocks of survival.

A city that has produced so much and will go on bringing alive the magic of music and laughter, football, architecrure and culture showing that despite the poverty and bad times in its 800 years we have been brought up with an attitude from father to son, mother to daughter that says 'If things aren't working out today it will tomorrow.'

A brand new day. Yeah, we are Scousers and we are getting on with it.

No wonder we have two cathedrals in a place called Hope Street. We are the capital of hope, too.

A BRIEF HISTORY OF
Scousers

By Ken Pye

WE Scousers have been around for a very long time indeed, and the earliest evidence of human activity in the Liverpool area is prehistoric.

Evidence was found, seven miles to the north-east of the City at a site in Croxteth Park, which was once the family seat of the Earls of Sefton. Here, and dating from the Mesolithic period – about 6,000BC – around 550 flint tools were found. This shows that there was an encampment of hunter-gatherers settled here who, in small family groups, would have hunted the wild boar and deer that roamed the vast forests, which once covered the whole area. Whilst doing so, these wild and woolly Wackers would have had to keep a wary eye out for the wolves and bears that shared the territory with them!

Then, in the Neolithic age – around 5,000BC – small communities of Stone Age peoples began to settle in the areas now known as Childwall, Toxteth, Woolton and West Derby, where stone axeheads and arrowheads have been discovered. And, from that period onwards, many more primitive Scousers established themselves in the area, gradually becoming organised and tribal, and also much more sophisticated.

In fact, close to modern Calderstones Park, a large, chambered underground tomb was excavated by Victorian archaeologists in the 19th century. This was a Neolithic Chief's Tumulus that had originally been erected around 4,800BC. This means that this was therefore older even than Stonehenge – which itself is older than the Pyramids of Egypt! Stonehenge was built around 3100BC, and the oldest pyramid in Egypt is the stepped Pyramid of Zoser, which was constructed around 2600BC. The tomb was surrounded by irregular-shaped standing stones, with strange cup and ball and footprint markings engraved into them. These were the Calder Stones, which gave their name to that district, and six of the stones survive. These are now on display, in a special greenhouse, in the Harthill section of Calderstones Park.

The name Calder comes from the Anglo-Saxon word Galdar or Wizard, and so the mysterious stones also gave rise to stories about ancient Druidical rites and sacrifices taking place in the district. This is why the modern Druids Park, and Druids Cross and Druidsville Roads were given their names. However, such tales of magical ceremonies; of the imbibing of hallucinogenic herb extracts; and of naked orgies in the woods and fields around these parts of prehistoric Liverpool, are completely mythical and have no basis in fact: although I can't speak for modern times!

Then, after around 2000BC the Bronze Age came to Liverpool and, in the once independent village of Wavertree, bronze burial urns and a burial chamber from that period were discovered, again in the 19th century. Fortunately, many of these artefacts, together with others from our Liverpudlian ancestors, are currently on display in The World Museum Liverpool, in the City centre. These discoveries show that this area, on the banks of the River Mersey, has always been a place of desirable residence for a variety of communities.

During the Iron Age – around 700BC, and lasting up to the time of the Roman invasion of Britain, in AD43, the dominant local tribespeople were the Brigantes. They were of Celtic origin, and one of their fortified encampments was at the summit of Camp Hill in Woolton, thus giving this high hilltop its name.

These were a settled community who mixed farming with warfare. Not unlike modern Scousers, they were a fierce and proud people and, in the face of any enemy attacks, they were determined to defend their homes, farmsteads, and families. Just imagine these warrior Wackers; charging down Camp Hill; armed to the teeth with sword and spear; often completely naked and with their bodies smeared with blue, woad war-paint; loudly screaming as they dashed towards horrified Roman troops. Perhaps the fact that there is no evidence of Roman occupation at the top of Camp Hill shows that the Romans never came there at all. Or, perhaps the dreadful sight of such a flapping and flailing marauding mob, of hairy, nude Scousers, was sufficient deterrent to frighten off the advancing soldiers!

Nevertheless, the Roman invaders sent their troops across the length and breadth of what is now Merseyside, and there have been significant finds of Roman coins, as well as traces of a Roman road, particularly in the Liverpool districts of Grassendale and Aigburth. But, whilst they had no permanent settlements here, there were Roman camps in and around Liverpool, at places such as Woolton, Toxteth Park, Halewood and Knowsley.

Also, during the 1960s, when the area around Canning Place was being excavated to build office towers, which once occupied the site of the modern Liverpool ONE retail complex, the remains of a Roman galleon were discovered, buried deep in the ancient river mud.

This was once the original large inlet – or Pool – of the ancient village of Liverpool, and the Romans sailed their galleys and trading vessels up both the Mersey and Dee rivers.

With the later Romans came the first Christians and, by 325, England already had three Christian Bishops who were based at London, York, and Lincoln. It was this latter Bishopric that included all of what were to eventually become the counties of Lancashire, Merseyside and Cheshire. But, in the year 367, Picts, Scots, Angles, and Saxons invaded Britain in a joint attack, ravaging the countryside, overwhelming the native Britons, and setting back the development of Christianity.

The Romans had left Britain by this time, and the country was left to fend for itself, descending into what we now call The Dark Ages. Small communities of Anglo-Saxons then began to settle in areas that were to become the suburbs of modern Liverpool, and a tiny fishing community established itself on the banks of the Mersey. Although this hamlet was to eventually grow into the Liverpool of today, it was then too insignificant even to have a recorded name.

At the time of these early Saxon settlements, Britain was still largely a Pagan land, and it was to be another two centuries before the Christian religion began to gain a true foothold.

Even so, just beyond the end of Tithebarn Street in Liverpool City centre, and in the quiet cul-de-sac of Standish Street stands a well-kept piece of lawn. This is surrounded by low railings and shaded by trees. Here, as well as some memorial plaques and tablets, is a tall, sandstone cross, adjacent to a large, perspex box, containing a highly coloured, life-size Pieta. Here is believed to be the place from where, in AD 432 and on the instructions of Pope

Celestine, St Patrick preached his final sermon before setting sail on a treacherous voyage to Ireland, to convert the people there to Christianity.

Today, Britain is a country of many cultures and many faiths, but Christianity only began to fully re-establish itself here, after 597. This was because, in the year 596, Pope Gregory the Great was passing through the market in Rome.

Here, he saw some beautiful British slave boys being offered for sale and, asking where they came from, he was told, Anglia. He responded, Niente Angles, per Angeli – not Angles but angels. In the year 597, the Pope then sent his Bishop, Augustine, to lead a Roman mission to convert the whole of England to the worship of Christ.

By this time, the Saxons had become the dominant culture in the land, spreading right across Britain, including the area known as Mercia. This territorial Kingdom included what is now Liverpool and Merseyside, as well as Lancashire, Cheshire, Shropshire, and parts of North Wales.

Life then became more settled, and many communities established themselves in the district, farming the fertile land, and hunting in the two, very large forests that covered wide areas around Toxteth and West Derby. Indeed, the Saxon legacy is shown in the names of places such as Fazakerley, Garston, Toxteth, Hale, and Knowsley. Even the name Mersey, or Mersea, derives from the Anglo-Saxon name Meres-ig, which means sea-island, although Lake-Island or Pool-Island is probably a more accurate translation from the Old Saxon dialect. But, the relative tranquillity of Saxon Britain was soon to be shattered by a new series of invasions, because along came the Vikings.

These sea-born aggressors, from all over Scandinavia, ravaged Britain from the 9th century. But, it was the Danes specifically, who set their sights on North East and North Western England, and they were the race who exploited and subjugated the Wirral, Liverpool, and the wider Merseyside areas of that time. These Norsemen sailed their longboats up the River Mersey and the River Dee, and found rich pickings in the villages, farms, churches, and monasteries of the area.

But, after these periods of rape, pillage, and plunder, and like previous invaders, they too set up encampments and fortifications in the Liverpool and north Cheshire areas. Important archaeological discoveries have been unearthed all over the Wirral Peninsula and it is now known that one of the Vikings earliest landing places on Merseyside was at Meols, as well as at what is now Formby, further up the coast from Liverpool. These latest invaders had lookouts on Thurstason Hill and other high spots, and settlements all over the area, on both sides of the Mersey.

In and around Liverpool, it was the Vikings who gave names to Croxteth, Kirkby, Walton, Aigburth, Aintree, and Kirkdale, amongst many others places.

And, in West Derby, they erected a significant walled fortification to defend what was the hub of their captured local territory. The Vikings, as had the Saxons before them, eventually married local women and settled down, in significant numbers, to adopt quieter lives of farming and animal husbandry.

Life moved on for these early Medieval Scousers, and their outlying villages steadily grew and developed in size and significance, whilst Liverpool remained an irrelevant fishing community. In fact, this small collection of fisherman's huts on the riverbank, only became important following the next, and most complete invasion of Britain; the Norman Conquest of 1066.

In that year, the armies of William the Conqueror began to completely subjugate the country, changing the face of Saxon Britain. They brought with them a new language, a new political system, and a new stratified social structure, built on wealth and class – the Feudal System. Even though the people living around the Mersey and the Dee were in a backwater of England, many Saxon communities, such as Childwall, Woolton, Wavertree, Croxteth, and West Derby, appear in the Domesday Book.

William had ordered this total survey of the value of his new domain in 1086, and it remains as a most remarkably thorough and detailed record of the Feudal System, and of the economic structure of England, as these then existed in the late 11th century. However, this was more than a simple record of the wealth of England, as it gave William a detailed analysis of how he could extract income from his new colony. The book was so named, because it was regarded as a final and irrevocable authority. There was to be no appeal against it, any more than there would be on the day of the Last Judgement before God; hence Domesday!

However, Liverpool was too unimportant to merit an entry in William's great account book. Indeed, there are conflicting opinions about where the name Liverpool comes from. However, the word liver either means muddy pool, or it is a derivation of laver, meaning a type of seaweed. Pool means haven, and this refers to the tidal pool that was a broad inlet that flowed inland from the River Mersey, beneath what is now Canning Place and South John Street, as far as Whitechapel. The 'Pool' was fed by many streams, which ran down from hills that surrounded the original hamlet of Liverpool, and this was the safe-harbour for ships, around which the Town of Liverpool was to grow.

However, the collection of cottages eventually become significant enough to warrant a name, and the history of Liverpool truly began, in 1207, when King John granted a charter to tiny Leverpul. This granted its citizens certain rights and benefits, as Burgesses, in the Town and Borough.

John used his new Town, and its large and safe Pool, as a base from which to launch his invasion fleets of Ireland. And, the reigns of that Monarch, and of his descendants, saw the fishing village steadily expand as a centre of shipbuilding, trade, and commerce, and, in due course, of political and strategic importance. Also, as the size of the population slowly increased, so too did the number of farms that surrounded Liverpool, each one providing food and clothing, and horse-powered transportation, for the people. Even so, Liverpool throughout the Middle-Ages consisted of only seven major streets with, by the 16th century, some additional connecting alleyways and tracks.

But, by the time of the outbreak of the English Civil War (1642-1651), the Town was the commercial and political centre of the Hundred of West Derby, with even more farms and large Baronial estates, a still increasing population, local trading guilds, and a developing merchant class – the first posh Scousers! Liverpool's Castle, built in the 13th century and held by the Molyneux Family who later became the Earls of Sefton, dominated the area, at what is now Derby Square. The Tower of Liverpool, standing on the site of what is now Tower Buildings, at the bottom of Water Street, was held by the Stanley family, who later became the Earls of Derby.

During this period, Liverpool was not a Parish in its own right. In fact, and up to the 18th century, the church for the Town was St Mary's Walton-on-the-Hill. However, the Medieval Chapel of St Mary del Quay, standing at the bottom of Chapel Street and directly on the river's edge, had been the local place of worship for people. Today the site of Liverpool Parish Church of St Mary and St Nicholas, for centuries this very ancient site has been a place of Christian worship and prayer, for Liverpool fisherman and seafarers, and for their families: Together they asked for God's blessing before sailing the perilous oceans of the world and, after their voyages, would give thanks for a safe return.

Besieged, and changing hands a number of times between the Roundheads and the Cavaliers in the Civil War, the Town of Liverpool was destined to become the most significant trading capital of the British Empire, after London. This really began in 1715, with the construction of the world's first enclosed wet dock, on the in-filled Pool of Liverpool, in and around what is now Canning Place. From this time, and well into the 20th century, entrepreneurial and industrious Scousers built more than 150 wet and dry docks, and the warehouses and factories to support them, all along the Mersey waterfront on both sides of the river, but chiefly in Liverpool.

It was during the 18th century too, that Liverpool began to develop into a hub of communication and transport, with the development of mail and passenger coaches and turnpiked roads, and the construction of the first canals. A hundred years later, in the 1830s, the first passenger railway in the world was built between Liverpool and Manchester. Within a decade, a network of railway tracks, for people and goods, was beginning to criss-cross Britain. And, it was the 19th century in particular, that saw the Town's wealth and population grow at a phenomenal rate. In fact, it was in 1880 that we officially became the City of Liverpool.

International shipping burgeoned from the Port, and a small but significant section of the people became very wealthy, from trade in commodities such as cotton, tobacco, and sugar, and, of course, from the Slave Trade. At the same time however, vast sections of the population lived in densely packed areas of squalor and poverty, especially after the influx of hundreds of thousands of Irish Immigrants, escaping from the Great Potato Famine of 1845 and 1846.

Here too, came the Welsh, the Scots, and people seeking their fortunes from right across the rest of Britain. Because of our dominating and worldwide shipping trade, people also came to settle here from all over Africa and the Middle East; from Continental and Eastern Europe; from the Indian Sub-Continent ; and from Asia. Many stayed here, but millions more used Liverpool as a stopping-off point, on their journeys to the New World.

And, Liverpool also saw hundreds of thousands of people from overseas, passing through its docks in the mid 20th century, but, not for trade or emigration, but to fight the greatest war to have ever afflicted our Country; World War Two.

In the battle against Hitler and his Nazis, and against the imperial ambitions of Japan, Scousers lived, fought, suffered, and died to preserve freedom and democracy. And, it was from September 1939 until May 1945, that Liverpool played a particularly vital role in the defence of Britain and her Empire. Indeed, no fewer than 1,747,505 Servicemen and Servicewomen passed through Liverpool's Docks, on their way to and from the battlefields of the world. But we also had a very specific role to play because, throughout the conflict, Liverpool was the location of the secret underground headquarters of the Western Approaches Naval Command, from which the Battle of the Atlantic was directed, fought and eventually won.

Liverpool was the most severely bombed City outside London, especially during the May and June Blitzes of 1941: Scousers braved the destruction of their homes, and faced injury and loss of life on a massive scale.

Altogether, there were 79 separate air-raids during the Blitz, and it was estimated that, out of the almost 300,000 homes in Liverpool at that time, around 200,000 were damaged – 11,000 of those being destroyed. The centre of the City lay in waste and the full length of the docks were heavily damaged also. Throughout the City and its suburbs there were 15,000 Blitzed sites and, between July 1940 and January 1942, the Luftwaffe bombing-raids over Liverpool killed over 4000 people, and injured more than 10,000.

After the end of the War, Scousers had to try to rebuild their lives and their shattered City but, it was at this time, that international shipping and its allied trades and services began to go into rapid decline. We were so dependant on these as our major source of income and employment that, throughout the late 1950s and the following decades, our descent into economic collapse, unemployment, and social instability was almost total. By the end of the 1980s, things were about as bad as they could get.

But then, the will, the indomitability, and the sheer hard work of Liverpudlians began to re-assert itself. Added to this was our intense and remarkable strength of community, and our sense of humour, and then, throughout the 1990s the tide began to turn. Scousers fought hard to create a new Liverpool; one that would draw on its heritage and its multi-cultural roots, rejoice in its vibrant and creative present, and boldly face the 21st century with commitment and optimism, but above all, with passion and pride.

Throughout our history, the millions of people who have passed through Liverpool; and the hundreds of thousands who made this outstanding City their home, brought with them their languages, their customs, and their faiths. This melange of humanity has made Liverpool one of the most dynamic, exciting, culturally rich and diverse communities in Britain.

This is a legacy that we all benefit from today, and one that makes Scousers the unique, strong, caring, welcoming, humorous and human people that we are.

The world of entertainment has always been well served by Scousers.
Not only actors and film stars but comedians and broadcasters - including high profile disc jockeys, TV presenters as well as writers and journalists.
Some have sadly departed but others are still making their mark.
Many made their names on stage or on TV, others became international stars thanks to film.
Scouse disc jockeys helped find new talent and shaped the careers of the bands and artists of tomorrow.
And it certainly looks as though there's plenty more stars waiting in the wings.

ENTE

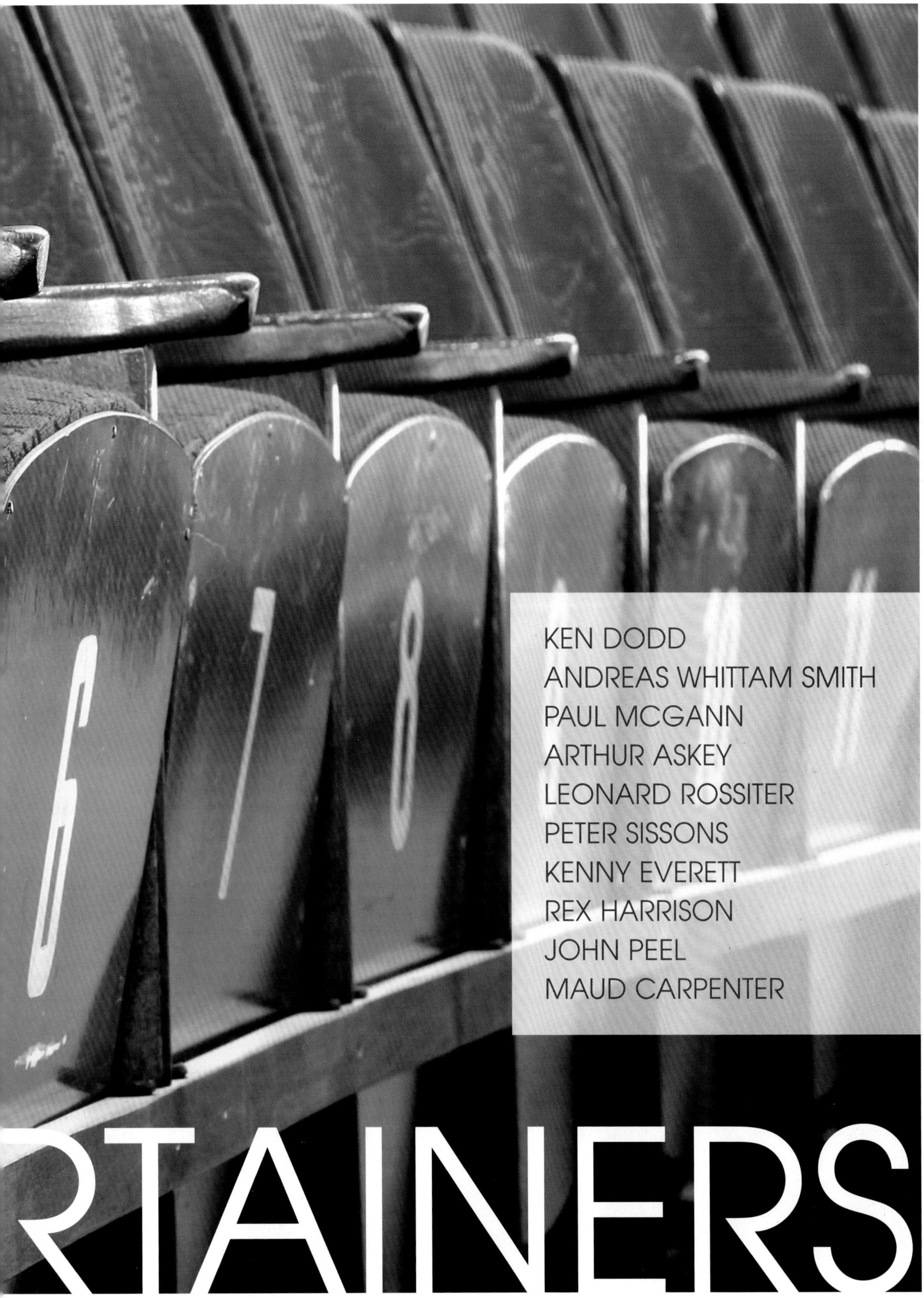

KEN DODD
ANDREAS WHITTAM SMITH
PAUL MCGANN
ARTHUR ASKEY
LEONARD ROSSITER
PETER SISSONS
KENNY EVERETT
REX HARRISON
JOHN PEEL
MAUD CARPENTER

RTAINERS

KEN DODD

"Doddy re-opened Liverpool's Royal Court in the 1980s by breaking the world joke-telling record with more than three hours of non-stop gags"

HE'S known as the funniest man in the business. Not just by the public, but by his fellow comedians.

Ken Dodd, 80 next November, is still at the top of the bill.

The playwright John Osborne, who wrote Look Back in Anger, once took the entire cast of the National Theatre to a Ken Dodd performance to learn about timing.

And the doyen of British theatre critics, Michael Billington, has likened Doddy's greatness to that of Laurence Olivier and Paul Schofield.

Not to be outdone, Ken did once tread the boards at the Liverpool Playhouse as Malvolio in Shakespeare's Twelfth Night.

His television appearances have been many. He is the only celebrity to do a second programme of An Audience With.

Doddy re-opened Liverpool's Royal Court in the 1980s by breaking the world joke-telling record with more than three hours of non-stop gags.

His glittering career has included two seasons at the London Palladium, where the audience included the then prime minister and MP for Huyton, Harold Wilson.

Doddy is the self-styled Squire of Knotty Ash, a nostalgic tribute to his family home in Thomas Lane, where he grew up as one of three children of a coal merchant, Arthur Dodd.

But his son - Kenneth Arthur - was destined for a unique sort of fame, enjoyed in the company of the Diddymen and the ventriloquist's doll Dicky Mint, to which he would sing the tear-jerking song, Sonny Boy.

As a singer, Doddy has enjoyed a multi-million disc-selling profile.

In 1965 the ballad Tears went to number one. The tickling stick-wielding troubadour has since had more than 20 other Top 50 entries, at times including two simultaneous top 10 hits.

Showered with honours, including the OBE and the Freedom of Liverpool, this is the man other comics call the guv'nor.

ANDREAS WHITTAM SMITH

"In 1977, he became the first editor of a new broadsheet newspaper, the Independent"

ANDREAS Whittam Smith, educated at Birkenhead school, is best known as the founding editor and first chief executive of the Independent newspaper.

But he also enjoyed high profile attention when he served for four years as president of the British Board of Film Classification, a period which overhauled guidelines to protect children but also relaxed rules for adults, allowing more graphic sex films to be rated.

His most recent senior appointment has been as the first church estates commissioner, overseeing management of church investments.

Whittam Smith's main interest in a distinguished journalistic career had been financially based.

After leaving Birkenhead to study at Oxford university, he joined the Stock Exchange Gazette, moving to the Financial Times in 1963.

After a move to the Times, he became deputy city editor and then city editor of both the Daily Telegraph and the Guardian.

In 1977, he became the first editor of a new broadsheet newspaper, the Independent, still known for its individualistic approach to news, often centred on Third World and green issues.

In the 1987 British Press Awards he was named Journalist of the Year.

Andreas Whittam Smith was particularly proud of his time at the BBFC. He said: "It is now seen as an open and accountable organisation, with a set of guidelines which reflect public opinions. That is not to say the board is above criticism. I appreciate not everybody shares our view that adults should be able to make their own viewing decisions."

His achievement was to make film classifications advisory rather than mandatory, while acknowledging that content information must be clear to help parents to make informed decisions.

Under Whittam Smith's leadership, new rules on hardcore sex films came into force, in response to a landmark legal ruling to allow some real sex scenes, as long as films were sold by licensed premises.

As chair of the church commissioners, Andreas Whittam Smith became responsible for the management of a £4bn investment portfolio.

The aim was to take financial problems away from bishops and the clergy, allowing them to devote more time to their ministry.

Whittam Smith holds an honorary doctorate from Liverpool university and is a fellow of Liverpool John Moores university.

PAUL MCGANN

A MEMBER of Liverpool's acting dynasty, Paul McGann has been a regular on screen for 25 years.

One of four acting brothers, he shot to fame when he appeared alongside Richard E Grant in the cult movie Withnail And I in 1987.

The previous year he had come to public attention playing the eponymous heroin Alan Bleasdale's controversial war series The Monocled Mutineer, but it was Withnail which made him a household name.

Paul has been in demand on the big and small screen throughout his career, starring in dramas like the BBC's adaption of Dickens' Our Mutual Friend, Hornblower, and the film Alien. He became the eighth Dr Who in 1996 for a joint US/UK production about the timelord but it never became a series.

Born in 1959, Paul was brought up in Kensington, Liverpool, with three actor brothers Joe, Mark and Steve, and a sister, Clare. He was a pupil at Cardinal Heenan Catholic high school and on the advice of a drama teacher went on to study at RADA.

The four brothers have acted together in the TV series The Hanging Gale in 1995, about the Irish potato famine, and performed in the West End musical Yakety Yak. Joe starred in the successful TV comedy series The Upper Hand, while Steve has appeared in the soap Emmerdale. Mark is perhaps most famous for playing John Lennon in the Everyman's award-winning musical Lennon and starred in the film John and Yoko.

"Paul has been in demand on the big and small screen throughout his career"

ARTHUR ASKEY

BESPECTACLED and diminutive funnyman Arthur Askey - he stood only 5ft 3in - was known to millions as Big-Hearted Arthur.

He was the first comic (together with Richard Murdoch) to make radio a distinctive medium for humour.

Their show, the prototype sitcom, Band Wagon (1938), was based on the premise of the duo living in a flat at the top of Broadcasting House, where visitors included Mrs Bagwash and her daughter Nausea, as well as Lewis the goat.

Arthur had made his professional debut in 1924, soon becoming a regular feature of summer seasons at leading seaside resorts.

For more than 50 years, Dingle-born Askey was a stalwart of British showbiz.

Prior to that, as a pupil at Liverpool Institute, he was to sit at the same school desk as Sir Paul McCartney - albeit decades apart.

The coincidence was discovered by the former Beatle who found the carved initials AA, and later sent the comedian a message, only to have his hunch confirmed.

It was Ken Dodd, who called Arthur "the funniest man I ever met off-stage".

Doddy persuaded the British Comedy Society to erect a plaque inside Lipa to the man whose catchphrases included "before your very eyes" and "hello playmates".

After leaving the Institute at 16, Arthur became a clerk at the city's education offices in Sir Thomas Street.

The son of a book-keeper, he then joined a concert party and began touring the music halls. An abiding image is of Arthur performing his busy bee song.

Yet it was Band Wagon which made Arthur Askey a true star. The series was later turned into a TV show, and Askey went on to launch a film career, making several light-hearted morale-boosting films during the war before returning to radio and the place he loved most - the stage.

He also had a television show called Before Your Very Eyes, as well as performing in numerous pantomimes. In the 1970s he became a panelist on the New Faces talent show.

He stopped working after losing blood circulation in both legs and had to have them amputated. He passed away a few years later in 1982. His own sign-off phrase speaks volumes: "I thank you".

"For more than 50 years, Dingle-born Askey was a stalwart of British showbiz"

LEONARD ROSSITER

"Rossiter had a reputation for being a perfectionist"

THERE are precious few performers who can combine comedy genius with distinguished and critically acclaimed acting.

But Leonard Rossiter certainly did that rare double in style.

Born in 1926, the son of John and Elizabeth Rossiter, Leonard grew up in the family home above his father's barber shop in Cretan Road, Wavertree, and attended Granby Street primary and the Collegiate.

He began acting when he picked up a girlfriend from her amateur dramatics class and was challenged to do better when he criticised her and her fellow performers.

He soon gave up his job in insurance to enrol in repertory theatre and turned professional at the comparatively late age of 27.

After learning his trade Rossiter's big break came in the early 1960s when he won roles in top British films including This Sporting Life and Billy Liar.

But it was as Rigsby - the landlord of a block of seedy bedsits - in 1970s sitcom Rising Damp that he made the massive leap in public consciousness.

Rossiter had a reputation for being a perfectionist and sometimes being difficult to work with.

Following Rossiter's untimely death in 1984, Reginald Perrin co-star Bruce Bould said: "Occasionally, before a recording, Len would blow up at somebody.

"Usually there was a very good reason and if sometimes there wasn't you could understand that all that nervous energy and tension had to go somewhere, and it was a small price to pay for the superb performances he gave."

PETER SISSONS

"He earned his foreign correspondent's spurs in Biafra in 1968, where he was wounded by gunfire"

AFTER almost 40 years in the business, Peter Sissons is one of the country's best known and most liked television news presenters.

Having worked for ITN, Channel Four and the BBC, he has gathered the kind of experience which marks him out as a tried and trusted deliverer of news.

Born at Smithdown Road hospital in Liverpool in 1942, he grew up at the Sissons' family home in Ingleton Road, near Penny Lane.

He went to Dovedale primary school and the Liverpool institute where he was head boy, and studied alongside Sir Paul McCartney, with whom he still keeps in touch and counts as a close friend, John Lennon and George Harrison.

While Messrs McCartney, Harrison and Lennon were destined for music superstardom, Sissons had his heart set on more academic pursuits and after leaving school he went on to read philosophy, politics and economics at University college, Oxford.

News and current affairs was his first love and he took his first job as a writer at ITN in 1964, becoming a reporter three years later. He earned his foreign correspondent's spurs in Biafra in 1968, where he was wounded by gunfire.

His first role as a news anchor came in 1978, when he began presenting ITN's News At One.

When Channel 4 was launched in 1982, Sissons was chosen to present their flagship 7pm news programme and in 1984 he was named Best Front Of Camera Performer by the Broadcasting Press Guild.

He joined the BBC in 1989 as presenter of Question Time, as well as joint presenter of the Six O'Clock News, and has been with the corporation ever since.

In 2002 he sparked controversy by failing to wear a tie when announcing the death of the Queen Mother. His response to the protests was curt "The reporter should not become part of the story."

Married with three children, he now lives in Kent.

KENNY EVERETT

TO millions, Kenny Everett was the face behind a cast of outrageous characters, a loveable clown who transformed radio with his irreverent and anarchic style and who influenced some of the biggest names in broadcasting today.

But away from the TV and radio studios, Crosby-raised Kenny was a sad and sometimes desperate man, tormented by inner demons.

Born Maurice Cole in Seaforth on Christmas Day 1944, Kenny was the son of a devout Catholic tugboat skipper, who dreamed of becoming a priest. After 12 years of marriage to clairvoyant Audrey Lee, he realised he was gay and set up home in a threesome with a Russian soldier and a Spanish waiter. He later said that coming to terms with his sexuality led him to attempt suicide.

Kenny's career was also a stormy series of highs and lows. Despite making his mark by developing a variety of daft voices and comedic personas at Radio London, he was publicly sacked after he poked fun at a religious broadcaster while covering the Beatles tour around America.

He joined the BBC when Radio 1 was launched, but was again sacked when he joked that the wife of the transport minister had passed her driving test by giving the instructor a fiver.

After a stint on London's Capital Radio he withdrew from public life when his Russian lover, Nicolai Grishanovitch, died of Aids in 1990. Following a series of newspaper reports Kenny admitted that he was HIV positive.

Kenny's career spanned, and helped to shape, the key moments in broadcasting history: pirate radio, the birth of Radio 1 and the start of commercial radio. On television, he entertained the nation with his oddball sketches, a cast of characters that included the punk Sid Snot and the drag queen Cupid Stunt and the catchphrase, "All in the best possible taste".

After he died of an AIDS-related illness in 1995, his family donated his private studio where he created much of his radio work to LIPA, to encourage young people in Merseyside to follow in Kenny's footsteps.

"Born Maurice Cole in Seaforth on Christmas Day 1944, Kenny was the son of a devout Catholic tugboat skipper"

"Harrison's debut in 1925 was a disaster, with a complete mix-up of lines"

REX HARRISON

HE hated being called "sexy Rexy," but like Henry VIII he did have six wives, plus a severe jolt to his Hollywood career when an affair with actress Carole Landis ended with her suicide.

But on stage and screen, Huyton-born actor Sir Rex Harrison (real name Reginald Carey Harrison) was the epitome of the suave and debonair theatrical charmer.

But it all happened almost by accident. At 16, Harrison wasn't sure what he wanted to do. As he told the ECHO: "I just had a vague feeling that I didn't want to work in an office."

His father was a friend of one of the board members of the Liverpool Playhouse and pulled a few strings. His son was hired: "I got 30 shillings a week, which wasn't bad money in those days."

Harrison's debut in 1925 was a disaster, with a complete mix-up of lines. The director, William Armstrong, advised him to give up.

Instead, he went to London, landed a role in the comedy Charlie's Aunt, and his career was under way.

So much so that it was to become an international success, capped by an Oscar for playing Professor Higgins in the 1964 movie My Fair Lady (repeating his stage success where he had created the role).

But even his Hollywood days had some mixed blessings.

He had an unsuccessful screen test for Warners in 1936, but during the mid-40s became contracted to Twentieth Century Fox.

Other film highlights included Major Barbara (1940); Blithe Spirit (1945); The Rake's Progress (1946); Anna And The King Of Siam (1946) and Cleopatra (1962).

His first marriage was to teacher Colette Thomas in 1934. He later wed actresses Lilli Palmer, Kay Kendall, Rachel Roberts and Elizabeth Harris, with a final marriage to Mercia Tinker.

He died in 1990, aged 82, from cancer.

"It was the
Fab Four who,
indirectly, helped
launch him on his
road to success"

JOHN PEEL

THE fact that there is now an annual John Peel Day tells you all you need to know about the son of a Liverpool cotton trader who was born John Robert Parker Ravenscroft.

Countless people whose lives were enriched by the influential broadcaster and writer - musicians whose careers he helped launch, or fans of his radio shows - felt bereft at his passing.

He was born in Heswall Cottage Hospital a few days before the outbreak of the Second World War and died, aged 65, in October 2004.

Always on the lookout for new and exciting music, the father-of-four and fanatical Liverpool FC fan championed countless acts over a 40-year period, not least David Bowie, Marc Bolan, The Smiths and the White Stripes.

In Merseyside, the likes of Echo and The Bunnymen, Pete Wylie, The Teardrop Explodes, Half Man Half Biscuit and The La's were all inspired by and supported by Peel.

And it was the Fab Four who, indirectly, helped launch him on his road to success. Peel was working as a DJ in Dallas, Texas, when Beatlemania hit the States - and the geographical "connection" proved useful.

Peel, who also gained access to a police press conference in the immediate aftermath of John F Kennedy's assassination by claiming to be a Liverpool ECHO reporter, returned to England in 1967 and joined the pirate station Radio London, before transferring to Radio 1.

He remained there for the rest of his life, the only survivor of its original line-up.

He also presented Home Truths on Radio 4 and wrote for The Observer and the Radio Times.

As his wife Sheila said: "He had a wonderful command of the English language and a lot of people have said that when they've been reading his words it was as if he was in the room talking to them."

MAUD CARPENTER

"Maud ruled with a benevolent rod of iron. What she said went"

IN an age when many theatres are run by legions of managers and directors, the story of Maud Carpenter seems like an anomaly.

But as general manager and licensee of Liverpool Playhouse for half a century - from its foundation as Britain's senior repertory in 1911 through to her retirement in 1962 - she overshadowed all, including the artistic directors and the actors, many of whom became very famous.

These included Mrs Patrick Campbell, Dame Sybil Thorndyke, Noel Coward, Rex Harrison, Michael Redgrave, Robert Donat and Rachael Lawrence.

Maud ruled with a benevolent rod of iron. What she said went.

The grande dame didn't like her actors walking to the stage door. She once instructed a group of wannabe thespians that "it would be better if they were seen arriving by taxi ... this is what the public wants."

Maud also told the actress Jean Boht that "it would be good if the cast were seen taking tea at the Adelphi."

To Maud, the image given to patrons was as important as what happened on stage.

"The trouble was," recalls Jean Boht, "we were all on dreadful wages and tea at the Adelphi cost one shilling and sixpence."

Nevertheless, Maud Carpenter had started out at the bottom herself. Her first wage was 12 shillings a week to run the box office. Twelve years later, she was running the whole show. But for all that, she used to tell a tale against herself.

While she was standing in as temporary secretary for the great director Basil Dean, she rushed into the auditorium to ask for his autograph.

"He was rehearsing the company and when I approached him, he turned around and said 'Go to hell!'

"When I returned to the theatre for evening duties, he asked me where I had been.

"I replied: you told me to go to hell, so I went home."

Maud Carpenter was awarded the OBE in 1954. Such was her popularity, that on retiring friends collected £550, more than half a year's wages for most people at the time.

STILL MAKING WAVES
RIVER MERSEY

By Tony Martin

THE Mersey has claimed its place as one of the great rivers of the world against all the odds.

Like a boxer punching above his weight, the river – a little like the people who live on its banks – faces the world with confidence and maybe a little arrogance.

It is only 60 miles long, rising near Stalybridge in the Pennines and was once a much humbler second cousin to the ports of Chester and Parkgate.

But the Mersey, whose name came from its status as the northern boundary of the ancient kingdom of Mercia, is a survivor and came to the fore when the Cheshire ports silted up and America wanted trade.

Even so, Liverpool and its river still struggled until 1715 when the Old Pool was enclosed in the world's first successful commercial dock and the river's mile-wide, fast-flowing waters and 30ft tide were tamed.

From then on the Port of Liverpool never looked back. From the original Old Dock, the Mersey has developed cargo links with hundreds of countries, from Ireland to China.

And like the tide that goes out and comes in, the Mersey and Liverpool have both influenced the world and been influenced by it, whether it is The Beatles and the Merseysound of the 1960s or the cosmopolitan nature of Liverpool's population. From its role as a major port of the British empire to a key link in transatlantic liner travel, the Mersey has made its mark.

VIGILANT
LIVERPOOL

Many proud Scousers have their ashes scattered over the Mersey. • Gerry Marsden's self-penned 'Ferry 'cross the Mersey is played each day on the Ferry cruises • Frankie Goes to Hollywood made their own cover ve

Pete Wylie Liverpool's legendary singer from the Mighty Wah! Has a daughter called... Mersey.

Phil Redmond created a series set in and around the River called Waterfront Beat •

...to swim the River Mersey for charity

Scouser Sian Boardman has a major ambition...

Scouser Sian Boardman at the time

sey themed' songs around at the time

A painting in 1875 by Atkinson Grimshaw, of Liverpool from Wapping, shows an evening scene on the quayside with a wide cobbled street; a line of brightly lit shops and taverns face the waiting ships and the waiting world. As a trading nation, Britain's ports have always played a vital role, and Liverpool as a gateway to the western world saw its lifeblood as ships, great and small.

Before the 1972 Seaforth container terminal, there were seven miles of docks on the Liverpool side alone from Gladstone in the north to Herculaneum in the south, with 27 miles of quays, while across the river, Birkenhead added more than nine miles of quayside. Ships and shipping lines abounded, and tens of thousands of men worked on the docks and at the Cammell Laird shipyard.

Cammell Laird

- The Cammell Laird shipyard in Birkenhead was for many years one of the most famous names in world shipping.

- Founded in 1828 by Scotsman John Laird and Sheffield steelmaker Cammell, at its peak the shipyard employed 20,000 people. It made ships as famous as the second Mauretania, the largest ship to be built in England at the time.

- One of the yard's greatest days was May 3, 1950, when more than 50,000 people watched the then Queen launch aircraft carrier Ark Royal.

- One of its saddest was in June 1939 when the submarine Thetis failed to return from its first diving test in Liverpool Bay. It left Cammell Laird with 103 men, naval and civilian, many local; only four got out before the escape hatch jammed and Thetis went to its watery grave.

As well as cargo, there was a big trade in people too, none more so than when emigration, particularly from Ireland, was at its height.

Between 1830 and 1930 some nine million emigrants sailed from Liverpool for America, many from Waterloo dock.

For an average fare of six guineas, people headed in hope to the New World, leaving behind all they had known.

Of course, not all ships using the Mersey were heading out into the great oceans. The first ferries on the Mersey were operated by the Benedictine monks of Birkenhead Priory from as early as 1150. Ferries at Seacombe and Tranmere were recorded in Elizabeth I's time and even today, when the Mersey tunnels both rail and road take most traffic, a ride on a Mersey ferry is a great way to see the river and the buildings that are famous around the world.

The ferry route from Woodside is classed as a royal highway, and passengers can see the proof in the crown emblem at the top of the gangway posts. And let's not forget here to mention the skill of the crews that carry thousands of people across the Mersey with its current that can run at six knots. Piloting a 460-ton ferry is, as one skipper remarked, like 'driving a bus on ice'.

Mind you, this would have been no joke if he had been around in 1881 and 1895, for in those years freak cold weather led the Mersey to freeze over.

For all the centuries of trade centred on the port, its undoubted hey-day was the era of the great transatlantic liners that plied their way between Liverpool and Boston or New York for decades until the mid-1960s.

It could be said to have started with one man, Samuel Cunard, who in 1840 came to Liverpool after his firm's steamships had won the contract to carry the mail. Passengers soon followed and over the decades the liners cut the travelling time from Liverpool to North America from 28 to three-and-a-half days; Cunard and its great rival the White Star line (before they combined in 1934) competed for passengers with Cunard ships known for speed and White Star (including Titanic) known for luxury.

Liverpool's landing stage was once called one of the wonders of the world. The 2,534ft hinged wooden deck, floating on 200 huge iron pontoons, was moored to the river by chains, booms and passenger gangways.

At the southern end was the Pier Head, and this was joined to the much-longer northern Princes stage where the great liners tied up. Like the reverse of a coin, these years saw the opposite effects of emigration to America, when the US and its ideas filtered back to the Mersey. From the influence of the Hollywood stars arriving in Liverpool on the liners to the crewmen who brought back music and fashions, the culture of the States arrived here. Music from records brought back by merchant seamen – popularly known as the Cunard Yanks – undoubtedly influenced the Liverpool sound, with Paul McCartney and John Lennon just two of the many teenagers whose eager young ears listened to early rock and roll from American stars.

Time has moved on and, while some of our docks have swapped trade for tourism, the Mersey and the people who live by it are still making waves.

I SUPPOSE I am an adopted Scouser – I was born in Birkenhead but my life as a photographer from the early 60s has always been in Liverpool.

I met my wife at the Liverpool Echo and my four children were all born at the wonderful Oxford St Maternity Hospital in the centre of the city.

From the first morning ferry trips to work in 1962 to today, the river and the Liver Buildings give me a special feeling – a warm glow, the sniff of ozone – Liverpool has a special smell.

I have photographed thousands of Scousers – some of them not too keen to have a camera poked in front of them but most love to have their picture taken. "Take our pic mister, will it be in the papers?" one child asked, with a greasy hot finger pressed against the lens. They often make me smile, the irony of life in Liverpool is always surprising and unique to this city.

Stephen Shakeshaft

Top left	The streets of Toxteth in 1965. Kids play on the cobbles – there was no adventure playground. They interrupted their game of soccer to ask: "Take our picture, mister"
Bottom left	Edge Hill in the 1960s. Houses waiting for demolition had many stories of Liverpool family life in each of them. Where would this dear lady go? Her kitchen was her refuge from the bulldozers
Right	Betty's paradise. Her terraced home about to be demolished, Betty sat covered with a blanket to protest under the majesty of Liverpool Cathedral

Left   This July evening, Liverpool was cooling from another boiling hot day. I jumped from the car on seeing this man and his dog walking home down Rodney Street

Right   Shanks's last match at Wembley. I walked onto the pitch behind him – the man with a crew cut and the swagger – when suddenly he was mobbed by tearful men who could not disguise their sadness

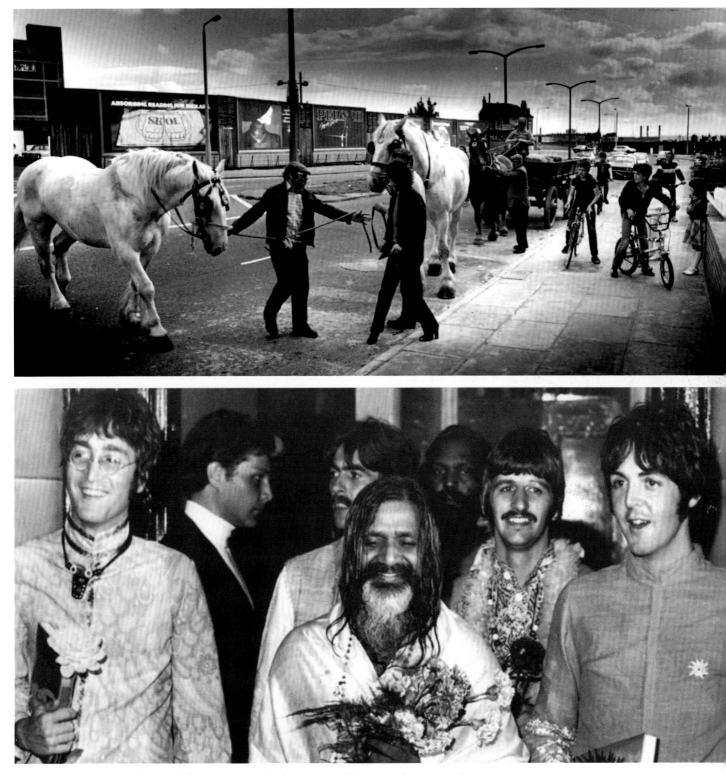

Top   Stagecoach, Kirkdale – swapping the horses to pull the carts for Liverpool carters
Above   The start of the end of the Beatles – Bangor 1967. Brian Epstein was found dead in his London flat and the Beatles
              were in Wales to attend a seminar with the Maharishi. On Sunday evening he waved them off – a sad end to a
              peaceful bank holiday weekend of meditation

Many Scousers have become household names thanks to their work beyond the call of duty – past and present.
Men and women who thought of others before themselves.
From the Crimean War to the First and Second World War conflicts there have been outstanding people from soldiers to sailors and civilian brave hearts who, on many occasions, saved so many lives.
The work of the Merchant Navy and of those individual members of the armed forces is not forgotten nor are the social reformers who took risks with little thought of their own welfare.
And there's the politicians who, to this day, are fighting the good fight.
Scousers have always had a real fighting spirit and sense of survival.

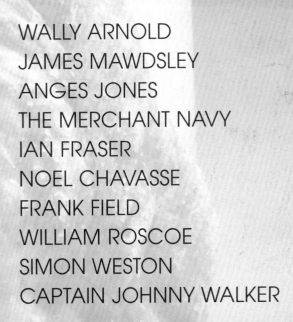

WALLY ARNOLD
JAMES MAWDSLEY
ANGES JONES
THE MERCHANT NAVY
IAN FRASER
NOEL CHAVASSE
FRANK FIELD
WILLIAM ROSCOE
SIMON WESTON
CAPTAIN JOHNNY WALKER

OURAGE

WALLY ARNOLD

WALLY "Stoker" Arnold survived one of Merseyside's greatest maritime disasters.

Born in Lower Tranmere, he first hit the headlines when he was leading stoker in the submarine Thetis, constructed at Cammell Laird, when she went out on her sea trials in Liverpool Bay 1939.

Stoker Arnold was one of four men saved from the vessel when she sank.

He had spent 12 years in submarines and had just returned from China when he volunteered for the Thetis.

A few years before he had been in another submarine incident in the Mediterranean, when his vessel was stuck on the sea bed for 36 hours.

In that tragic summer of 1939 a major rescue operation to save the lives of the 99 men on the Thetis trapped inside came to an abrupt end.

For three days, just 38 miles from land, the men on board battled the effects of carbon dioxide poisoning, waiting for a rescue which never came.

Conditions on board were extremely cramped, with the submarine carrying 103 men – twice the number she was designed to carry.

Many aboard were engineers from Cammell Laird, with only 69 of the crew being sailors.

Stoker Arnold was in the third compartment and immediately realised something was wrong.

His son Derek Arnold said: "He knew something was wrong when he felt a blast of air go past him, most unusual in a submarine."

Lt Woods, Stoker Arnold and two other men managed to escape through a hatch, yet four men died attempting to escape using the same route.

"Arnold once told legendary Echo columnist George Harrison that he had 'all the luck in the world, otherwise I would not have survived'"

The cruiser he joined after Thetis was torpedoed in the Atlantic and his vessel was sunk in Crete. He clung to a raft for hours until he was picked up by a British destroyer.

Arnold, who died at the age of 68 in 1974, was one of the true Merseyside maritime heroes.

JAMES MAWDSLEY

JAMES Mawdsley shocked the world when he left his home and family, travelled across the world to certain imprisonment, and laid his life on the line for a foreign and faraway cause.

The 33-year-old pro-democracy activist from Ormskirk spent 14 months in a Burmese prison cell, subjected to torture, beatings, hunger strikes and solitary confinement.

He gained worldwide recognition for his stance against the dictatorship responsible for genocide against minority nations on the borders of Burma. After a campaign he was freed and returned to a hero's welcome.

"James was imprisoned after he set out to draw international attention to the plight of the Burmese people"

Initially he went to the Thai-Burma border to teach English in a jungle camp, before staging a one-man protest. He chained himself to railings and was deported within 10 hours of his arrest.

He went back to Burma, giving out leaflets demanding the release of all political prisoners. This time he was interrogated and tortured, spending 99 days in jail.

On his release he again distributed pro-democracy leaflets and was sentenced to 17 years in prison for sedition and illegal entry, before being freed after 14 months.

James's interest in Burma began when he was 13 by the arrival of a young boy, Aung Lin, at his school. They became friends and Aung Lin told him about his country and the suffering of its people. His tales of genocide, rape and repression spurred James to make his first trip into Burma to join the fight for democracy.

"I wanted to go to Burma and confront the military regime, I wanted to make an appeal to them to put down their guns," said James.

"It seemed an impossible, even foolish task but, he reasoned: "One person may indeed make little or no difference. But that is not a reason to avoid trying"

Since his return from Burma James has been on the Conservative campaign trail in Ormskirk and has said he may consider pursuing a seat in Parliament.

AGNES JONES

AGNES Jones, a nurse trained by Florence Nightingale, worked and died among the ill, poor and destitute of Victorian Liverpool.

She turned her job from the expected "closing the eyes of the dying" into a revolutionary approach to education, nutrition and hygiene.

After education in Dublin and England, she studied nursing in Bonn where she was to learn revolutionary ideas in health care.

She later returned to work in a Dublin hospital, but spent most of her time working with the poor and homeless.

> "By 1862, she had become a student of Florence Nightingale at St Thomas's Hospital, London, and in 1865 became the first matron to be appointed head of a medical institution"

She recruited 65 women to help in her work. Soon other hospitals across the country followed her example.

Donegal-born Agnes, today remembered in a stained-glass window in Liverpool's Anglican Cathedral, was brought to the city at the personal request of philanthropist William Rathbone.

She worked here from 1865 to 1868, before succumbing to fever herself.

> "Her funeral was a massive outpouring of grief, the coffin being taken in an open carriage from the Brownlow Hill workhouse – now the site of the Metropolitan Cathedral – to the Pier Head, from where it sailed to Ireland for burial at St Mura"

Now a movie is to be made about Agnes, one of the city's largely unsung heroes.

It will feature in the Irish strand of the city's 08 Capital of Culture calendar.

Scriptwriter Felicity McCal says: "We are beginning a cross-border campaign to achieve an artwork memorial to this truly remarkable woman. We have even traced descendants of her wayward brother in New Zealand, more than 140 years after the family was assumed to have become extinct."

In the movie, Agnes will be played by Derry actress Bronagh Gallagher – aka Berni, the upfront member of the band in another feted film, The Commitments.

THE MERCHANT NAVY

THE terrible statistics of World War II alone speak for themselves. During the Battle of the Atlantic, 35,000 merchant crew sailing to or from Liverpool lost their lives.

Before the end of the First World War I, when the UK sailed more than half of the global tonnage, the official name was the Merchant Service. It was changed to the Merchant Navy by the royal proclamation of George V, in recognition that the service had sailed valiantly alongside the Royal Navy's fighting ships.

And so this continued to be the case, with the Merchant convoys responsible for keeping up the supplies of food and war materials which kept Britain "breathing" during her darkest hour.

Meeting up as they would in Halifax, Nova Scotia, the merchant ships would sail forth across the ocean, often paying the same terrible price as Royal Navy shipping. In all, 2,600 merchant ships were sunk during the last war.

A memorial to their crews and to other merchant seamen, pictured at its unveiling by John Prescott, stands at the Pier Head.

In 2006, a special project, The Cruel Sea, set up by the Liverpool Everyman/Playhouse company, paid tribute to the Merchant Navy,

following recorded interviews with the crews who served.

For the first time, the memories of black and racial minority veterans, who accounted for 20% per cent of recruits, were also acknowledged.

The gesture redresses the balance of a study carried out in 2000 which did not profile these forgotten heroes.

More than 700 seamen were inverviewed from Liverpool's Chinese, Somali, Caribbean, Malaysian, West African, Arab and Yememi communities.

"All played their part in the magnificent service and sacrifice of the Merchant Navy. All are commended today"

IAN FRASER

DIVING pioneer Ian Fraser won the Victoria Cross, the highest award for gallantry in the face of the enemy that can be awarded to British and commonwealth forces.

Lt Cmdr Fraser, who lives in Wallasey, was born in 1920. At 24 he became a lieutenant in the Royal Naval Reserve in World War II.

He was awarded his VC for his part in a midget submarine attack in the far east.

On July 31, 1945, while in command of a sub in the Straits of Johor, Singapore, Ian Fraser went to attack a Japanese heavy cruiser, which was reached after a hazardous journey through mined waters.

The challenge, undertaken with acting leading seaman James Magennis who also received the VC, was to fix limpet mines to the underside of the enemy ship.

The men succeeded. Fraser slid the submarine under the Japanese ship to sabotage the vessel before making for home.

"His VC citation read: 'The courage and determination of Lieutenant Fraser are beyond all praise. Any man not possessed of his relentless determination to achieve his objective in full, regardless of consequences, would have dropped his charge alongside the target'"

"The approach and withdrawal entailed a passage of 80 miles through water which had been mined by both the enemy and ourselves, past hydrophonic positions, over loops and controlled minefields and through an anti-submarine boom."

After the war Ian Fraser realised that frogman-style diving (now called scuba diving) could aid many sorts of underwater work that old-fashioned gear had become unsuitable for.

He and some associates set up a demonstration in a large aquarium tank at Belle Vue zoo in Manchester.

This aroused so much interest that he was able to use the show's takings to set up commercial diving organisation Underwaterwork.

NOEL CHAVASSE

NOEL Chavasse is Liverpool's most courageous son. A serviceman whose legendary valour is still spoken of almost a century after his heroic deeds, Chavasse is one of only three soldiers to have been awarded two Victoria Crosses.

During World War I, Chavasse was a captain with the Royal Army Medical Corps, British Army attached to the 10th Battalion of The King's (Liverpool) Regiment.

His first VC was awarded in recognition of his actions on August 9, 1916, at Guillemont, France, when he attended to the wounded all day under heavy fire

With little consideration for his own safety he continued searching for wounded comrades in front of enemy lines throughout the night.

The following day, Chavasse and a stretcher bearer carried an urgent case 500 yards to safety, despite coming under heavy shell fire.

He was wounded but the same night, along with 20 volunteers, he rescued three injured men from a shell-hole 36 yards from enemy trenches and collected many identity discs.

Altogether he saved the lives of 20 wounded men.

General de la Billiere said of his bravery: "Noel Chavasse never killed anyone, nor did he even fire a shot in anger."

Chavasse's second award was made in the summer of 1917, at Wieltje, Belgium.

Though severely injured early in action while carrying a wounded officer to the dressing station, he refused to leave his post and in addition to his normal duties, went out repeatedly under heavy fire to attend the wounded.

"During this time, although practically without food, worn with fatigue and faint from his wound, he helped to carry in badly wounded men, being instrumental in saving many who would otherwise have died in the bad weather"

Chavasse died of his wounds in Brandhoek at the age of 33. He is buried at Brandhoek New Military Cemetery.

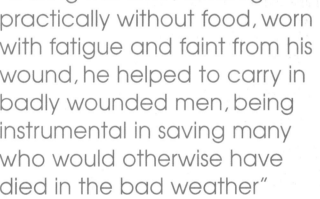

FRANK FIELD

FRANK Field is a politician who has never been scared of thinking – or saying – "the unthinkable".

The Labour MP for Birkenhead since 1979, who was born in London on July 16, 1942, is a long-standing campaigner for social and welfare reform – and someone who has often attracted big headlines for his big ideas.

He was appointed by Tony Blair – and asked to "think the unthinkable" – as minister for welfare reform after New Labour swept to power in 1997.

But he was at the Department for Social Security as Harriet Harman's number two for just 15 months (be blamed Harman and chancellor Gordon Brown for wrecking his radical reform plans).

In Blair's first cabinet reshuffle, Harman was sacked and Field resigned, declining to accept a move offered by the PM in the process.

"A passionate supporter of self-help, hard work and tough love, Field's controversial proposals have included making neighbours from hell live under a motorway fly-over, docking people's housing benefit and giving local communities the power to go directly to the courts to get troublemakers arrested"

Regarding the welfare state, he asked: "Why is it so terrible to say there should be a contract for receiving welfare? You have to turn up to work and behave in a certain way in return for having a job, so why not for welfare?"

He has also called for disaffected pupils to be allowed to get jobs at 14 and work for two years before being given the option of returning to education – and suggested "bouncers" be employed to stand guard over lessons in a bid to clamp down on violence against teachers.

A former director of the Child Poverty Action Group and Low Pay Unit, Field actually began his political career as a Young Conservative, but left the party in protest at its stance on apartheid.

He is also an unapologetic admirer of Margaret Thatcher.

He said: "She's in a league of her own. You can admire someone because they deliver"

Field, a practising Christian, is chairman of the Churches Conservation Trust and a member of the General Synod.

WILLIAM ROSCOE

"POET, etcher, biographer, linguist and botanist. There was no end to the talents of William Roscoe"

But it is for his work as a reformer – he was considered the founder of Liverpool's cultural life – and his involvement in the abolition of the slave trade, which led him to become one of the city's most famous sons.

Born on March 8, 1873, he was the son of an innkeeper in Mount Pleasant.

He had a love of learning and a passion for beauty. It was a trip to Florence and other Italian cities which inspired him to do all he could to counter the ugly and brutal materialism of a town still engaged in the slave trade.

To William Roscoe, the city owes the Botanical Gardens, originally located at the top of Mount Pleasant; the Athanaeum which opened in 1799, and the Royal Institution dating from 1817.

It was said that the Institution was the outcome of Roscoe's dream to build, in the middle of Liverpool, "a place which should be a focus for every intellectual interest, a perpetual radiator of sane and lofty views on life and a reminder of the higher needs and aspirations of men".

As a member of parliament, though only for a short time, he had the honour and great courage to vote for the Act of 1807 which ended the slave trade.

For that highly charged vote, however, he was welcomed back with sticks and brickbats.

He did not return to Westminster but continued his beneficent work for Liverpool – work of lasting value. He was given the honour of Freeman of the city.

He died, aged 79, in 1831, but his legacy and, indeed, his name lives on in roads, institutions and schools.

William Roscoe's body is buried in a small public garden in Mount Pleasant, not far from the spot where he was born.

WILLIAM ROSCOE, 1753

SIMON WESTON

WHEN Simon Weston set sail for the Falkland Islands in 1982, little could he have known that the experience would change his life for ever.

Having already served his country in Northern Ireland, Germany and East Africa, the Welsh Guardsman was part of the task force which set sail for the South Atlantic with one aim – to recover the Falklands from invading Argentine forces.

Weston was with 3 Company of the Welsh Guards on the afternoon their virtually undefended troopship Sir Galahad was bombed at low level by four Argentine jets.

Stocks of petrol stowed on board magnified the fireball that engulfed the ship.

For the British, it was the most disastrous episode of the war as 51 soldiers and sailors lost their lives.

Weston somehow survived – despite suffering terrible burns to half his body.

His injuries were so severe though that he had to undergo numerous operations to repair the physical damage.

"In the eyes of the British public Weston became the embodiment of the never-say-die attitude as he refused to be beaten by his injuries, while also displaying a positive attitude which belied the gravity of his personal situation"

After rejecting the extensive plastic surgery which might have helped him return to something like his original appearance, Weston set out to give hope and inspiration to others in a similar situation.

Despite being a native of Wales, Weston became an adopted Liverpudlian, setting up the Weston Spirit charity in the city in November 1988.

The charity now has 11 centres at sites throughout the UK, all of which help thousands of youngsters lead fuller lives.

He remains a tireless worker for the Royal British Legion and the Royal Star and Garter Home. His charitable work earned him an OBE in the 1992 Queen's Birthday Honours.

CAPTAIN JOHNNY WALKER

CAPTAIN F J "Johnny" Walker was a naval hero in the mould of Drake or Nelson.

In short, he was the ace German U-boat killer, based in Bootle, who helped mastermind victory in the Battle of the Atlantic.

Winston Churchill had admitted that without triumph in this particular sea battle, Britain was in danger of losing the war.

> "Walker himself jubilantly reported to friends on Merseyside, where he was based for sailing from Gladstone Dock: 'They have given me a free hand and I'm going to show them what I can do'"

In the process, he became U-boat killer number one.

His name today is associated with two particular sloop ships, Starling and Stork.

Like other vessels in the same pack, they were affectionately known as "Walker's chicks" because all were named after birds.

At present, the last surviving example, Whimbrel, is berthed in Cairo and the subject of a £2m appeal to bring her back to the Mersey.

As one campaigner put it: "The price of victory has been paid with the lives of the men who died.

"Now it is our turn to repay the debt by bringing the last of Walker's ships back to its true home port."

Frederick John Walker took as his signature tune A Hunting We Will Go. Each time he returned to the "sheltering arms" of Gladstone Dock (a term he used in a letter dated March 6, 1942), the melody would ring out from the quayside.

Captain Walker's most dramatic gesture was to order the hoisting of the General Chase, which could be decoded as "every man for himself".

In the whole of British naval history, this had only happened twice before: it was used by Drake when he chased the Spanish Armada from the Channel, and by Nelson when he defeated Napoleon's fleet at the Battle of the Nile.

A statue of Johnny Walker stands proudly at the Pier Head, looking out to sea.

When Walker died on July 8, 1944, aged just 48, in the old Liverpool naval hospital, the death certificate recorded cerebral thrombosis.

But to his friends and his men there was no doubt that Captain Walker had burned himself out in the selfless service of his country – and more truthfully had died of exhaustion.

MUSIC

THE Beatles might have been four lads who shook the world - but Liverpool had started to shake, rattle and roll even before John, Paul, George and Ringo took centre stage.

Billy Fury, born plain old Ronald Wycherley in 1940, was known as the British Elvis - and he enjoyed staggering pop music success.

In fact, he had more hit singles in the '60s than the Beatles did, and spent an amazing 280 weeks in the charts.

Fury remains a legendary figure on the Liverpool music scene and beyond - and his legacy, and that of the Beatles, has certainly lived on in what the Guinness Book of Records dubbed the 'pop music capital of the world'.

Music seems to flow in the veins of Liverpool people - be it a sing-along at a family party; a night on the karaoke or a trip to one of the many live music venues that have thrived in the city over the years.

The 60s, of course, produced the Beatles - but also hugely successful acts like Gerry and the Pacemakers and The Searchers.

Some of the best known pop songs of the era - like You'll Never Walk Alone, How Do You Do It and Sweets for my Sweet - emerged from region, spreading the Merseybeat sound far and wide.

The Beatles, and the solo careers of the band members, went on of course to span decades - always ensuring a Liverpool twang or turn of phrase was hovering somewhere in the charts.

One of the most successful bands of the 70s was The Real Thing - the soul/disco group formed by the Amoo brothers that enjoyed massive hits with catchy tracks like You To Me Are Everything and Can't Get By Without You. Eddie Amoo had also played in The Chants, who appeared with the Beatles at the Cavern in 1962.

The late 70s and early 80s in Liverpool were dominated by the Eric's club scene. Teardrop Explodes, led by Julian Cope, became well-known with their hit Reward, and Echo and the Bunnymen formed in 1978. Ian Broudie was also involved in the Eric's scene, and went on to form hit-making pop band The Lightning Seeds.

The Icicle Works, Echo and the Bunnymen and the Mighty Wah! were all notable successes in the 80s - and frontmen Ian McNabb, Ian McCulloch

Anticlockwise from top:
Billy Fury, the Searchers,
two young punks on a night
out at Eric's nightclub,
Echo and the Bunnymen
and The Lightning Seeds

and Pete Wylie are all still gigging and recording, either with their bands or as solo artists. Over the water, OMD were also making waves. Other notable pop writers from the Wirral included Elvis Costello, later the Boo Radleys and cult heroes Half Man Half Biscuit.

Mainstream chart dominance came again in the form of Frankie Goes To Hollywood. Singer Holly Johnson led the band in a parade of smash hits like Relax and The Power of Love.

Dead or Alive also charted with You Spin Me Round (Like A Record) – a single that enjoyed a recent resurgence following Pete Burns appearance on Celebrity Big Brother.

The Farm were a Liverpool band who formed in the mid-80s – but their best known hits came at the time of the 'Madchester' scene, with songs like Groovy Train and the anthemic All Together Now. In the same era The La's came up with one of the most memorable songs of the time – if not ever. There She Goes is still to be found on playlists and jukeboxes around the globe.

In the 90s came the Britpop explosion, and Liverpool and its Lomax club certainly had its share of attention, hosting gigs by the likes of Oasis before they reached the height of their fame.

Homegrown talent also came to the fore. Cast was a band formed by John Power after he left The La's. They enjoyed several hits and John continues to write and play.

Clockwise from top: Elvis Costello, the Zutons on stage, the Coral, The original kine-up of Atomic Kitten and Space

Space was another high-profile band of its time, and tracks like Neighbourhood and Female of the Species are still often to be heard on TV.

Mel C of the Spice Girls continued to fly the pop flag for the region. Sporty Spice was often to be seen in her Liverpool FC kit, and was always keen to talk about her home at the Albert Dock.

Continuing the pop princess theme, Atomic Kitten – originally Kerry Katona, Natasha Hamilton and Liz McClarnon, later Jenny Frost – were phenomenally successful with several number one hits like Tide Is High and Whole Again.

In more recent times bands like The Coral from the Wirral, and The Zutons, have combined commercial success with credibility and helped to kick-start the live music scene.

This area has produced more than its fair share of musical talent – and with the likes of Candie Payne; the Sonic Hearts; Jade Gallagher; The Hot Melts and The Rascals on their way up, the Mersey Sound shows no sign at all of shutting up.

Liverpool Firsts

by Catherine Jones

LIVERPUDLIANS have always been inventive, creative and forward-thinking.
It is no surprise then that the city has led the way in so many fields -
health, education, welfare, transport, art and business.
So here are just a selection some of Liverpool's 'firsts'.

Health

- The world's first public health officer.
  Doctor William Duncan, a physician at Liverpool Infirmary, was appointed the world's first
  Medical Officer of Health on January 1, 1847.
  Duncan recognised that there was a clear link between housing conditions and the outbreak
  of diseases such as cholera, smallpox and typhus.
  He worked with borough engineer James Newlands to tackle the problems of poor housing
  and sanitary provision.

- The United Kingdom's first purpose-built ambulance service.
  A horse-drawn ambulance service was set up in 1884, based at the Northern Hospital.
  Two years later the Royal Southern Hospital was presented with a horse and ambulance and a
  fund was instituted for maintenance purposes.
  The horse and driver could be ready within a few minutes of being called.
  Liverpool also had the country's first motorised fire engine which was based at Hatton Garden
  Fire Station in 1902.

- Liverpool's School of Tropical Medicine became the world's first when it opened in 1898.
  It was successful in discovering that malaria could be passed on by the bite of the mosquito, and in
  1902 the School's Professor Ronald Ross became the first Briton to win a Nobel Prize for Medicine.

- In 1776 Matthew Dobson, of Harrington Street, a physician at the Liverpool Infirmary between
  1770 and 1780, discovered the link between sugar and diabetes.
  By evaporating the urine of a diabetic patient, Dobson was the first to prove the presence of
  sugar in urine. He also discovered the excess of sugar in blood.

- In 1896 Professor Oliver Lodge of Liverpool University used x-ray photography to take an image
  of a bullet which was in a boy's wrist.
  It was the first time an x-ray had been used for surgical purposes in the country.

- Liverpool established Britain's first children's hospital, Alder Hey, as early as 1848 - four years
  before Great Ormond Street Hospital in London was opened.

- The first training of district nurses.
  In 1862, the Liverpool Training School and Home for Nurses was established. The district nursing
  system was implemented in Liverpool and later spread throughout the country.

Welfare

- The first public wash-house in the country.
  In 1842, Britain's first public wash-house was opened in Frederick Street, instigated by the work of Kitty Wilkinson and her husband Tom during the cholera epidemic.

- The world's first Age Concern branch.
  What is now an international movement had its birth in the city in 1928 when a welfare body was set up by social campaigners, including pioneering MP Eleanor Rathbone.
  Almost 80 years after the Liverpool Personal Service Society created its Old People's Welfare sub-committee, the charity has more than 470 branches, including some in Spain, the Ukraine, Barbados and New Zealand.

- Britain's first charity to prevent cruelty to children.
  On a trip to American in 1881, Liverpool banker Thomas Agnew visited the New York Society for the Prevention of Cruelty to Children.
  Has was so impressed that on his return he set up a similar venture in Liverpool in 1883, the Liverpool Society for the Prevention of Cruelty to Children.
  It was the forerunner of the NSPCC.

- The first animal welfare society in the UK was begun in Liverpool in 1809.

Transport

- Speke airport was the first provincial airport in the country when it officially opened in 1933.

- The first intercity railway service.
  When it opened in 1830, the Liverpool and Manchester Railway became the first in the world to run locomotives. It was also the scene of the world's first passenger fatality when William Huskisson was run over by Stephenson's Rocket in September 1830.
  Crown Street opened as the world's first public railway station on September 15, 1830, as the Liverpool passenger terminus of the railway.

- The world's first overhead electric railway, which became known as the Dockers Umbrella, was opened by the Marquis of Salisbury in February 1893.

- Liverpool was the first port in the world to install a radar-controlled ferry system and port radar, in 1948. The port radar was set up in Gladstone Dock and could monitor all shipping in the river and approaching channels.

- Britain's first steamroller was bought by the Liverpool Corporation in 1867. It weighed 30 tons and was built by Thomas Aveling of Rochester.

There have been many famous Scousers who are known for their distinctive work covering all aspects of life.
Some were born here and others are 'adopted' but they have all left their mark.
They have a common bond: they inspired people with their work. Some with their paintings and some with their sculptures.
Some produced photographic images, too, recording Scouse lives.
There is the power of poetry from the war poets to the best-selling Mersey Sound anthology. There are novels - fact and fiction - and there's the playwrights who create a world of escapism.
We have top broadcasters and musicians who continue to fly the flag, entertaining with their Scouse wit.
And there's the buildings and world famous architecture from the majestic to the innovative.
They are all individuals influenced by Liverpool whose works speak volumes to the world.

ROBERT TRESSELL
WILFRED OWEN
GILES GILBERT SCOTT
ARTHUR DOOLEY
E CHAMBRE HARDMAN
ADRIAN HENRI
SHIRLEY HUGHES
BRIAN JACQUES
WILLY RUSSELL
ROGER MCGOUGH

ARTISTS

ROBERT TRESSELL

"By 1945 Tressell was being hailed as one of the architects of Labour's landslide election success"

IN a churchyard at the rear of Walton jail lies the grave of a man whose writing helped alter the political landscape long after his death. Robert Tressell died in poverty in 1911 and was buried in a mass grave along with 12 other paupers.

But by 1945 Tressell, whose real surname was Noonan, was being hailed as one of the architects of Labour's landslide election success.

The reason was simple – the book he had written, The Ragged Trousered Philanthropists, a 1,600 page hand-written manuscript, had become the bible of the Left.

His account of how capitalism operates in the workplace is a socialist critique par excellence and remains as relevant today as it did when it was first written.

Tressell was actually born in Dublin in 1870 and was the youngest of five children who grew up in a wealthy household by the standards of that time.

He spent time in Cape Town and Johannesburg, where he found work as a decorator and it was while in South Africa that his interest in trade unionism and socialism was first displayed.

In 1901 Tressell left South Africa with his wife and family and came to England. Six years later he had a row with his employer about taking too much time over a job, and walked out. During 1908-9 Noonan remained politically active, but his health got worse. "Wun Lung", as he called himself, lost time at work, and the workhouse beckoned.

Even so, politics remained important. He was no public orator, but he could win close-quarter arguments on the bench and at work, against all-comers.

He needed extra income and The Ragged Trousered Philanthropists was completed by 1910. Noonan signed it "Robert Tressell", for fear of reprisals, but he failed to find a publisher.

That August he came to Liverpool, supposedly to make arrangements to emigrate to Canada.

Initially, he found lodgings in Erskine Street. But in November he was admitted to the Royal Liverpool Infirmary and on February 3, 1911, he had died of phthisis pulmonalis – a wasting of the lungs associated with tuberculosis – and cardiac failure.

Almost a century later, Robert Tressell's legacy still lives on.

WILFRED OWEN

"His poems, including Anthem For Doomed Youth, Futility and Dulce et Decorum Est, have marked him out as one of the great war poets"

REGARDED by many as the greatest of all war poets, Wilfred Owen spent his formative years in Birkenhead, attending Birkenhead Institute, before moving with his family to Shrewsbury when he was 14.

His early poems were largely romantic and imitative. Then came the war.

Lieutenant Owen was awarded the Military Cross for gallantry, but died on the banks of the Oise-Sambre Canal in France just a week before the end of the Great War.

Prior to his demise he had already stated his purpose: "My subject is war and the pity of war. The poetry is in the pity".

His poems, including Anthem For Doomed Youth, Futility and Dulce et Decorum Est, have marked him out as one of the great war poets.

He told of the fear, pain and mental anguish of the trenches and how it haunted him at a time when many people were ignorant of the true horrors of warfare.

Owen's poetry cut through much of the propaganda which fired these misconceptions and provided a counterbalance to the overtly patriotic work of fellow poet Rupert Brooke.

The bulk of Owen's work was written in Craiglockhart hospital, Scotland, in 1917 while suffering from shell-shock. It was while he was there that he met Siegfried Sassoon, already an established poet.

In July 1918, Owen returned to active service in France, although he might have stayed on home-duty indefinitely.

His decision was almost wholly the result of Sassoon's being sent back to England. Sassoon, who had been shot in the head in a so-called friendly fire incident, was put on sick-leave for the remaining duration of the war.

Owen saw it as his patriotic duty to take Sassoon's place at the front, that the horrific realities of the war might continue to be told.

Sassoon was violently opposed to the idea of Owen's returning to the trenches, threatening to "stab [him] in the leg" if he tried it. Aware of his attitude, Owen did not inform him of his action until he was once again in France.

Owen was killed in action at the Sambre-Oise Canal just a week before the war ended and news of his death reached his family on Armistice Day.

GILES GILBERT SCOTT

"Scott himself was present at the topping out ceremony for the tower, but never lived to see his completed dream"

GILES Gilbert Scott was only 22 when he won the design competition for Liverpool's Anglican Cathedral.

The project occupied him, on and off, for well over half a century until his death, aged 79, in 1960.

John Betjeman called the cathedral "one of the great buildings of the world," which indeed it is. St Paul's, London, would fit inside Liverpool Cathedral, surpassed in size only by St Peter's in Rome and the cathedrals of Seville and Milan.

One of Scott's other great designs - a dot by comparison - is the British red telephone box, derided as a blot on the landscape when it first appeared in 1924, but later acknowledged as one of the country's distinctive treasures.

Today, one of those boxes stands inside Liverpool Cathedral, as testimony to the creative genius of a man who also designed Battersea Power Station and Waterloo Bridge, and who was put in charge of the rebuilding of the Houses of Parliament after wartime bomb damage.

Scott's original design for Liverpool Cathedral showed two west end towers (as with Westminster Abbey or Notre Dame Paris). The final plan, with the massive 331ft central tower, emerged after several modifications. However, Scott's vision for a massive cave-like structure, not too light, endured, despite the early interference of senior architects such as G.F. Bodley, whose much fussier style is seen as a major influence of the cathedral's Lady Chapel, the first part of the building to be brought into use.

The main cathedral was consecrated in 1924 (after 20 years' building) and the enormous enterprise only completed in 1978.

Scott himself was present at the topping out ceremony for the tower, but never lived to see his completed dream.

The cathedral features the highest Gothic-style arches ever constructed, and the highest and heaviest peal of bells in the world. The 10,000-pipe organ set another global record.

Scott is buried outside the western entrance – a Roman Catholic who produced the worldwide Anglican church's greatest edifice.

But what a legacy, famously described thus by poet laureate Betjeman: "Suddenly one realises, that the greatest art of architecture, that lifts one up and turns one into a king, is the art of enclosing space."

ARTHUR DOOLEY

ARTHUR Dooley famously described himself as the chairman of a limited company.

For someone who was once a self-confessed anarchist, it sounded somewhat conventional, especially as his chosen work outfit was a dirty bobble-hat and overalls.

The man who used to mould Dunlop tyres for a living, moulded a new career in art, providing important, mainly religiously inspired, sculptures for cathedrals, churches and public spaces.

Among his many pieces was a homage to the victims of Hillsborough.

At 60 he declared: "An artist of my age has only just got started. You are only just maturing."

Arthur enjoyed what he called "the only real type of industrial sponsorship in Britain."

Liverpool Exhaust Supplies gave him gallery space and an office. He then drew a salary and sold his work. When it came to office paperwork, he sat behind a desk surrounded by computer software and proudly wore the blazer and tie of the Irish Guards, in whose ranks he had served for nine years.

Dooley, who died in 1994, supported the workers' takeover of the Fisher Bendix plant, and campaigned for the revival of the south docks and the demolition of the tower blocks, in the days when it was not fashionable to criticise planners.

He later stood for the city council, in Everton, as an independent Save Our City candidate.

He saw Liverpool as the prototype creative centre two decades before anyone had heard of Capital of Culture. He believed sculpture, painting and writing could perpetuate the success which pop music had begun.

When he gained television celebrity, including being chosen as the subject of This Is Your Life, Arthur Dooley relished the idea of having bypassed normal qualifications and certificates and would tell academic snobs: "My degrees are in the work I have done."

That output was often roughly hewn, and described by one leading critic as being "sort of Henry Moorish, but with a personal, distinctive and angular style." The philosophy remained the same: "Everyone has got eyes and hands and a sense of touch, which is why I will always say that anyone can be an artist."

At 60 he declared: "An artist of my age has only just got started. You are only just maturing"

E CHAMBRE HARDMAN

E CHAMBRE Hardman, Liverpool-based photographer extraordinaire, will forever be remembered for his astounding image Birth of the Ark Royal.

This was a picture of the newly-built giant gleaming aircraft carrier on the slipway at Cammell Laird, seen over the rooftops of Birkenhead terraced houses.

Also forever etched into the minds of disciples of this particular lensman is a picture of the winter cityscape, taken from the steps of Liverpool Museum.

The irony, of course, is that Chambre Hardman's express fortes were portraits – often of the famous – as well as country landscapes and mountains.

During a career spanning three generations, he built up a vast collection of thousands of indexed monochrome negatives, all stored in the house in Rodney Street he shared with his photographer wife Margaret, who had been his studio assistant since she was a teenager.

Their home has recently become a museum to the art E Chambre Hardman promoted, ever since his early days as a member of London's exclusive art salon set, when he got to know Yousef Karsh, the great portrait photographer, and Cecil Beaton.

Rather than the ultra-realism favoured by photographers such as Henri Cartier-Bresson and Donald McCullin, Hardman preferred what he termed "treatment and craft" over subject. A soft-focus impressionist approach gave a gentle warm tone, providing the edge for long-term viewing, he believed.

One of the things learned from Karsh – a valuable tip once he had set up as a portrait photographer in Bold Street with former Indian Army pal Kenneth Burrell – was that people were frightened by cameras with huge black focussing hoods.

Karsh himself had a golden hood, while Chambre Hardman chose emerald green (could this have been in tribute to his Irish upbringing)?

The Rodney Street house is not only fascinating for its direct links with photography, but also because it epitomises an era of lifestyle.

The time capsule still has the Hardmans' hats hanging on hooks, and the tinned contents of the kitchen cupboards remain undisturbed.

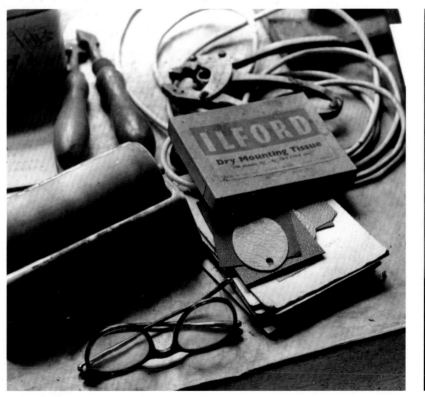

"Adrian Henri returned to Liverpool, never again to leave. In 1965, he had turned his back on the trendier London scene, saying there was nowhere else he preferred to be"

ADRIAN HENRI

ADRIAN Henri, poet, painter, playwright and bon viveur: Liverpool's single most enduring everyman as artist up to the time of his death, aged 68, in December 2000, on the eve of which he was granted the freedom of Liverpool, in company with fellow scribes Roger McGough and Brian Patten.

The Mersey Sound – their joint compilation of self-penned rhyme – became the biggest selling poetry anthology of all time.

No wonder Mo Mowlam suggested that Adrian should be poet laureate.

He used to joke that he thought this was tough on Tennyson, who came from an era when poetry was taken seriously and rated as being of national importance.

But the Liverpool trio always argued that they had helped restore the prestige of poetry.

As Adrian Henri said: "By playing with pop music, television and the whole business of image, we showed how poetry had to reach people, and not just in a few slim volumes."

Born in Birkenhead, the grandson of a seaman from Mauritius, Henri studied fine art in Newcastle and went on to teach in Preston, Manchester and Liverpool.

He was also proud of his time as a fairground worker, "a world where the smell of engine oil mixes with that of fried onions – terrific training for life."

Adrian Henri returned to Liverpool, never again to leave, in 1965.

Unlike McGough and Patten, he had turned his back on the trendier London scene, saying there was nowhere else he preferred to be.

In 1972, he was a major prizewinner in the Liverpool John Moores Exhibition, and later became president of the Merseyside Arts Association and the Liverpool Academy of Arts, as well as being awarded honorary degrees by Liverpool University and Liverpool John Moores University.

He counted among his many friends and work associates John Lennon, George Melly, Allen Ginsberg and Willy Russell.

The Liverpool Scene was more than a mere description of the city's cultural revolution during Adrian Henri's heyday.

It was in fact a wide-ranging poetry and music band which also included Andy Roberts, Mike Evans, Mike Hart and Brian Dodson.

Four LPs were issued, all heavily featuring Henri's poetry, and the first produced by John Peel.

Other great moments included a 1969 tour with Led Zeppelin.

"Her distinctive graphic style is a combination of pen and ink, watercolour and gouache. Her sketchbook drawings are done very quickly – "almost at the speed of seeing"– and used as a visual and memory reference for storyboards and finished illustration"

SHIRLEY HUGHES

SHIRLEY Hughes is one the world's best loved children's authors and illustrators.

For almost 40 years, her picture stories featuring characters such as Alfie and Dogger have thrilled children and adults, with their tales of growing-up and everyday discovery.

Born and raised in West Kirby, Shirley, 78, is the daughter of local businessman TJ Hughes who founded the renowned store. Her wartime childhood was spent drawing, playing and making up stories and games with her two sisters. Encouraged and inspired by visits to the Walker Art Gallery, she developed a lifelong interest painting and illustration.

After a year at Liverpool Art School studying costume design, Shirley moved on to the Ruskin School of Drawing & Fine Art in Oxford. It was there she began to always carry a sketchbook with her, drawing figures from her daily life. She soon settled in Notting Hill, London and concentrated on book illustration, initially for other authors.

Her distinctive graphic style is a combination of pen and ink, watercolour and gouache. Her sketchbook drawings from are done very quickly, "almost at the speed of seeing", and used as a visual and memory reference for storyboards and finished illustration.

The characters in Shirley's books, including Alfie, Annie Rose, Lucy and Tom are purely fictional, an imaginary combination of the children she has observed over the years, whether in parks and play areas or in her own family. She builds her stories around the everyday dramas that impact upon a child's world, such as a new pair of Wellington boots or a lost toy – such experiences that may seem minor to adults but are important to little ones.

Shirley holds a number of awards, including the Kate Greenaway Medal (1977) for Dogger Eleanor, the Farjeon Award for services to children's literature (1984) and an OBE for services to children's literature (1998).

She is married and has three grown-up children and seven grandchildren. Her daughter, Clara Vulliamy, is herself a picture book creator. "We don't comment on each other's work too much," laughs Clara. "Although occasionally I'll ask for an opinion and, very sparingly, she'll make some suggestions... there's nobody's respect I'd rather have. As an illustrator, she is second to none."

BRIAN JACQUES

BRIAN Jacques was born into a Liverpool Irish family on the eve of World War II and grew up near the docks.

He began reading at an early age and was specially keen on adventure stories by writers such as Daniel Defoe, Sir Henry Rider Haggard, Robert Louis Stevenson and Edgar Rice Burroughs. From the age of ten, Brian attended St John's School where one of his teachers, Austin Thomas, introduced him to poetry and Greek literature. "Because of him," remembers Brian, "I saved seven shillings and sixpence to buy The Iliad and The Odyssey at this dusty used bookshop."

After leaving school at 15, Brian set out to find real-life adventure as a merchant seaman. He travelled to many exotic places, but in the 1960s and with the Beatles causing a worldwide sensation, Liverpool was the place to be. Brian, his two brothers and three mates formed a folksinging group called The Liverpool Fisherman. Brian has also backed Roger McGough's band The Scaffold. He has life membership of The Cavern nightclub.

Brian, 66, wrote his first book, Redwall, for the children at the Royal Wavertree School for the Blind. He first came into contact with the children through delivering their milk.

"I didn't have a typewriter and I was skint, so I went and bought dozens of 30p pads and sat up all night," he says.

It was immediately snapped up by a publisher, and there are over seven million copies of the 14 Redwall books in print.

He continues to visit the children at the school for the blind and has set up a literary award for children's writing in Merseyside.

Brian has two grown sons who live close by in Liverpool. He often finds inspiration for his novels when taking his west highland terrier Teddy out for a walk in Stanley Park. He writes in his garden under an umbrella on a manual typewriter.

He is proud of his Liverpool roots: "I was born and bred in Liverpool and that's the place I'll die. I have never considered myself patriotic English but I'm a patriotic Scouser."

"Brian, 66, wrote his first book, Redwall, for the children at the Royal Wavertree School for the Blind. He first came into contact with the children through delivering their milk"

WILLY RUSSELL

WILLY Russell is the creator of world famous plays and films such as Educating Rita, Shirley Valentine and the musical Blood Brothers.

Born in Whiston in 1947 he left school with one O-level in English and was a hairdresser for six years.

He held various other jobs, including stacking stockings in the Bear Brand warehouse and cleaning girders in the Ford car factory at Halewood.

He originally began writing as a songwriter in the folk idiom in the early 60s, performing at local folk clubs playing in a semi-pro capacity on the same kind of circuit where Billy Connolly and Barbara Dickson played.

He also had his own group The Kirkby Town 3.

At 20 he decided to complete his education, went to college and became a schoolteacher in Toxteth.

Willy married Annie and became more interested in drama.

He was inspired to be a serious writer when he saw a production of John McGrath's Unruly Elements at Liverpool's Everyman Theatre in 1971.

His first play, Keep Your Eyes Down, was produced that year, but he made his name with John, Paul, George, Ringo … and Bert, a hit musical commissioned by the Everyman about the Beatles.

Two of his best-known plays have female protagonists, Educating Rita and Shirley Valentine.

Willy Russell's other huge theatrical success has been Blood Brothers about twins separated at birth and brought up in completely different environments.

It continues to enjoy a very long run in London's West End and played a two-year run on Broadway. The British touring version continues to play to packed houses across the world.

Willy has also enjoyed success with the Words on The Run troupe comprising the late Adrian Henri, Roger McGough, Brian Patten and Andy Roberts.

He released his first CD Hoovering the Moon in 2003 and went on a sell-out UK tour called In Other Words & Singing Playwrights with writer Tim Firth.

Willy continues to live in his home city and is working on a wide range of projects including TV and film.

"He was inspired to be a serious writer when he saw a production of John McGrath's Unruly Elements at Liverpool's Everyman Theatre in 1971"

ROGER MCGOUGH

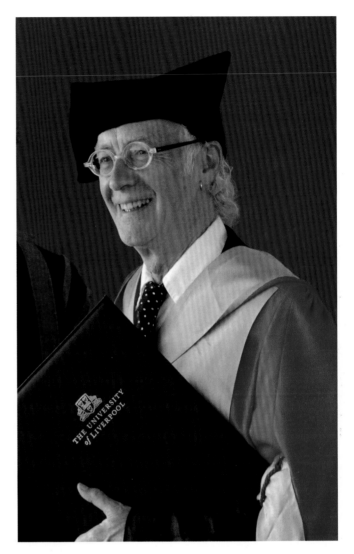

"He was later responsible for much of the humorous dialogue in the Beatles' animated film Yellow Submarine, although he did not receive an on-screen credit"

POET, singer and broadcaster Roger McGough was born in Litherland and educated at the University of Hull at a time when the chief librarian there was Philip Larkin.

Roger returned to Merseyside in the early 1960s and met up with Mike McGear and John Gorman, both talented entertainers; together they formed the Scaffold, reaching No 1 number one in the UK singles chart in 1968 with their version of Lily The Pink and having a successful TV career with Score With The Scaffold.

He was later responsible for much of the humorous dialogue in the Beatles' animated film Yellow Submarine, although he did not receive an on-screen credit. He is particularly proud of this achievement in a long and varied literary career.

McGough, with Adrian Henri and Brian Patten, published two best-selling volumes of verse entitled The Mersey Sound.

McGough won acclaim as one of the Mersey Poets of the 1960s and 70s, along with his great pal Henri.

In the multi-varied troupe GRIMMS he worked on numerous books, broadcasts and gigs. In 1978 McGough appeared in All You Need Is Cash, detailing the career of the spoof Beatles band the Rutles.

One of mould-breaker McGough's more unusual compositions was created in 1981, when he co-wrote an "electronic poem" for radio called Now Press Return. Again he was and is always making poetry accessible to everyone of all ages.

McGough won a Cholmondeley Award in 1999, and was awarded the CBE in June 2004.

He holds an honorary MA from Nene College of Further Education, and was awarded an Honorary Degree from Roehampton University in 2006.

He was Fellow of Poetry at the University of Loughborough (1973-5) and Honorary Professor at Thames Valley University (1993). His has written his autobiography called Said And Done which explores his fame and his life from Liverpool to international success.

Roger was honoured with the Freedom of the City of Liverpool along with his beloved Mersey Poets.

He currently hosts BBC Radio's most popular arts programme, Poetry Please.

McGough has been called "the patron saint of poetry" by Carol Ann Duffy and 'Liverpool's own Poet Laureate' by the Liverpool ECHO.

SILVER SCREEN

LIVERPOOL could one day be the UK's film capital such is our movie reputation, from writers to directors, producers to stars and of course our fantastic locations.

Forget London and Hollywood – why can't we have our own sign on a hill saying Scousewood?

Liverpool and movies are old friends. Film producers love coming to the city just as TV crews are now seen everywhere. Writers want their work filmed here, from Alan Bleasdale and Jimmy McGovern to Frank Cottrell Boyce. Liverpool is a much sought-after supporting star.

Here's some movies with that Liverpool connection:

Gumshoe (1971)
A detective film starring Albert Finney as a bingo caller who loved the work of Humphrey Bogart. Acting out his fantasy he inadvertently stumbled across a real life murder mystery. Set against a Liverpool backdrop, this Scouse sleuth spoof was directed by Stephen Frears.

The Magnet (1950)
An Ealing Comedy about a schoolboy who swindles another lad out of his prized magnet. And he ends up poles apart and feted as a local hero but guilt rears its head. It brought together director Charles Frend with Ealing stalwart writer TEB Clarke who with Passport to Pimlico and the Lavender Hill Mob scripted some of post war Britain's most enduring and inventive comedies.

Dancin' Thru' The Dark (1989)
Willy Russell's screen adaptation of his stage play Stags and Hens boasted another witty script. Real people and not stereotypes.

A bride to be finds herself celebrating her hen night at the same place as her impending hubby's stag do.

Matters are thrown into more disarray when her ex appears on the scene.

Ferry Cross The Mersey (1965)
A UK film with Brian Epstein at the helm featuring Gerry and The Pacemakers, The Fourmost, The Black Knights, Cilla Black, Earl Royce and the Olympics and The Blackwells.

With 14 songs, Liverpool location footage included: Birkenhead Market, Locarno Ballroom, Adelphi Hotel, the Pier Head, the Mersey Tunnel and, of course, the world famous Cavern Club. A real fight broke out at the Locarno Ballroom and was kept in the film. Another scene in Frank Hessy's music store featured hundreds of real fans pushed up against the windows while Gerry and the Pacemakers played inside.

OTHER notable films made in and around here include:
Hilary and Jackie and Grow Your Own (2007) written by Frank Cottrell Boyce

The Waterfront (Richard Burton) 1950

Violent Playground (1958, filmed amid the Liverpool tenements starring Stanley baker)

These Dangerous Years (1957) starring Dingle's Frankie Vaughan

Distant Voices, Still Lives (Terence Davies)

No Surrender (Alan Bleasdale)

Letter to Brezhnev (1985) starring Margi Clarke and written by brother Frank and directed by Chris Bernard

Liam and Priest (Jimmy McGovern) and John Lennon In his Life (Colin McKeown)

51st State (2000)

Dead Man's Cards (2006)

The Parole Officer (Steve Coogan 2006)

Across the Universe, a romance using Beatle songs (2006)

Hunt For Red October (starring Sean Connery)

Young Sherlock Holmes (Spielberg)

In the Name of the Father (Pete Postlethwaite)

Let Him Have It (Mark McGann)

Lazy Bones (Lee Evans)

Yentl (produced by and starring Barbra Streisand)

SCOUSERS

by
Peter
Grant

Gerry and the Pacemakers filming Ferry Cross The Mersey and, inset, the crew of Neil Fitzmaurice movie Going Off Big Time

MERSEYSIDE MOVIE MAGIC

 Scouser Arthur Askey made a string of box office smashes now released on DVD.

 Rita Tushingham in A Taste of Honey.

Ken Dodd appeared in Kenneth Branagh's film version of Hamlet.

Paul Barber starred in hit movies The Full Monty and Dead Man's Cards.

The Beatles in Help and Hard Day's Night and Let It Be with a cameo appearance in Yellow Submarine (written by Roger McGough).

The Beatles had many solo projects. Lennon in How I won the War and his own hit film Imagine; Ringo in the Magic Christian and Caveman; George in the Concert for Bangladesh – he went on to save Monty Python's Life of Brian and make a success of his own company Handmade films. Paul produced Give My Regards to Broad Street and appeared as himself in Eat the Rich.

Bill Kenwright has his own successful film arm, making Don't Go Breaking My Heart starring Jenny Seagrove and Anthony 'ER Edwards'

Paul McGann starred in cult classic Withnail and I with Richard E. Grant.

Neil Fitzmaurice, star and co-writer on Phoenix Nights, created film Going Off Big Style.

And who can forget movie legend Rex Harrison – Oscar winning star of My Fair Lady, The Rake's Progress and Cleopatra – born in our very own Huyton.

SPORTING SCOUSERS

By Alan Jewell

WHEN it comes to a shared social interest, football dominates the hearts and minds of this city like little else, even music.

However, it would be erroneous to categorise Liverpool as a one-sport city, even if, at times, the obsession feels suffocating.

Merseyside is home to the Grand National that can now surely claim to be the biggest annual one-off sporting event in Great Britain.

The spruce fences of Aintree present a captivating spectacle. More than any other, this horse race appears to guarantee drama, providing a slew of wonderful stories as heroes and heroines appear from the most unlikely sources.

Three-times winner Red Rum (the most famous horse of all) was trained locally, at Donald 'Ginger' McCain's Birkdale stables, and was frequently allowed a canter on Southport sands.

When 'Rummy' went to that great stable in the sky in 1995, he was buried at the winning post.

> "The National, first run in its present form in 1839, has long been the biggest betting day of the year, while the three-day festival continues to grow in popularity"

The expansion and modernisation of Aintree has seen crowds rise in recent years. It's a far cry from the 1970s and early '80s when attendances plummeted and a series of 'final' Grand Nationals were run.

In 1975 racecourse owner Bill Davies tripled admission prices and the entire meeting could only muster 40,000 people: as losses mounted, plans were put in place to move the race to Doncaster.

A public appeal helped the Jockey Club purchase the course from Davies in 1983 and it's grown ever stronger since. By 2005 National day alone drew 70,850.

It was another form of horsepower that attracted what is believed to be the largest crowd recorded at a single-day sporting event on Merseyside. In the early 1950s the then owner of Aintree, Mirabel Topham, decided to maximise revenue by building a three-mile motor racing circuit within the grounds. Featuring corners named 'Becher's bend', 'Tatts corner' and 'Melling crossing', it opened in 1954 and first staged the British Grand Prix the following year, when British icon Stirling Moss, driving a Mercedes, just held off the challenge of team-mate and world champion Juan Manuel Fangio to win by a fifth of a second.

This feat was surpassed two years later on a weekend when the talk of the nation was the execution of Ruth Ellis, who was hanged for murdering her lover, David Blakely – a racing driver. As in 1955, between 100,000 and 150,000 people were estimated to be there. Those present in '57 ignored a bus and coach strike to witness Moss share driving duties with Tony Brooks to win in a Vanwall. It was the first time a British driver-car combination had won a Grand Prix.

Aintree, never popular with motor racing's hoi polloi, hosted its final British GP in 1962, though club races continued in 2007.

Boxing has traditionally been a strong thread in the sporting fabric of Liverpool. From Nel Tarleton, a featherweight who fought 145 times in a 20-year career, to modern day world champion Derry Matthews, heroes of the ring have made a particular impact.

Kirkby-born light-heavyweight world champion John Conteh was one of Britain's foremost sportsmen of the 1970s, and had his final fight at the famed Liverpool Stadium in 1980. The only purpose-built boxing venue in the country, it opened in 1932 and was demolished in 1987. Despite the stadium's sad demise, scouse boxers continued to prosper and the 1990s saw Paul Hodkinson and Shea Neary claim world title belts. Neary thrillingly stopped fellow Liverpudlian Andy Holligan in a 1998 fight held in Stanley Park, which was memorably dubbed 'The nark in the park'.

Amateur boxing is thriving in Liverpool and the city hosts the 2008 European Amateur Championships at the new indoor arena at the Kings Dock. While significant professional bouts have traditionally taken place elsewhere, often in Manchester, the creation of the arena offers a stage for significant fights, in the same way that bigger musical acts are anticipated to be headed in this direction.

Golf is another sport in rude health on Merseyside. The 2006 Open Championship was staged at the Royal Liverpool course in Hoylake, its first visit to this challenging links in 39 years.

A total of 230,000 people watched Tiger Woods's emotional victory, weeks after the death of his father and mentor, Earl. It was a record attendance for an Open in England and the vocal nature of the galleries found favour amongst the players, who were not accustomed to hearing shouts of encouragement along the lines of "Come on, Tiger, lad." Thomas Bjorn, one of Europe's leading golfers, remarked afterwards: "It is the people who have made this week and it has felt very much like a people's Open as the spectators have been magnificent." The tournament is expected to return to Hoylake within ten years but it will be back on Merseyside much sooner than that: the 2008 staging at Royal Birkdale, near Southport, neatly coinciding with the Capital of Culture year.

The region is also home to the 2007 rugby league World Club champions, St Helens, although whether they would appreciate being described as 'scousers' is doubtful. Saints, the dominant club in the Super League era, achieved a clean sweep of domestic honours in 2006 and were voted the BBC's team of the year. One of their most promising players is James Graham, from Maghull, who became the first Liverpool-born man to captain Saints and represent Great Britain during that successful season.

Rugby Union is more of a fringe sport, even if the Liverpool club (now known as Liverpool St Helens) were formed as long ago as 1858. Players from this area have represented England with distinction over the years, notably Mike Slemen (later a PE teacher at Merchant Taylors school in Crosby), Austin Healey and Matt Dawson, a World Cup winner in 2003. Dawson went on to become a team captain on 'A Question of Sport', where one of his predecessors was John Parrott, snooker's world champion in 1991.

Olympic pentathlon gold medallist Mary Peters, whose greatest moment came at the Munich games of 1972, was born in Halewood but moved to Ballymena, Northern Ireland, aged 11. More recently, Steve Smith was a fine competitor in the high jump, medalling at the World Athletics Championships and 1996 Olympics before a ruptured Achilles tendon brought a premature end to his career.

Wirral cyclist Chris Boardman caused a stir at the 1992 Barcelona games by winning gold in the 4000 metre individual pursuit aboard a striking carbon-fibre bicycle made by Lotus, the sports car manufacturer. He showed there was much more to him than this machine by going on to break the one-hour world record three times and achieve success in the Tour de France.

It's a sign of the times that a mention of Cricket in Liverpool is likely to bring to mind the image of an orange-tinted young woman tottering down Mathew Street as she struggles with the weight of her shopping bags. It wasn't ever thus.

"The Liverpool Cricket Club in Aigburth, which hosts a Lancashire first-class match more summers than not, was celebrating its 200th anniversary in 2007"

The undisputed greatest cricketer of all time, Sir Donald Bradman, appeared there for the Australian tourists in 1930, while a few years earlier Everton footballers Jack Sharp and Harry Makepeace also represented England in Tests. Few scouse cricketers have played to a high level but all-rounder Tom Smith, born on Boxing Day, 1985, had an impressive debut season for Lancashire in 2006 and was part of the England Academy squad in the winter of '06/'07.

"Another sporting occasion that is growing in popularity is the Liverpool International Tennis Tournament, which takes place in June at Calderstones Park. It features an attractive mix of retired 'legends' and young prospects"

In the pool, Stephen Parry achieved a bronze in the 200 metres butterfly at the 2004 Athens games, while there are high hopes for teenager Francesca Halsall, who is from Southport and trains at Everton Park Sports Centre. In 2006 she won two silver medals at the Commonwealth Games and a gold at the European Championships.

Another young woman who is turning potential into achievement is gymnast Beth Tweddle. By the age of 21 she was the most decorated British gymnast of all time: already a Commonwealth and European Champion, in 2006 she won gold in the uneven bars discipline at the World Championships, which helped her earn third place in the vote for the BBC's Sports Personality of the year. Although born in Bunbury, Cheshire, she has been adopted as a scouser, having trained at the City of Liverpool Gymnastics Club since she was a young girl, while going on to study at John Moores University.

John Moores himself, the founder of the Littlewoods empire, set up the first football pools in 1923. Sport and gambling has always gone together in Liverpool, as the Grand National demonstrates.

After all, its first winner was a horse named Lottery.

And as this recollection of Sporting Scousers comes to an end here's bit of extra time – who can forget... Mel C Sporty Spice...?

Projections of the past at St George's Hall

SCOUSE WIT

BILLY BE
PAUL McCAR
ALLAN WILLIAMS
PETE PRICE CARM
LORD MAYOR JO,
STAN BOARDMAN ,
BILLY BENNETT ALAN
BESSIE BRADDOCK BII
PAUL McCARTNEY ALL
PETE PRICE CARMEL HE
LORD MAYOR JOAN LAI
STAN BOARDMAN ARTH
BILLY BENNETT ALAN BLE/
BESSIE BRADDOCK BILLY
PAUL McCARTNEY ALLA
PETE PRICE CARMEL HEL
LORD MAYOR JOAN LANG
STAN BOARDMAN ARTHUR .
BILLY BENNETT ALAN BLEASD,
BESSIE BRADDOCK BILLY BUTLI
PAUL McCARTNEY ALLAN WII
PETE PRICE CARMEL HEF
LORD MAYOR JOAN LAI
STAN BOARDMAN AI'
BILLY BENNETT ALAN B
BESSIE BRADDOCK BI
PAUL McCARTNEY A
PETE PRICE CARMEL
LORD MAYOR JOAN
STAN BOARDMAN
F

"I was born here and have been through the good times and bad times. I was here when nobody had any money and have seen how the city has re-built itself.

Liverpool people are special because you can knock them down but they will always get straight back up. They are resilient and will always fight back from what people say." Us Liverpool people have a different sense of humour, one which I will never see anywhere else."

2007 Lord Mayor Joan Lang

"I love the place and I love the people, their warmth and their depth of feeling."

John Carmel Heenan
former Archbishop of Liverpool
and Archbishop of Westminster

"I've never understood how people can give us stick on what they see in a fictional programme like Brookside. The thing I love most about Liverpool is the sense of humour and the music. Liverpool people are so quick witted and no-one else can compete with that."

Billy Butler
BBC Radio Merseyside Presenter

AND WISDOM

"Liverpool keeps my feet on the ground.
I am a Scruff from Speke."

Paul McCartney

"Liverpool is my life blood.
It has given me an incredible career and its people have given me the most joy. Without Liverpool my life would be very empty.
I look though my lounge window every day and see the greatest waterfront in the world. I wake up with that view every morning and go to bed with it every night.
Sat in the Radio City tower, I look out over the rooftops and seeing the sun set over the Mersey cannot be beaten."

Pete Price
broadcaster

"I represent the common people – and there's no one more common than me."

Billy Bennett
Scouse Music Hall comedian who dressed in a red sash and carpet slippers on stage

"Being a Scouser means you are a survivor. You put up with all kinds of setbacks and laugh in the face of adversity. It's a great mechanism to say 'yeah, well tomorrow's another day.' You get on with it and that's why I think we have produced so many great comics because we have an in-built ability to use humour in a positive way."

Stan Boardman
Comedian

"They put a plaque on the wall of the house where I was born. It says, 'condemned.'"

The late great **Arthur Askey** on a visit back to his native Dingle

"I think I made a mistake."

Allan Williams, the manager who gave the Beatles away, when asked what he thought now about his decision to part company

"Liverpool is just like a film set."

Alan Bleasdale
playwright and author

Bessie Braddock, Labour MP could not retort with a Scousism on this true incident. In the post war House of Commons:

"You are drunk, Mr Churchill."

"Yes, Mrs Braddock, but you are ugly and I shall be sober in the morning."

"I was born and bred in Liverpool and that's the place I'll die. I have never considered myself patriotic English but I'm a patriotic Scouser."

Brian Jacques
writer

There's no business like Scouse business and when it comes to inventors and engineers we are up there among the leading lights whose forward looking and versatile talents helped create industries to boost the local and national economy.

Many of the seeds our business people have sewn remain vibrant enterprises to this day.

There have been the business brains and innovators who created multi-million pound empires.

The shopkeepers who turned ideas into massive job creation industries.

Ship builders, MPs and leading progressive journalists.

There have been impresarios who helped build the careers of some of the world's greatest artists.

And there's the engineers and thinkers who helped build livelihoods and seal the city's reputation.

Scouse Power, indeed.

FRANK HORNBY
SIR JOHN MOORES
MICHAEL JAMES WHITTY
DAVID LEVY
ALASTAIR PILKINGTON
BRIAN EPSTEIN
SAMUEL CUNARD
SIR TERRY LEAHY
WILLIAM HESKETH LEVER
MACGREGOR LAIRD

BUSINESS

FRANK HORNBY

FRANK Hornby, creator of Meccano, millionaire and MP for Everton, was the son of a Liverpool merchant.

Young Frank originally followed his father into work as an imports clerk.

His deep love of engineering and inventions led to the building of a workshop in his garden, where he would try to develop a perpetual motion machine and models of working submarines.

While the sub dived very well, it failed to surface.

After marriage, becoming a father and continuing in his day job, the wish to innovate and invent returned.

On the journey home one evening, after watching the workings of a crane, he came up with an idea to entertain his two young sons.

FRANK HORNBY
1863–1936

> "On the kitchen table he cut out strips of copper, joining them together with miniature nuts and bolts bought from a watchmaker.
>
> The result was a very basic crane – and Meccano was born"

By 1901 Frank had been granted the patent for the idea, and the new construction toy proved a winner in an age when children showed the same fascination for the new everyday technologies that their counterparts show today for computers.

Meccano was first manufactured in a cramped workshop above a city shop using hand presses, a lathe and a small gas engine for power.

Within two years, Hornby had bought five acres of land at Binns Road and built his factory.

Meccano instruction manuals were prepared in no fewer than 14 languages.

After World War One, the Board of Trade wanted to reduce German imports, and suggested Hornby turn his hand to manufacturing toy trains.

The result was the Hornby trains, originally clockwork, but later electric.

Dinky cars followed in the 1930s, taking advantage of a new process for casting metal, using a zinc alloy.

Frank Hornby died in 1936, having served as MP for Everton from 1931 to 1935. He is buried at Maghull, his home for many years.

SIR JOHN MOORES

THROUGHOUT the world there are several universities named after historic figures.

But Liverpool is unique in having a campus bearing the name of a legendary figure who had so much contemporary impact on the region.

Eighteen months later, he transferred to Liverpool where he set up a small football pools company with two friends – who took the name "Littlewoods" from a relative.

By the third season in 1927, the company had 20,000 regular customers.

"Sir John Moores was to become Liverpool's most famous entrepreneur, adopting the philosophy that anything is possible if people really want it and are prepared to work hard.

Hence the university's call to its students to 'dream, plan, achieve'"

John Moores was born in Eccles in 1896, the eldest of eight children.

By his 36th birthday he was a self-made millionaire, and shortly before his death, aged 97, in 1993, he was one of the wealthiest men in Britain.

But his rise to riches had very humble beginnings. He was just 14 when he left school to start work as a post office messenger, studying telegraphy in his spare time.

During World War One, he used those skills to serve in the Royal Navy, but once back in civvy street, he moved to work for a cable company on the south coast of Ireland.

There he built up a small shopping club to provide goods for people living in remote areas.

As a precaution, in case this new-found fortune ever floundered, he handed over the pools business to his brother Cecil, and decided to revive his shopping club idea.

Littlewoods Mail Order used a database of names from the pools company, and sent catalogues to their homes.

The idea was a surefire hit, and within four years, the first chainstore was added to this growing empire.

After the war, the Littlewoods Organisation continued to thrive with more than 100 stores and six different home shopping companies. Sir John retired as group chairman in 1977, but remained on the board.

He was a major shareholder in both Everton and Liverpool football clubs, and is also remembered as founder of the Liverpool John Moores Painting Exhibition, the UK's leading contemporary painting prize.

MICHAEL JAMES WHITTY

"MICHAEL James Whitty was the father of modern-day journalism in Merseyside"

But this amazing Irishman was also distinguished in other areas of public life.

Born in Nicharee, Co Wexford in 1795, Whitty went to London in 1821 and started as a journalist. His career included editorship of the London and Dublin Magazine, described as the best periodical of its day.

In 1821 he became editor of the Liverpool Journal, and in 1836 he became the founder and first head constable of Liverpool Police and Fire Brigade, a post he held until retirement in 1844.

It was then that he founded the Liverpool Daily Post.

It followed a pledge he made in parliament that changed the face of newspaper publishing. Michael Whitty told a select committee of MPs that the Stamp Act, under which newspapers were taxed, was restricting enterprise.

He promised that if the act was repealed he would bring out a paper with a cover price of just one penny.

He was true to his word, and on June 11, 1855, the first eight-page issue of the Daily Post was published.

The enterprise ran from a small printing shop at 29 Lord Street, which was also the home of the Liverpool Journal which Whitty now owned.

"The Post went from strength to strength"

In 1869, Edward Russell was appointed editor, a position he held for almost 50 years.

Subsequently, the Liverpool Echo was born in 1879 – six years after Whitty's death – funded by Alexander Jeans, who had been manager of the Daily Post.

Michael James Whitty was buried in Anfield cemetery.

DAVID LEVY

LIVERPOOL'S most famous shopkeeper founded a shopping empire which became the biggest retail operation in Britain.

David Levy, the son of a Jewish merchant in London, came to the then booming Liverpool in 1838 to make his fortune as an ambitious 15-year-old. When he arrived he Anglicised his name from Levy to Lewis and signed up for an apprenticeship with Lord Street tailors Benjamin Hyam and Co.

At the age of 23 he chose a site on Ranelagh Street to set up a boys' clothing shop, no more than 24 feet long with a single front door. From these humble beginnings he built the Lewis's empire piece by piece. Along the way he created three rules which would govern the running of all his later shops:

All goods were marked in figures at the lowest selling price – no haggling was allowed. This was unusual for a time in which market trading was still the norm.

All items could be later exchanged, provided they were not worn or damaged.

All goods were bought and sold for cash – no bartering was allowed.

Lewis's became a marker leader – along with its original slogan: "Lewis's are friends of the people".

It was the first department store in the world to install a Christmas grotto and use full size display mannequins within its windows.

The shop went from strength to strength and David Lewis opened Bon Marché in Church Street, selling ladies' fashions.

He teamed up with his wife's nephew Louis Cohen and began to build a national chain of Lewis's stores with new shops in Manchester, Sheffield and Birmingham.

But the enormous 10 floor flagship store which dominating one end of Lime Street was always his primary concern. He lived in the city until his death in 1885 and paid for a hospital, a hotel and a club to be built in his name.

"When his original store was destroyed in the blitz of May 1941, it was rebuilt from the rubble and the store which still bears David Lewis's name remains one of Liverpool's most recognisable landmarks"

ALASTAIR PILKINGTON

THERE can't be many engineering marvels born from doing the washing up.

But doing the dishes provided the inspiration for Alastair Pilkington's eureka moment which changed the way glass is made around the world.

The St Helens scientist hit on the idea of changing the way glass was made as he helped his wife Patricia clean up after dinner. He saw a plate floating on the soapy water and wondered whether the same science could be applied to glassmaking. He tried it, it worked, and he set up a workshop in his garden shed to develop his ground-breaking idea.

At the time he worked as a technical officer for Pilkington Brothers, although he was no relation of the original Pilkington family.

"It took seven years of hard work to prove to the world that he was right about his new process, and the cost of developing it brought his employers close to financial ruin"

Before this innovation, quality glass could only be made by the costly and wasteful plate-glass process. Because there was glass-to-roller contact, the glass surfaces were marked. They had to be ground and polished to produce the parallel surfaces which bring optical perfection in the finished product.

But Pilkington's invention made the company more than £600m. Today, more than 80% of the world's flat glass is made by his process. He was honoured with a knighthood in 1970 and was made chairman of Pilkington glass.

Sir Alastair was educated at Sherborne School and Trinity College, Cambridge, and came to work at Pilkington in 1947 after serving with the Royal Artillery during World War II, and later fought in the Mediterranean, where he was taken prisoner after the fall of Crete.

Sir Alastair retired as chairman of Pilkington at the age of 60 and played an important part in community life. He was closely involved in the creation of the first enterprise agency in the UK – the Community of St Helens Trust – from which grew Business in the Community, of which he was the founder chairman.

He also served as chancellor for Liverpool University until his death in 1995 aged 75.

BRIAN EPSTEIN

BRIAN Epstein, the businessman who managed The Beatles, was born into a Jewish family in Childwall.

When he was only six, his father Harry moved the family to Southport in an attempt to protect them from the wartime bombing of Liverpool.

But five years later, young Brian was back in the city centre, where he was introduced to his lifelong great love – music.

In 1945, his mother Malka (known as Queenie) took him to a Liverpool Philharmonic Orchestra concert, and his fascination with the classical repertoire began.

Brian began his working life in the family business, as a shopkeeper, overseeing the North End Music Stores in Whitechapel.

And that is the way his life may have stayed if a customer had not come to request a record called My Bonnie, by Tony Sherridan, featuring a group called the Beat Brothers.

Brian tracked down the band, famously attending a lunchtime session at the Cavern Club in Mathew Street, a stone's throw from his record shop.

He was introduced to The Beatles by the legendary Cavern DJ Bob Wooler, and was so captivated by their music that, against the advice of his friends, he became their manager.

> "He transformed the Beatles into a more professional outfit, banning them from swearing or eating on stage. In the spring of 1962 he won them a recording contract, and within two years Beatlemania had taken America by storm"

Meanwhile, NEMS had been transformed from a small family business into a multi-million pound organisation.

Epstein also signed, among others, Gerry and the Pacemakers, Cilla Black and Billy J Kramer.

But after The Beatles ceased touring in 1966, Epstein's role in their day-to-day lives was minimal, and a year later drug dependency took him to the verge of a nervous breakdown.

In August 1967, Brian Epstein died in London, aged 32, from an overdose of a sleep-inducing drug.

He is buried in the Jewish cemetery in Long Lane, Aintree.

SAMUEL CUNARD

BORN in Halifax, Nova Scotia, Samuel Cunard was a civil engineer who came to Britain to operate a fast mail service using steamships between the UK and America.

A highly successful entrepreneur, Cunard had volunteered for service in the 2nd battalion of the Halifax Regiment of militia and rose to the rank of captain.

"Once in Britain he set up a venture to bid on the rights to run a transatlantic shipping company between the UK and North America. Successful in his bid, the company would eventually bear his name, becoming Cunard Steamship Limited"

"Samuel Cunard (1787-1865) was the founder of perhaps the best-known shipping line in the world, which had small beginnings in Liverpool"

In 1840 the company's first steamship, the Britannia, sailed from Liverpool to Boston, Massachusetts, with Cunard and 63 other passengers on board, marking the beginning of regular passenger and cargo service.

Built in 1840 Britannia was Cunard's first purpose-built Atlantic liner.

She was way ahead of sailing ship competition in terms of passenger accommodation and speed but there were some disadvantages to this ultra-modern mode of transport.

Because she was designed for speed, passengers had to put up with some inconveniences. The noise of the engines and the smoke on deck from the belching funnel were very unpleasant.

However, compared with contemporary sailing ships, her passenger accommodation was considered luxurious – small cabins for the 115 people on the main deck below.

There was also a dining saloon and cows were carried on deck to ensure supplies of fresh milk.

It was used by popular author Charles Dickens and his wife on a voyage from Liverpool to Boston USA in 1842.

He wrote in his American Notes: "Nothing smaller for sleeping in was ever made, than a coffin."

Cunard Steamships Limited went on to absorb Canadian Northern Steamships Limited and its principal competition, the White Star Line, owners of the ill-fated Titanic.

After that, Cunard dominated the Atlantic passenger trade with some of the world's most famous liners.

In 1859, he was created 1st baronet by Queen Victoria.

He died six years later, in 1865, but the Cunard building which bears his name to this day was not completed until 1918.

SIR TERRY LEAHY

HE spent his childhood living in a pre-fab in Childwall Valley and council properties in Netherley and Lee Park and was first paid by Tesco to stack the shelves of one of its London stores.

Today, he's the ever-expanding company's super-successful chief executive, a knight of the realm and freeman of the city of Liverpool.

> "Born in Liverpool's Oxford Street maternity hospital on February 28, 1956, Sir Terry Leahy, who passed his 11-plus to get into St Edward's College in West Derby, is living proof that hard work pays off"

He studied for a degree in management science in Manchester and stayed in the city to work for the Co-Op as a product manager, remaining with the company for 18 months.

Sir Terry, whose father reared and trained greyhounds, joined Tesco in 1979 as a 23-year-old marketing executive.

But in typically modest fashion, he claims he was taken on by default: "I started in the marketing department but I didn't even get the job. There were two people interviewed – and I came second. The other person was so good they offered him another job in the company, as a buyer."

He displays even more modesty when talking about the clubcard – commonly viewed as being a Terry Leahy invention after he introduced it to Tesco in 1995.

"It wasn't a new idea," he says. "I stole it off Bury Co-Op. There had always been a dividend stamp, but Bury Co-Op tried to make it electronic. All the good ideas are already out there."

The married father-of-three, who lives in North London, says he "couldn't get a better job", while one commentator said that if you cut him he would "bleed Tesco".

When he heard this, the lifelong Evertonian told the Echo: "That must be the brand colours, blue and red – but it'd be mostly blue!"

Sir Terry is not exaggerating. In 2004, he was unveiled as a special advisor to the club.

WILLIAM HESKETH LEVER

IF William Hesketh Lever had ever had to write his own CV it would have been a mighty tome. His list of accomplishments and achievements would have included:

"Social reformer, philanthropist, soap boiler, MP, self-made millionaire, friend of Kings and Prime Ministers and Lord of the Western Isles.

Not bad for a grocer's son"

Lever held ideas and beliefs that were well ahead of their times, such as the welfare state, votes for women and workers' rights.

He was also a leading exponent of enlightened self-interest, in which the business owner improved conditions for his workers, the payback being that the employees were fitter and healthier and therefore worked harder to the benefit of the business.

He was born in Bolton in 1851, but Lever will forever be associated with Port Sunlight, the model village he created to house the Lever Brothers' workers on Wirral.

At the heart of the village is the Lady Lever Art Gallery, now part of National Museums Liverpool, which contains some of Britain's greatest art treasures, a prime example of how Lever fused his love for business and art.

Although one of the pioneers of the multi-national company, Lever was immersed in the Port Sunlight community and even took Sunday school classes every week.

Lever was a lifelong supporter of William Gladstone and the Liberal cause, and was often called upon to contest elections for the Liberal party.

He served as Member of Parliament for one of the seats in the Metropolitan Borough of Wirral between 1906 and 1909, using his maiden speech to the House of Commons to urge Henry Campbell-Bannerman's government to introduce a national old age pension, as he already provided for his own workers.

He was created Baron Leverhulme in June 1917, and Viscount Leverhulme in November 1922, the hulme section of the title being in honour of his wife, Elizabeth Hulme. He died on May 7, 1925.

MACGREGOR LAIRD

"WHEN the likes of Winston Churchill and the Prince of Wales hold a dinner in your honour 71 years after your death you must be a person of some note"

The person in question on this occasion was MacGregor Laird, the Merseyside man who opened the door to the riches of Western Africa for his native Britain.

Born in Greenock in Scotland in 1809, a year prior to his family moving to Merseyside, Laird was not destined to follow in the footsteps of his elder brother, John, who built up the business at Cammell Laird which his father had begun.

Inspired at an early age by the adventures of explorer Richard Lander, MacGregor had his sights set on Africa.

At the age of 23 he got his chance. He organised the construction of two small vessels – the Alburkah and the Quorra – and engaged his hero Lander as leader of the expedition.

Laird went with the expedition, along with 48 Europeans, all but nine of whom died from fever or, in the case of Lander, from wounds.

Laird went up the River Niger to the confluence of the Benue, which he was the first white man to ascend. He did not go far up the river but formed an accurate idea as to its source and course.

This expedition opened up African trade but MacGregor was always a virulent opponent of the slave trade, which he regarded as little more than piracy and an affront to human rights.

On two separate occasions he gave evidence to Parliament on the subject and was always outspoken in his criticism of slavery.

His hope was that developing mercantile trade with Africa it would lead to the end of the slave trade.

A little known fact about MacGregor Laird is that he also designed the river steamer "Ma Roberts" for Dr David Livingstone's famous expedition to the Zambezi.

Top   Paddy's Market on Great Homer Street in the early 70s. Merchant seamen walked from the dock road to buy
           a new suit for five bob – today 25p!
Above   Liverpool Cathedral. Paul McCartney listens to his Liverpool Oratorio rehearsal with the Philharmonic Orchestra

This Dingle rag and bone man asked: "Why do you want to take a picture of me?"
I remember the thrill, as a child, of getting a goldfish in exchange for a pile of old clothing from the rag and bone man

Top left   His hands attracted me to him at first, then his soft voice, explaining the skill of a master craftsman. Thomas Murphy, the last stonemason to work on Liverpool Cathedral

Top right   This Dock Road landlady called time every night always wearing a different hat. Real Liverpool class with real Liverpool humour

Above   Soccer in Liverpool is a religion. This was a field off Stanley Road in Kirkdale one Sunday morning – the tobacco warehouse in the background – but it could have been a cup tie at Anfield for the atmosphere

Dear Lizzie. "Here you are love, here's an apple for your dinner". Lizzie Christian stood in all weather in Williamson Square at her fruit stall. A real Liverpool face and a smile that made your day

Day trippers...tickets to ride – super Scouse outings

By Tony Martin

Sefton Park

The 269-acre Sefton Park was designed in 1867 by Parisian Edouard Andre and Liverpool architect Lewis Hornblower to blend the natural landscape of the area with two branches of a tributary of the Mersey, creating ornamental watercourses and rock features with cascades, grottoes and stepping stones leading to a seven-acre lake. It opened in 1872 and won a place in Liverpool people's affections that remains strong today.

With is Grade II * listed Palm House, from 1896, Sefton Park, one of the largest city parks in England, is a great place for a family day out. Its distinctive winding paths, carpets of bluebells and woodland bring a sense of rural peace in the heart of a great city.

WHAT shall we do today, mum, dad? That perennial cry of the child in the fondly remembered, long days of summer was usually met with the same response.

We'll go to the seaside.

And what a choice of seaside we have. For Liverpool and the towns that surround it are fortunate that our coast is both accessible and safe.

In Sefton, from the end of the docks at Seaforth to Southport there are 22 miles of coast, while Wirral is an entire peninsula of seafront opportunities, with the beach at West Kirby a jewel in its crown.

Yet there's more than one way to spend a day out in the fresh air.

Discounting a day trip to our near neighbours such as the Lake District and North Wales, the opportunities for that outdoor experience are rich and varied.

No matter where you live, there will be a park nearby, then for the price of a bus or train ticket the opportunities are endless, be it the grounds of Speke Hall where the Victorian gardens sit in splendour by the banks of the Mersey with views of the Welsh hills, or Croxteth Country Park, which since 1986 has been the city's largest public open space with 530 acres of woodland surrounding the magnificent former home of the Earls of Stanley.

A walk along the newly revamped Otterspool Prom or a trip on a Mersey ferry, a two hour journey through Beatles land on the twice daily Magical Mystery Tour; a visit to Parkgate or a Mersey meander along the banks of the Leeds-Liverpool canal. So much to see and do on our doorstep.

But it is our local parks that are our most familiar escape routes from the urban sprawl. And what a fine necklace of green our city wears. Liverpool's three famous Victorian gems, Stanley, Newsham and Sefton parks share the crown with Birkenhead Park.

Birkenhead Park takes the accolade as the first publicly funded park in Britain. Featuring 125-acres it make other parks green with envy.

Designed by Joseph Paxton, it had great influence far and wide; its design was substantially copied for New York's Central Park. On the day Birkenhead Park opened, April 5, 1847, 10,000 people went through its gates. It may not attract such crowds today, but it is still a magnificent friend to the lover of open spaces.

In Liverpool, the 100-acre Stanley Park has been described as the most architecturally significant of the city's great parks; it opened in 1870 but has had its ups and downs while the later Newsham Park has probably never outdone that day in 1891 when Buffalo Bill Cody chose it to stage his Wild-West show with Annie Oakley and Sitting Bull.

But Sefton Park was and remains one of the city's best-loved open spaces.

Railways changed the face of Britain and brought travel into the mass market and, while some parts of the great Victorian rail network may have declined, they have left a legacy of leisure for us all to enjoy. The old Cheshire Lines rail line on north Merseyside is now part of the 216-mile coast to coast Trans Pennine Trail and is a magnet to walkers and cyclists.

On the Wirral, another former railway has become a route to roam that thousands enjoy every year.

For more than 70 years from the height of the Victorian era to the early 1960s a busy railway ran from Hooton, near Chester to West Kirby. Now this 12-mile Wirral Way forms the backbone of the splendid Wirral Country Park, the first designated country park in Britain.

Seven miles of the route run alongside the Dee Estuary, a haven for seabirds. A good place to start an outing is the country park visitor centre at Thurstaton, if for no other reason than to pick up a leaflet highlighting the delights of this park of contrasts. From the sheltered inland quiet of the Wirral Way where badgers and foxes hunt in the shadows to the 60ft cliffs overlooking the Dee where you can enjoy the sights, sounds and smells of the sea, this park is a true oasis of peace.

The more adventurous could consider a walk across the mud flats at low tide to the isolated sandstone Hilbre Islands (it must be stressed that this walk must be taken with great care after checking tide times and route with the proper authorities).

To the north of the Mersey lies the Sefton coast where beaches, marshes, dunes, woods and heaths form a ribbon of tranquillity and opportunity for walkers and birdwatchers alike.

From the 670-acre Ainsdale and Birkdale sandhills nature reserve, one of the largest areas of wild dune left in Britain, to the Gormley iron men in Crosby and the red squirrels and pinewoods of Formby, this truly is a region surrounded by the great outdoors.

Parkgate

It is sometimes called the port that the sea forgot, but Parkgate on Wirral has been charming visitors for centuries and still does. Two hundred years ago, Parkgate was the main port between England and Dublin, but today is a different story.

It has a proud history, with Horatio Nelson's mistress, Emma Hamilton (a blacksmith's daughter from Ness) once holidaying in Parkgate for a month, taking regular dips in the sea to cure a skin complaint. The composer Handel is believed to have put the finishing touches to his Messiah while in Parkgate, before sailing to Dublin for its premiere. He is rumoured to have stayed at the George Hotel, whose building has now been incorporated into Mostyn House School, with its distinctive half-timbered facade.

Today, thousands of people enjoy a promenade along the front at Parkgate sampling either an ice cream or native shrimps and cockles from the shops. Although the estuary has silted up, with the tide only coming in twice a year, Parkgate is still a must-see day out.

Clockwise from far left: A fisherman on the lake at Sefton Park, a fun day out at Croxteth County Park and a spot of kite flying at Sefton Park

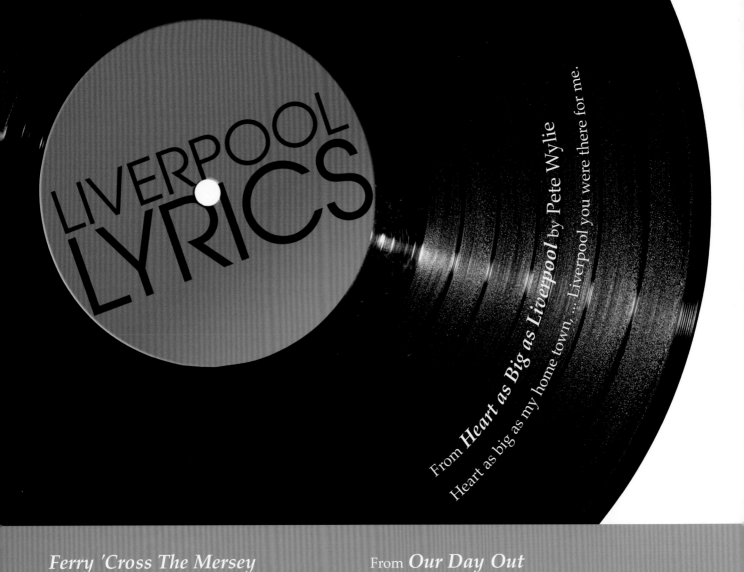

LIVERPOOL LYRICS

From *Heart as Big as Liverpool* by Pete Wylie

Heart as big as my home town... Liverpool you were there for me.

Ferry 'Cross The Mersey
by Gerry Marsden

Life goes on day after day
Hearts torn in every way

So ferry 'cross the Mersey
'Cause this land's the place I love
And here I'll stay

People they rush everywhere
Each with their own secret care
So ferry 'cross the Mersey
And always take me there
The place I love

People around every corner
They seem to smile and say
We don't care what your name is boy
We'll never turn you away

From *Our Day Out*
by Willy Russell

The Mersey Tunnel is three miles long
and the roof is made of glass,
so that as you are driving through
you can watch the ships sail past,
there's a plughole every five yards
that's opened every night,
it lets in lots of water
and it washes away the..da da da diddly da da da.

From *Maggie Mae* (traditional)

Oh dirty Maggie Mae
They have taken her away and she'll never walk
down Lime Street anymore
Oh the judge he guilty found her
For robbing a homeward bounder
That dirty no good robbing Maggie Mae
T'was in the Port of Liverpool where they took me to.
Two pound two a week that was my pay.

From *'Long Haired Lover From Liverpool'*
by Little Jimmy Osmond

I'll be your long haired lover
from Liverpool
And I'll do anything you say
I'll be your clown or your puppet
or your April Fool
If you'll be my sunshine daisy
from L.A

From *Penny Lane*
by McCartney / Lennon

Penny Lane is in my ears
and in my eyes.
There beneath the blue
suburban skies
I sit, and meanwhile back…

From *Strawberry Fields*
by Lennon / McCartney

Let me take you down,
'cause I'm going to Strawberry Fields.
Nothing is real and nothing to get hungabout.
Strawberry Fields (forever).

From *Oliver's Army*
by Elvis Costello

Hong Kong is up for grabs
London is full of Arabs
We could be in Palestine
Overrun by a Chinese line
With the boys from the Mersey
and the Thames and the Tyne

From *I am the Greatest*
by John Lennon

When I was a little boy
way back home in Liverpool
All my friends told me I was great

From *The World in One City*
by Pete McGovern

Senior Citizens are marching throughout Liverpool;
they're starting all over to go back to school,
to study computers and using the mouse,
and taking "A" Levels in "Classical Scouse."

The Leaving of Liverpool (traditional)

It's not the leaving of Liverpool that's grieving me
But my darling' when I think of you.

From *In My Liverpool Home*
by Pete McGovern

In my Liverpool home,
in my Liverpool Home,
We speak with an accent
exceedingly rare;
We meet under a statue
exceedingly bare.
If you want a cathedral,
we've got one to spare
in my Liverpool home

From *You Are Here*
by John Lennon

From Liverpool to Tokyo
…what a way to go.
From distant lands,
one woman one man
Let the four winds blow

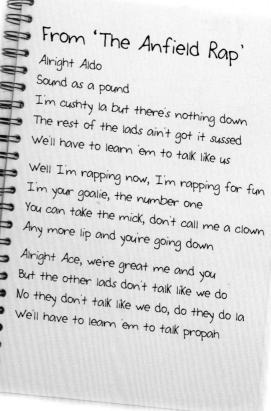

From 'The Anfield Rap'

Alright Aldo
Sound as a pound
I'm cushty la but there's nothing down
The rest of the lads ain't got it sussed
We'll have to learn 'em to talk like us

Well I'm rapping now, I'm rapping for fun
I'm your goalie, the number one
You can take the mick, don't call me a clown
Any more lip and you're going down

Alright Ace, we're great me and you
But the other lads don't talk like we do
No they don't talk like we do, do they do la
We'll have to learn 'em to talk propah

A green and pleasant day at Knowsley Hall Estate

TALENT IN THE

LIVERPOOL has fallen in love with The Beatles... for the second time.

The 60s lunchtime Cavern groupies, reared on soft drinks and hard rock, are today's grand parents.

Now, after years of indifference, they have been replaced by an international brigade of tourists, engaged and entertained by a hard-nosed business brief that puts £200m a year into the Merseyside economy.

Good enough reason to like The Fab Four or, as they now are, Paul and Ringo.

John and George (together with Hamburg Beatle, Stuart Sutcliffe) have joined the saints, leaving us mere mortals to consider the largely local indifference to their names during three lost decades of enterprise on the home front.

Part of the reason for that vacuum was a perhaps understandable frustration on the part of those left behind, at the concept of Liverpudlian creativity being limited to a relatively small handful of groups who inhabited a Mathew Street cellar, and later, during the 70s and 80s, other bands who took over Eric's club in the same street.

There was more to Liverpool than rock 'n' pop, even though the city had produced the single most successful entertainment phenomenon of all time, and topped it up with the most number one hit records ever to be produced by any other individual city, including New York.

Resentment?

Well, not really. More a case of exasperation at the ignorance of the masses (ie those outside the city who thought Liverpool was a one-track musical sensation).

What about the Royal Liverpool Philharmonic, Britain's second oldest symphony orchestra? Or the Playhouse, the longest established repertory in the world? The Everyman producing some of the UK's finest acting talent. Or the UK's first legit public art gallery of note, the Walker?

And that was just for starters.

The architectural stage on which Scouse life was enacted included the Anglican cathedral and the world's greatest neo-classical building, St George's Hall.

All this in a relatively small city - barely more than a mile across at its centre - but with the cosmopolitan feel of a giant village, where people actually knew each other.

How apt that when the Capital of Culture judges came to town, the Echo ran a picture of all 12 panel members, with the headline: If you see these people today - Smile!

The judges themselves loved that sense of connection, just as the panel chairman, Sir Jeremy Isaacs, turned down an opportunity to go to the opera at the Empire in favour of a pub comedy tour featuring local stand-up Keith Carter, as the 'scally' shell-suited Nige.

Isaacs even went so far as to admit that Carter's caustic take on life in the Pool had contributed to him casting his vote in favour of Liverpool.

And ALL the judges said that the prize had been won by the people of Liverpool, a sort of honorary republic on the outskirts of normality, beyond the tried and tested.

Of course, there was a great lineage of troopers - from the comedians of old like Rob Wilton, Ted Ray and Arthur Askey, through to today's veterans like Ken Dodd and Micky Finn.

ART OF THE CITY

By Joe Riley

Just as there were the Mersey poets - led by Adrian Henri, Roger McGough and Brian Patten, a trio whose 60s poetry anthology has still never been outsold by any others.

And who would want to forget the visual artists: Don McKinlay, Sam Walsh and George Jardine, or a leading ceramicist like Julia Carter Preston, whose father, Edward, had provided most of the statues in Liverpool Cathedral?

And what about Arthur Dooley, the rough and tumble ex-guardsman who produced great sculpture and became the subject of an early edition of television's This Is Your Life?

Against this gigantic backdrop of talent, new voices were heard, especially in the theatres: Willy Russell and Alan Bleasdale leading the troops in a stand against wall-to-wall middle class British sitcom which prevailed in most other cities.

Bleasdale made the transfer to television, as did Jimmy McGovern. All of a sudden it seemed that if Liverpool writers and actors were not taking up small screen space, Scousers were either making the news (football, music, politics etc) or actually reading it such as Livedrpool Institute old boy Peter Sissons.

When we were competing against other British cities for the 2008 Euro prize (remember that Belfast was the early favourite and Newcastle the final bookies' choice), the Echo published a supplement with the title: 100 reasons why Liverpool should be Capital of Culture.

And once again, it was Jeremy Isaacs, in a rare moment of impromptu comment, who said: "Yes, and you could probably produce another supplement of another 100 reasons."

Acknowledgement, if ever there was, that he and his team had found themselves confronted and challenged by an extraordinary city.

One that through its unique sense of togetherness and solidarity could claim to be the true powerhouse of UK arts and creativity in a way that London - an amalgam of districts connected by Tube - could not possibly challenge in its own right.

Here, like in no other place in this country, is the humour of survival and the promise of future excellence cohabiting and continuing to flourish.

It has not always been easy. The past 30 years have seen all our theatres, as well as our art galleries and the Philharmonic threatened with extinction, not helped for a long period by a city council which spurned heritage and culture.

How times have changed, although funding, it has to be said, is only now just coming up to speed for a prosperous future.

The Capital of Culture prize has not only fire-proofed those institutions once almost certainly doomed, it has provided a springboard for them to revive.

The world, of course, still sees and hears The Beatles.

And long may that continue as one of the reasons (together with football) why this city needs no international passport for its reputation to travel to the four corners of the earth.

The year 2008 will offer both Europe and indeed a global audience, a new and expanded way of viewing this vibrant village on the banks of the Mersey - which like all the great cities of the world, stands on a great river.

Scouse: The Dish and the Diction By Ken Pye

LIVERPUDLIANS find fun in food and in sharing it with family and friends. Of course, our local delicacy, and from which comes the name of our dialect and community, is Scouse. Contrary to popular opinion however, our traditional local dish is not related to either Irish Stew or Lancashire Hot Pot, being in fact of Scandinavian seafaring origin. Indeed, 18th century sailors would have the dish – these seafarers called it loblolly.

This name derives from a combination of two Norwegian words, meaning to eat noisily and broth.

The word scouse itself, is a shortened form of the word lobscouse – an amalgamation of the Danish word lapscouse and the Dutch word lapskous , both meaning spoon meat.

The meal was ideal to eat at sea, because it could be very quickly prepared using cheap or leftover cuts of meat, such as lamb. Plain root vegetables such as potatoes and onions,

which were inexpensive and readily available, would then have been roughly chopped and added to the meat. Covered with water and seasoned with salt, this could then be left to stew slowly on a hob, without needing to be watched, for an indefinite period, thus making is an ideal meal for sailors.

Scouse was not only quick, cheap, and easy to produce, but it was tasty, warming, and nourishing, especially in cold and stormy conditions. On shore, it became the food of sailor's families and of poorer people, for the same reasons, and because the basic recipe could vary depending on the ingredients that were available.

Now, in the 21st century, Scouse is once again a popular dish. Once the food of the poor, it can now be found on the menu of many cafes, restaurants and clubs all over the City.

Why not try making it yourself with my own foolproof and simple recipe?

KEN PYE'S TRIED AND TRUSTED SCOUSE RECIPE

Dice enough meat, either stewing beef or shoulder of lamb as preferred, to feed your guests (say 4-6ozs for each person). Do not over-trim the meat, because the fat thickens and flavours the broth. Place the meat in a large, heavy, cooking pot; Scouse is stewed on a hob, not baked or casseroled in an oven.

Next, chop roughly enough large Spanish onions, to give each person half an onion. Then slice enough large carrots, to give each person about half a carrot. Add these to the pan.

Coarsely dice 1 large potato for each guest and add to the pot. It is important that the potatoes should be old potatoes such as King Edwards or Maris Pipers, which will collapse or lob during cooking.

Season to taste with salt and white pepper, and pour enough cold water into the pan just to cover all the ingredients.

Leaving the cooking pot uncovered, bring the mixture to a boil, stirring occasionally, and then reduce the heat to a simmer. Now cover the pot, and continue simmering until the potatoes have fallen, again stirring occasionally. Check the seasoning.

Keep cooking gently until the meat is tender and the broth has thickened. If it has not thickened enough, and just before the meat begins to fall apart, you can rapidly raise the heat and reduce the stew.

You will now have a basic, but tasty and nutritious Scouse that can be reheated easily if necessary. This makes it a good dish to prepare in advance of a family meal or party. Scouse also freezes and defrosts well, so you can make lots of it, and save it for those cold and rainy days!

Today, it is perfectly acceptable to add an appropriate stock to the stew before cooking and, if using beef, perhaps an Oxo cube or dessertspoon of Bovril would boost the flavour. A lamb or chicken stock cube in the broth for a lamb Scouse is also a good idea, as is the addition of a few good dashes of Worcestershire Sauce, in the final twenty minutes or so of the cooking. This will really lift the flavour, but these suggestions, of course, are all a matter of taste, so experiment a little; the stew can stand it!

Whichever way you prepare your Scouse, and whatever your ingredients, how you present and eat it is critical! Serve great scoops of the broth on large, warm dinner plates, and make plenty of it, because everyone will want seconds. Ensure that there is plenty of crusty bread on the side, to dip into the Scouse and to wipe your plate clean with afterwards. Pickled red cabbage and sliced beetroot are essential side dishes.

If you are on your own and need cheering up, a good pan of Scouse will do it every time: It has that home-cooked, mother-used-to-make taste which we all need to pick us up from time-to-time.

Bon Appetit!

There are many street names and plaques adorning walls dedicated to famous innovators who have helped shape the city as we know it.

From famous astronomers to radio pioneers to health workers and those who made important breakthroughs in what were deemed incurable diseases.

Social reformers, teachers and university heads are recognised throughout the city from clock towers to libraries.

Our inventors' sacrifices, both personal and financial, to make a difference have been great.

These are the Scousers who decided to get up and do something to realise an ideal – of benefit to all society.

INNO

JOSEPH ROTBLAT
CLAIRE DOVE
JEREMIAH HORROCKS
SIR RONALD ROSS
WILLIAM POBJOY
JANET HEMINGWAY
PETER TOYNE
WILLIAM RATHBONE
SIR JAMES ALLANSON PICTON
OLIVER LODGE

OVATORS

JANET HEMINGWAY

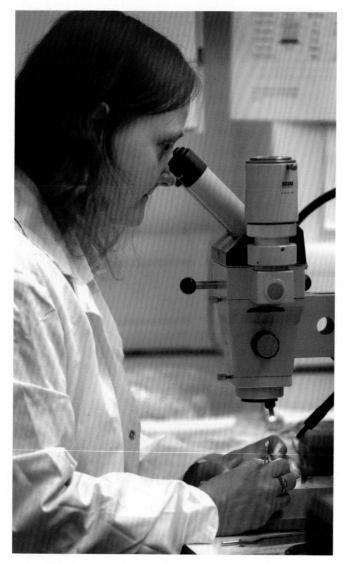

PROF Janet Hemingway's pioneering work continues to save lives around the world.

She is at the forefront of a global fight to eradicate malaria - a disease which kills more than two million children a year, most of them in the central belt of Africa.

As the first female boss of the prestigious Liverpool School of Tropical Medicine, she heads a world-class team of researchers working to treat and cure diseases around the globe.

At the moment she is handling the biggest grant the school has ever received - £28m from the Bill and Melinda Gates Foundation.

The school, founded in 1898 by Liverpool shipowner Sir Alfred Lewis Jones, was the first of its kind in the world. It has been a leader in the field ever since, collecting accolades from across the globe.

One of the most famous was in 1902 when Sir Ronald Ross became the first British winner of a Nobel prize for medicine when he discovered that malaria is carried by mosquitoes.

The school's scientists also developed the first drug to treat malaria and pioneered treatments for sleeping sickness and relapsing fever.

More recently their work was instrumental in discovering the links between insects and river blindness and conducting research into new organisms which affect HIV.

They continue to save lives, often in war-torn countries, including Afghanistan, Eritrea and Sierra Leone. Despite working in grave danger, the school's scientists persevere against great odds to sustain crucial treatment and control programmes.

Professor Hemingway, 49, originally trained in genetics, before moving into insect molecular biology.

She has one teenage daughter, Charlotte, and works to encourage more women into science. "It's tough for women in science - there are less than 1% at my level," she said. "It's probably because the career track is not geared to having a family."

She is also keen to foster links with universities and hospitals around the world - more than 500 students from over 70 countries are welcomed each year.

"As the first female boss of the prestigious Liverpool School of Tropical Medicine, she heads a world-class team of researchers working to treat and cure diseases around the globe"

OLIVER LODGE

> "Lodge befriended George Holt, the Blue Funnel Line shipping magnate, and in 1904, Holt bankrolled the city's first physics lab"

OCCASIONALLY, the time comes to correct the accepted record of history.

And here is a case in point. Radio was not invented by Marconi as most people think.

Although the Italian played a significant role in the birth of wireless transmission, it was Oliver Lodge who made the first transmission - in Liverpool - on August 14, 1894.

He successfully beamed radio signals from Liverpool University's Victoria Tower in Brownlow Hill to Lewis's city centre store.

Lodge was the first professor of physics at the university. The department opened on the site of the former lunatic asylum in 1881 (it was then University College Liverpool).

It was later incorporated into the university, which received its charter in 1903.

Even in those days there was a big debate over funding, but luckily, Liverpool's pre-eminence as a city meant wealthy entrepreneurs were willing to stump up the cash.

Lodge befriended George Holt, the Blue Funnel Line shipping magnate, and in 1904, Holt bankrolled the city's first physics lab.

Lodge's influence was to be immense in helping to raise the profile of physics. Born at Penkull, Staffordshire, he studied at the Royal College of Science and at University College, London, before accepting the Liverpool post in 1891.

Nine years later - after the immense breakthrough with radio signalling in Liverpool - Lodge became the first principal of the new university in Birmingham.

His work there included preparing the way for the theory of relativity.

But it was the wireless connection which proved to be his lasting legacy, including two ground-breaking books, Signalling Across Space Without Wires (1897) and Talks About Wireless (1925), very much a retrospective, as he was then aged 75.

Even so, an autobiography appeared six years later.

Lodge was elected a Fellow of the Royal Society in 1887 and awarded the society's senior medal in 1898. He was knighted in 1902, and lived until the grand old age of 91.

Scholarships continued to be given in Lodge's name at Liverpool. Among recipients were Joseph Rotblat the nuclear physicist.

JEREMIAH HORROCKS

UNTIL comparatively recently far too few people were aware of the genius of Otterspool-born Jeremiah Horrocks.

Horrocks Avenue in Speke is named after the man and their are plaques in his honour at both the Ancient Chapel of Toxteth (where he is buried) and the church of St Michael-in-the-Hamlet.

But ask the average man in the street what Jeremiah Horrocks was famous for and the odds were you would get nothing but a blank look.

That was until a surge of publicity gave the man who discovered the transit of Venus the prominence he undoubtedly deserved.

Now recognised alongside the likes of Sir Isaac Newton and even Galileo, Horrocks was an astronomer of outstanding ability.

Born in 1619, his father was a watchmaker and the family were deeply religious Protestant Puritans.

Jeremiah was a brilliant scholar and won a place at Cambridge University at the age of 14. By then he was already well-versed in Greek, Latin and the Scriptures.

Using the data from his Venus discoveries he went on to find that the sun was in fact gigantic, with a volume more than a million times that of the Earth.

He also showed that the planets Jupiter and Saturn were giants, totally opposing the biblical view that our own planet must be the grandest in creation.

His discoveries changed the way the whole solar system was viewed and were, given the times in which they happened, totally revolutionary.

Jeremiah Horrocks is now known as the "Father of British Astronomy"; he had a tragically short life (he was just 22 when he died) but he left a legacy which lives today.

Thanks to him, Venus transits can be predicted with accuracy. The most famous took place in 1769 when the British explorer Captain James Cook, sailed to Tahiti in order to observe it.

"Claire, Deputy Lieutenant for Merseyside, created Blackburne House, the Hope Street-based women's training organisation, and has spent more than 30 years championing women's education"

CLAIRE DOVE

CLAIRE Dove has pioneered services and training for women and championed equality on Merseyside.

Claire, Deputy Lieutenant for Merseyside, created Blackburne House, the Hope Street-based women's training organisation, and has spent more than 30 years championing women's education.

After giving birth to her fourth child at 47 she continued to combine motherhood with a stressful job.

Claire, with an MBE for her services to women's education, has been awarded an honorary fellowship of Liverpool John Moores University, a fellowship of the Royal Society of Arts and was voted nationally as an exemplary leader in regeneration.

It is a long way since her fight for equality began as a child.

"As the only black girl at my school, Lawrence Road, I will never forget a current affairs lesson when we were discussing Enoch Powell's Rivers of Blood speech," she has said.

"One kid stood up and yelled 'send them all back' and then, after seeing the look on my face, added 'except for Claire that is'."

After leaving school Claire struggled to find a job as a secretary, despite being well-qualified. "They would tell me the post had already been filled, which I knew was a lie," she has said.

Undeterred, she decided to set up her own employment agency which judged staff purely on their merits.

She also worked for the Martin Luther King Foundation, became a member of the Black Women's Liberation Movement and, in the 1980s, helped set up Liverpool Black Sisters.

Blackburne House remains one of the city's original and most successful social enterprises, thanks largely to the pioneering work of Claire Dove.

SIR JAMES ALLANSON PICTON

SIR James Allanson Picton was a prominent member of both Liverpool town council and the Wavertree Local Board of Health.

In Liverpool he was chairman of the Libraries Committee for almost 40 years.

As a mark of respect, one of the main library buildings was named after him in 1879, and two years later he was knighted by Queen Victoria in recognition of his "high attainments and public services".

Picton was a keen student of local history. His two-volume work Memorials of Liverpool remains one of the leading reference books on the city's buildings and personalities of the time.

He was also famously outspoken. On the opening of Jesse Hartley's Albert Docks in 1845 he said: "It is to be regretted that no attention whatsoever has been paid to beauty as well as strength. The enormous pile of warehouses is simply a hideous pile of naked brickwork."

Born in Highfield Street, Liverpool, in 1805, the son of a timber merchant, Picton became a well-known architect and surveyor.

He moved to Wavertree in 1848, having designed and built himself a house - Sandy Knowe - in Mill Lane.

Picton was a seasoned traveller and a talented linguist, being in the habit of touring different parts of Britain and Europe each summer.

He was also a literary scholar, and named his new house after the farm where Sir Walter Scott was brought up, in the Scottish border country. The polygonal sandstone extension, displaying the family arms, was built to house Picton's own private library.

He was a prominent local resident and when his wife Sarah died in 1879 after 50 years of happy marriage, he donated the Picton Clock Tower - at the junction of Childwall Road, Church Road North and the High Street - to the people of Wavertree.

It has been a local landmark for more than 100 years.

Sir James died at home in 1889. His legacy lives on in the libraries and local history centres of Merseyside.

> "Picton was a seasoned traveller and a talented linguist, being in the habit of touring different parts of Britain and Europe each summer"

WILLIAM POBJOY

THERE are teachers - and particularly head teachers - who are remembered for all sorts of reasons.
Are school days really the happiest of your life?

Thanks to the commitment and foresight of William Pobjoy, pupils at Quarry Bank school during the 50s, 60s and 70s could probably say they were, with a fair degree of accuracy.

William Pobjoy became a sort of honorary Mr Chips. When he retired in 1982, after 26 years in charge of the well-known comprehensive (and a further 10 years in the teaching profession) there were tears and regrets all around.

Here was a truly inspirational man who always wanted the best for his pupils.

Former pupils include entertainer Les Dennis, international novelist Clive Barker and Jude Kelly, now artistic director of London's South Bank complex.

Most famous of all the Pobjoy pupils was John Lennon, a name which caused the teacher, rather than the Beatle, some regret.

William Pobjoy was never allowed to forget how he had once caned Lennon. And he was the head teacher who went on to be the first in the city to ban corporal punishment.

He was to recall: "I knew from almost the very moment I did it, that the cane was not the right form of discipline for John Lennon."

That was during the 50s. By 1961, the cane had been outlawed at Quarry Bank.

"Quite simply, corporal punishment does not work," William Pobjoy was to insist.

"Take a look at school punishment books and you will see the same names cropping up time and time again."

For the rest of his career, he held firm to the principle that teachers should not be allowed to smack children. William Pobjoy had himself been a pupil of Fonthill Road school before going to Cambridge and getting a double first in modern and medieval languages.

"Here was a truly inspirational man who always wanted the best for his pupils"

"As vice-chancellor, chief executive and honorary professor, he presided over the only British university to be named in honour of a contemporary business icon"

PETER TOYNE

PETER Toyne is the Yorkshire butcher's son who wanted to drive a steam engine, but ended up in charge of Liverpool John Moores University.

As vice-chancellor, chief executive and honorary professor, he presided over the only British university to be named in honour of a contemporary business icon, Moores having founded the Littlewoods empire.

But it was Toyne who personally fronted the university's image, at one point raising £35m a year in addition to grants and fees.

There was no financial tie-in with the Moores family: "No megabucks, and we didn't even ask. We just wanted a role model for this generation. John Moores was the guy who did it for himself, and that's exactly what we're about."

Educated in Ripon, Peter Toyne progressed to teaching geography at Exeter University, a degree which he later joked helped him find his way around the 20-odd outlying buildings of the JMU.

His time in office saw much new building, as well as massive restoration projects, such as the North-Western hotel in Lime Street and the Bull Ring flats in St Andrew's Gardens.

He referred to this early regeneration as "the twin attack on buildings for academic use and student residence".

Peter Toyne called the debate over university league tables "stupid".

"What is certain," he said "is that degrees are different from what they were, and so they should be. What matters is that we are still taking people to the maximum of their capability. A first is still a first. A degree is a degree."

His great love as a child had been railways. Everyone else in his village worked down the pit: "That background is something that stays with me, and why I was happy to come to Liverpool and make all this available," he said.

Peter Toyne had first moved to Liverpool in 1986, when the JMU was still Liverpool Polytechnic.

Since then, he has served in many public offices, including High Sheriff of Merseyside and as chairman of the Royal Liverpool Philharmonic Society.

He was also chairman of Liverpool's successful Capital of Culture bid.

"Friends and colleagues
noted that he always had a
total dedication and fixed,
tireless focus on his work"

SIR RONALD ROSS

SIR Ronald Ross left a Liverpool legacy to be proud of. He was the man
behind one of the greatest medical breakthroughs of the 20th century -
a cure for malaria.

Travellers, holiday-makers and those living in countries where malaria is
common acknowledge his genius and life-long dedication and commitment
to never giving up on research.

The British-born physician became the first Briton to win the Nobel
Prize for Medicine in 1902.

Sir Ronald was awarded the Nobel Prize Laureate after
identifying that mosquitoes carry malaria - one of the
world's biggest killers.

He was born in Almera, Nepal, the son of an army officer
and studied at St Bartholomew's hospital in London and
entered the Indian Medical Service in 1881 inspired by
his father.

One of Ronald Ross's early jobs was as a ship's doctor.

Friends and colleagues noted that he always had a total
dedication and fixed, tireless focus on his work.

Yet apart from being a popular, visionary doctor he
was also regarded as somewhat of an 'eccentric',
a mathematician with a gift for poetry and writing
romantic stories - a world away from the vital work
he carried out in the laboratory.

His real life-enhancing and life-changing achievement
lay in his research work which would see him burn the
candles at both ends to reach his goal.

While investigating the belief by his contemporaries that
malaria was transmitted through mosquito bites, Dr Ross
discovered his true vocation to seek a cure.

By 1898 he had also worked out the life cycle of the malaria
parasite for birds.

He came to England in 1899 with his wife and family and lectured
and became professor of tropical medicine at the Liverpool of
School of Tropical Medicine.

He became Sir Ronald in 1911. From 1926 he directed the
world-renowned Ross Institute in London.

His award of the Nobel Prize in 1902 was the greatest
accolade bestowed on this man who captured the spirit of
pioneering research and the spirit of a changing Liverpool.

"The Rathbones were a Quaker family, and their wider remit was to include business interests in shipbuilding and timber trading"

WILLIAM RATHBONE

WILLIAM Rathbone (1787-1868), one of seven Liverpool luminaries from the same family bearing the same name, was a social reformer and politician, and is remembered for his work to improve sanitation in Victorian cities.

He lived in the family's ancestral home in Greenbank, now part of the Liverpool University campus, and became lord mayor at the age of 50.

In 1809 he had set up a merchant's business with his brother Richard, but after being elected to parliament as a Liberal MP for Liverpool in 1835, he began a career in public life.

He took a strong stance against bribery and other forms of corruption in local government elections, and was an active supporter of the Municipal Reform Act, passed the same year, which gave Liverpool its first truly elected councillors.

Rathbone worked with his wife, Elizabeth, and the social reformer Kitty Wilkinson, to establish public baths and wash-houses following the cholera epidemics which struck Britain in the 1830s.

Ironically, his most memorable contribution began with his own wife's illness.

William Rathbone was so impressed with the nursing care she received (at the family's expense), he thought the same standard should be enjoyed by others.

Thus he appointed the city's first publicly paid nurse, Agnes Jones (a student of Florence Nightingale), who was stationed at the workhouse for the poor on Brownlow Hill - now the site of the Metropolitan Cathedral.

The Rathbones were a Quaker family, and their wider remit was to include business interests in shipbuilding and timber trading.

They were also involved in the formation of the universities of Liverpool and Bangor (it was not until 1912 that the family branched out into stockbroking and investment management).

The wider family also included the actor Basil Rathbone, famous for his screen portrayals of Sherlock Holmes.

As for William Rathbone, a man who had done so much good for others, especially in the health field, it was ironic that he should die under the surgeon's knife, having agreed to experimental surgery in the latter stages of a serious illness, thought to be cancer.

JOSEPH ROTBLAT

"As war closed in, Rotblat returned to Poland to collect his wife, but she was too ill to travel. He never saw her again nor ever learned of her fate"

THE scientist and physicist Joseph Rotblat, working in Liverpool, was at the epicentre of man's most powerful transformation of the fates.

He had inadvertently given his genius to the development of the greatest terror known to human kind, before becoming one of the most persuasive opponents of its use.

And so the man who had helped make the atomic bomb, was awarded the Nobel peace prize in 1995.

Joseph Rotblat was the fifth of seven children born to a Jewish paper merchant, who distilled vodka in his Warsaw home after the family business crumbled in the Great War.

Joseph graduated in physics in 1932, and completed his doctorate as the Nazis rose to power.

In March 1936, he married Tola Gryn, and accepted the Oliver Lodge Fellowship at Liverpool University under James Chadwick, who had discovered the neutron.

As war closed in, Rotblat returned to Poland to collect his wife, but she was too ill to travel. He never saw her again nor ever learned of her fate.

Chadwick's team continued with their project and suggested an atomic bomb was possible.

Thus, in 1944, Rotblat joined the Manhattan project in Los Alamos, and worked on the programme which would result in the bombing of Hiroshima and Nagasaki.

Originally, he had feared that the Germans were developing their own bomb. But when it became evident that this was not the case, he returned to Liverpool. He left in 1950 to work at a London medical school.

Seven years later, Rotblat and other like-minded scientists met in Pugwash, Nova Scotia, and formed a group which would continue to campaign against nuclear arsenals.

Rotblat was knighted in 1998, and died on August 31 last year, at the grand age of 97.

His epitaph could be a quote about the atomic bomb he gave to the Echo in 1970: "One always hoped that it would not be used, or that one had made a mistake in the calculation and it would not detonate."

The Steble Fountain goes with the
flow as the Liverpool skyline changes

"LIVERPOOL Football Club is all about winning things and being a source of pride to our fans. It serves no other purpose."

– David Moores, Liverpool FC Life President

IT isn't just supporters of England's most successful football club that the Reds are a source of pride to.

Liverpool FC is a source of pride to the city of Liverpool.

Indeed, you could quite conceivably argue that, along with The Beatles, LFC has been the most important ambassador for Liverpool that the city has ever had.

With the Liver Bird upon their chest, the Reds have blazed a trail across Europe for over 40 years.

While John, Paul, George and Ringo were putting the Merseyside music scene on the map, Bill Shankly and his players were ensuring that Liverpool became recognised across the continent as one of the most successful sporting cities.

What's more, they had a backing group of thousands on the Spion Kop – the most famous terrace in football.

The arrival of Scotsman Shankly as Liverpool manager in December 1959 not only transformed Liverpool FC but

the face of sport in the city forever.

By 1964 he'd taken Liverpool from second division obscurity to champions of England and led them into Europe for the first time.

While Shankly was transforming the Reds' fortunes on the pitch, the Kop's inhabitants, collectively known as Kopites, were creating a new terrace culture that had never been witnessed in this country before.

Up to 28,000, predominantly Scouse, male, Liverpudlians would congregate behind one of the goals every other Saturday afternoon on the Spion Kop – a steep, banked, terraced area named after a battle on Spioenkop Hill in South Africa during the Boer War in 1900.

The Mersey Sound was not only resonating around the world but also around Anfield on the PA system before kick-off on a Saturday and with a couple of hours to kill before the game started, Kopites began to sing along to the

tunes, just as they would in Liverpool's pubs of a night.

Soon they were adapting tunes by adding their own lyrics, usually spontaneously, to reflect something that had happened during the match.

In a city famous for it's quick-witted inhabitants, all manner of songs and chants developed and with up to 28,000 all singing at the same time a truly unique, stunning and utterly mesmorising phenomenon ensued.

It was so amazing that the BBC's Panorama even came to film the Kop in 1964!

Over the years the passion, colour and noise of Liverpool's Kop has become one of the most famous spectacles in world sport.

There are no spectators on the Kop. Only participants. They were the original '12th man', backing the teams created by Shankly, Bob Paisley, Joe Fagan, Kenny Dalglish, Gerard Houllier and now Rafa Benitez to success after success.

These days fans at all kinds of sporting occasions sing and shout but that terrace culture was born by Scousers at Anfield and taken all over the continent as Liverpool conquered Europe time and time again.

Liverpool should be proud of the way the city united in the aftermath of the Hillsborough disaster, when 96 Liverpool fans were crushed to death in Sheffield at the beginning of the FA Cup semi-final against Nottingham Forest on April 15, 1989.

In the agonising days afterwards the city mourned as one. Shoulders to cry on came in two colours. Red and Blue. Liverpool and Everton. Allegiances were put aside. Rivalry forgotten.

Anfield was opened to the grieving public and the Kop and pitch became a collage of colour, filled with flowers, scarves, flags and shirts.

Appropriately, Liverpool's first league game after the disaster was at Goodison Park for the Merseyside derby and the season ended with an all-Merseyside FA Cup final at Wembley, the second in four years.

At both those finals in 1986 and 1989, supporters of both clubs stood together and a chant of 'Merseyside, Merseyside, Merseyside' echoed around the ground.

That wouldn't have happened with any other two clubs from the same city.

In truth, it might not happen these days if Liverpool and Everton got to the FA Cup Final as relations between the two sets of fans have weakened in recent times but those afternoons were two of the proudest in our city's history.

But perhaps more than anything, Liverpool is proud of Liverpool FC for the success it has brought to the city.

English football is considered by many to be the best in the world. It's certainly the most exciting.

So for Liverpool to be the most successful club England has ever produced is something the city is fiercely proud of.

Liverpool FC is famed around the globe and has fans worldwide but its heartbeat remains in the city.

18 league titles, five European Cups, three UEFA Cups, seven FA Cups, seven League Cups, three European

Super Cups and ten Charity/Community Shields have been brought to the city by Liverpool FC (so far!).

And to truly understand what that means you only need to look at the number of people who turned out on the streets of Liverpool in May 2005 to welcome home the team who had just won a 5th European Cup.

An estimated 750,000 people lined the route that Liverpool's open-topped bus travelled down the following evening with another 300,000 in the city centre near St George's Hall where the homecoming tour ended.

It was the biggest street party the city had ever seen. A whole community came out to celebrate.

That's what Liverpool FC means to this city.

As David Moores said, one of the two reasons for Liverpool Football Club's existence is to "be a source of pride to our fans."

It's more than that.

It's a source of pride to our city with its success and supporters acting as standard bearers for the whole of English football.

by Chris McLoughlin

Saturday night was bath night in this Edge Hill home in 1980. No bathroom – the kitchen sink was ensuite

Top   Arthur Dooley, ex-docker and a fantastic sculptor. Impatient with photographers, he told me to "Hurry up" as I
         asked him to go back to the docks for this picture
Above   Liverpool guru and playwright Willy Russell knows how the real Liverpool people think. Educating Rita, educating us

Above left	The Steble Fountain on William Brown Street. The children had walked from the tenement block behind the art gallery to cool off and play in the water on a hot August afternoon
Top right	Cilla back home. She had just hit the charts and she played her record at the Scottie Road flat for her mum
Bottom right	Ken and a little girl meet at a Claire House fundraiser. I was touched as Ken knelt to talk to the little girl, clasping his hands with a look of delight in his eyes

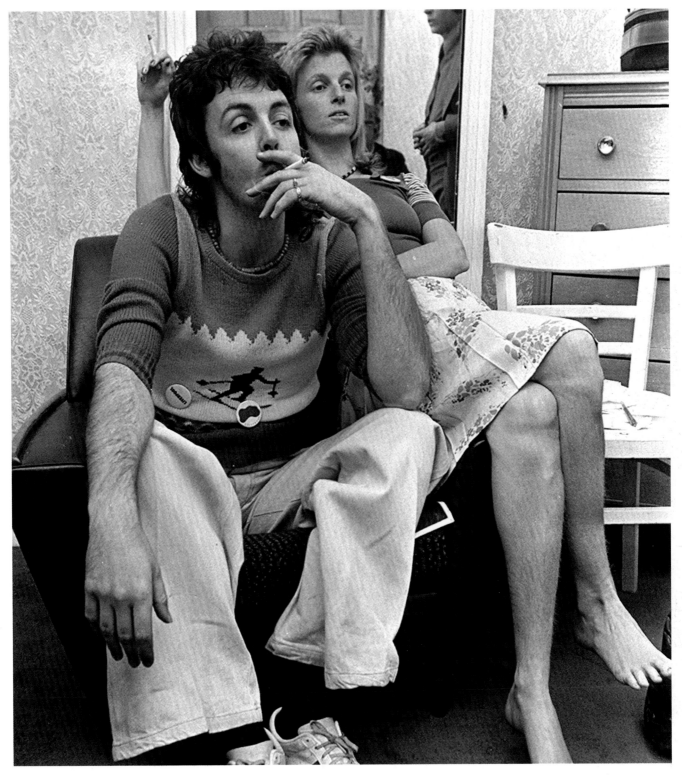

Behind the scenes with Paul McCartney and Linda at the Empire for their first tour with Wings. They sat on a Sunday afternoon in everyday wear – both smoking, both relaxed – as their children played tick in the corridors

D'you remember the buses then?
Tall, green and thin...
With an open platform at the back
That you'd jump on to get in

An' a half spiral staircase
That led up to the top
Where you could look out on the people
Or down into the shops
An' the seats all looked like leather
But you could tell that they weren't real
by the odd ciggy burn
And that "plasticky" feel

But upstairs was dead "Macho"
Meant for smokers and for "Men"
And the windows were all grimy
....no Clean Air Act then
And Downstairs was for mums with kids
Or people who had shopping
And you could swing around the
platform post
And jump off without stopping
And you'd be in Church Street
And savouring the smell
of the coffee up from Coopers
...The Kardomah as well.
.....None of it's there now...
... The Tatler....Woollies....gone
Just like the buses with the platforms
That you'd jump up to get on.

A CITY ON THE MOVE

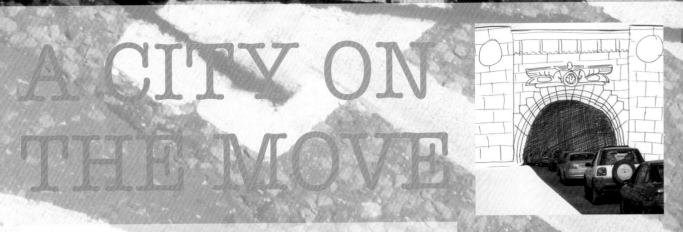

HOPPING onto the bus or train is a great way to explore the city and see Liverpool life all around you.
It really is a city on the move. Unless you're on Scottie Road in rush hour, that is.
We Scousers are a well connected bunch – we can get to London in about two hours on the train from Lime Street.
We can fly around the world from John Lennon Airport.
But wherever we may roam, there's nowhere quite like this Liverpool home.

A COMMUTER'S TRIBUTE
by Andrew Bonner

The Queensway Mersey Tunnel is a magnificent link between Wirral and Liverpool.
  Not only have I driven through it approximately four thousand times, but it's the only place where there's no point stressing if you're caught in traffic because you can't take a detour! If I add it up, I've spent at least a fortnight of my life down there.
  The tunnel is an amazing feat of engineering. I've been lucky enough to experience life underneath the road surface. It's a dark, dank, eerie world in the bottom half of the tube. I was amazed to see a small stream running down the middle. It appears my childhood fears of the tunnel leaking are actually true – albeit at a trickle!

Liverpool Loop Boogie   by Raphael Callaghan

When I've got a taste for travelling on a train
I go down to the station, book my ticket on Merseyrail
If you wanna go long distance well, that's cool
I'd rather go round and round on the Liverpool Loop

You can keep your Intercity, Motorail and Sealink too
I'd rather go round and round on the Liverpool Loop

You can buy your ticket ride the rails
from coast to coast
But I'll keep travelling
on the line I like
the most

If you wanna go long distance well, that's cool

I'd rather go round and round on the Liverpool Loop

Oh the Liverpool Loop is something we can be proud of
I'd rather ride on that train than in some plane
Up in the sky above

You can keep your Intercity, Motorail and Sealink too
I'd rather go round and round on the Liverpool Loop

The Liverpool Loop
The Liverpool Loop (mind the gap!)

We four kings of Liverpool are
George in a taxi, Paul in a car
John on his scooter, beeping his hooter
Following Ringo Starr

Scousers have roles in all walks of life – some high-powered, others working solidly behind the scenes.

Some may no longer live here but they made an impact that the city will never forget. Others carry on tirelessly championing work for the greater good.

From famous politicians to local legal stars there are those who aim to use their skill, contacts and expertise to achieve goals.

There are charity campaigners and writers who talk passionately about their subject matter to inspire and inform.

There's the commentators who speak out against injustice and the much loved and missed religious leaders who were happy to be called Scousers in their lifetimes.

And the social reformers and the entertainers whose common touch to communicate their passions hit the right chords with ordinary folk.

We may be champions in soccer and sport but Scousers are also gold medal winners in Liverpool's own league of selfless well-doers.

CH

CHERIE BLAIR
RICKY TOMLINSON
FIONA CASTLE
STEVE BINNS
DAVID SHEPPARD AND
DEREK WORLOCK
JOAN JONKER
REX MAKIN
KITTY WILKINSON
MARGARET SIMEY
SIR BOB SCOTT

AMPIONS

CHERIE BLAIR

SHE is known to legal colleagues and clients as Cherie Booth, eminent barrister and part time judge.

But it is as Cherie Blair, wife of former British Prime Minister Tony, that most of us recognise her.

Yet her career and her public life has been as influential in its own way as that of her husband.

She has a strong human rights background, fighting for a number of high profile causes.

"Many also see her as a role model for women, juggling both a successful career and four children"

Born in 1954, her father is the actor Tony Booth. Her parents' marriage broke down and she was raised by her mother, Gale.

She attended school in Crosby, including Seafield Convent Grammar, now part of Sacred Heart, and then studied law at the London School of Economics, graduating with a First Class degree.

She became a barrister in 1976, the same year in which she met a fellow lawyer, Tony Blair. The couple married in 1980.

Cherie specialises in employment, discrimination and public law, a stance which ironically has seen her represent claimants against the UK government, and has worked in the European Court of Justice.

In 2000 she also helped found Matrix Chambers, which specialises in human rights law.

As well as her legal work Cherie is active in a number of charities including Breast Cancer Care and Victim Support. She has also supported aids work in Africa.

Closer to home she is a patron of breast cancer charity the Lily Centre, based in Vauxhall, and is Chancellor Emeritus at John Moores University.

No stranger to controversy, she has weathered a flurry of unflattering headlines and photographs over the years.

Yet she guards the private lives of her children fiercely and enjoys close friendships with, among others, the Clintons. Indeed, Bill has urged her to stand as an MP. He said:

"If she wanted me to go ringing doorbells for her, I'd be happy to do it"

RICKY TOMLINSON

ACTOR, comedian, singer, banjo player, all-round entertainer, political activist, campaigner and fund-raiser – Ricky Tomlinson is all these things and more.

Above all, perhaps, he's a man of the people, a man who is never slow in championing Liverpool, the place and its people.

During his rich (and sometimes poor), colourful life, Ricky's love for and loyalty to the city has always shone through.

Not for him a move to a big posh pad in the Home Counties when fame came calling and the money began to roll in.

Ricky, who believes there is little difference between New Labour and the Conservatives, is currently supporting the campaign for a new workers' party.

He is also a central figure in the Justice for the Shrewbury Pickets group, which is fighting to clear the names of 24 men who received convictions after the 1972 national building strike. Ricky was jailed for two years in 1973, after being found guilty of unlawful assembly, affray and conspiracy.

In his autobiography, meanwhile, the former plasterer was brave and honest enough to confront an unpleasant part of his past when he spoke about his involvement with the National Front in the late 1960s, explaining that he had been poorly educated and politically naive.

As an actor, Ricky is possibly best known for his portrayals of Bobby Grant in Brookside and Jim Royle in The Royle Family. He has also starred in several films, including Mike Bassett: England Manager, and Raining Stones.

Ricky, however, is keen to put the world of acting in perspective, saying: "In the building game, we sometimes laid floors from eight in the morning until 6am the next day.

> "Acting is a piece of piss compared to that. I still don't regard myself as an actor... it has never seemed like a proper job. It's still like a game"

Late last year, Ricky showed his skills as a presenter, fronting an edition of Channel Five's Disappearing Britain series called When Coal Was King.

Who would play him if someone made a film of his life? He says: "Well, for the young Ricky, it'd have to be Brad Pitt – and, for the older Ricky, the wonderful Johnny Vegas!"

FIONA CASTLE

FIONA Castle was with her husband Roy every step of the way as he fought his brave battle against cancer and, at the same time, spearheaded the campaign for a lung cancer research centre in Liverpool.

Since he died on September 2, 1994, and although she is no longer associated with her husband's charity, she has continued to campaign for a cancer cure – and against smoking and passive smoking.

Her husband believed, as a non-smoker, that his cancer had been caused by the smoky atmosphere in jazz clubs where he played the trumpet. He was one of the first people to highlight something that is now commonly accepted – passive smoking is also harmful.

It may have taken time, but the ban on smoking in enclosed public places, which came into effect in July 2007, would have delighted Roy. As it does Fiona.

Her husband's wonderful legacy, of course, is the Roy Castle Lung Cancer Foundation Centre in Liverpool, which opened in May, 1998.

Fiona, meanwhile, the daughter of Dr William Dixon, lived in West Kirby until she was 14, attending Avalon School, Caldy – she later boarded at a ballet school in Surrey.

So there is more than one reason why Merseyside will always hold a special place for in Fiona's heart. Last October, she was back in the city to deliver the main address at the eighth annual ecumenical Pause for Hope service.

It was held at the city's Anglican Cathedral and organised by cancer charities including the Roy Castle Foundation, Alder Hey children's hospital, Macmillan Cancer Support, Marie Curie Cancer Care, the North West Cancer Research Fund, Merseyside Prostate Cancer Trust and the Woodlands Hospice.

Before devoting herself to family life, Fiona had a career in showbiz, having been introduced to Roy by their mutual friend, Eric Morecambe. She was a dancer and singer in pantomimes and summer seasons and also toured in musicals.

As well as sharing a rich life with Roy, Fiona shared a rich faith, and explained:

"Once Roy got cancer, he said, 'I can talk about my faith now because if it hadn't been real, it would have gone out of the window, but it is even more real to me now'.

My faith didn't waver either"

STEVE BINNS

IF ever a competition was launched to find Liverpool's truest champion Steve Binns would be one of the clear favourites.

Quite simply, there is barely a fact about his home city which Steve does not know – as countless tourists, journalists and Liverpool-philes can testify.

Anyone who has been taken on a guided tour of either the town hall or St George's Hall by Steve will able to vouch for the fact that he is one of this city's most passionate ambassadors.

As the city council's community historian, he spends much of his time talking of Liverpool's past while also extolling its virtues as a thoroughly modern city.

His guided tours are the stuff of legend with many a visitor having been wowed by his knowledge and his passion. And that's without even mentioning that Steve is blind.

"If ever there was a born fighter, it is Steve"

When he came into the world two months premature, he weighed just 2lbs 15ozs and as doctors battled to save his life, he was given too much oxygen and this cost him his sight.

As he points out: "It was the early 1950s and, if it had happened in more recent times, a good solicitor would have told us we had a good case to sue.

"But in those days, we just got on with things."

And get on with things he certainly did. After leaving school which, he readily admits, he hated, Steve went on to find work making wall brackets and later in a workshop for the blind.

But it was when he got a job in the council's PR department in 1990 that he really started to come into his own, particularly when he volunteered to take people on tours of the town hall – a task which he alone wanted to do.

In 1998, he became the city's community historian and six years later he was awarded the MBE for services to heritage.

"Modest and down to earth, Steve Binns may not like the fanfare of being listed amongst the greatest Merseysiders, but his place is undoubtedly deserved as he is a true champion of this region"

DAVID SHEPPARD AND DEREK WORLOCK

ANGLICAN bishop David Sheppard and Roman Catholic archbishop Derek Worlock formed a unique working partnership and friendship which helped transform the city's past tensions between the two communities during the so-called era of the "Orange and the Green".

Between them they forged an ecumenical understanding which also encompassed and befriended other faith groups in the city.

They were affectionately christened "fish and chips" by an admiring public.

David Sheppard was already famous as a former Sussex and England cricketer when he came to Liverpool in 1975 to be bishop.

Derek Worlock had worked in the East End parish of Stepney before moving to become Bishop of Portsmouth, and eventually coming to Liverpool a year later than David Sheppard, in 1976.

His instruction from Pope Paul VI was to "make sure that Liverpool did not become another Belfast".

Both archbishop and bishop were also closely involved with the community during the period of the Toxteth riots.

They once smuggled megaphones beneath their jackets to the leader of the black community who needed them to urge the crowds to disperse.

But their audiences didn't always listen. David Sheppard recalled a meeting with prime minister Margaret Thatcher in 1987 when she continually interrupted him. "It was like being heckled," he later wrote in his autobiography, pointed out that it was so often the peacemakers who got shot at.

He went on record as saying he was glad not to have been made archbishop of Canterbury.

"It would have been a murderous task to take on," he said. "The press were quite pitiless towards Robert Runcie and George Carey"

One of Derek Worlock's prime moments in office was welcoming Pope John Paul II to Liverpool in 1982.

The archbishop had formerly played an international role in church affairs, having advised the second Vatican Council on the role of lay people.

JOAN JONKER

IF she was writing a profile for one of the characters of her best-selling novels, Joan Jonker might have written: Feisty, intelligent, determined, funny, dignified… a champion and, above all, a lady.

But better than any fictional personality, the heroine this description would best describe is the woman herself.

For Joan, who became a best-selling author of around 20 books, was just as well known for her work fighting for the rights of victims of violence.

Great grandmother Joan, who died in February 2006 aged 83, was an enduring example of courage and selflessness, qualities that made the lives of thousands of people safer and better. She put her concerns into actions.

Joan founded Victims of Violence in 1976 after hearing about an elderly First World War veteran who had been beaten up and robbed in his home.

So outraged, she felt compelled to visit him and was inspired by his determination not to let the thugs win.

The charity grew into the only 24-hour service in Britain for such victims of violence, offering help and refuge.

Two hostels were set up in Kensington, primarily for elderly victims too scared to continue living in their own homes. Joan continued her work in spite of being a victim of crime herself, being mugged twice and burgled several times.

As she neared her 80s and, after fighting her own battle against cancer and undergoing several operations, Joan gave up the charity and it closed in 1999.

But her work as an author carried on apace from her home in Southport.

The many people she helped became friends of hers and she won numerous awards including an ECHO Mersey Marvel Award for for tireless efforts for others.

"Among the letters of praise she received was one from the late Princess of Wales and another from Ken Dodd, who supported the charity.

He said: "She was a lady of great integrity. She wasn't very tall but she was full of energy, drive and goodness"

REX MAKIN

THERE can hardly be a celebrity, politician, high-ranking police officer or, indeed, a gangster in Liverpool who does not have Rex Makin's number stored on their mobile phone.

In a legal career spanning almost 60 years, Rex – whose little-known first name is Elkan – has developed a reputation as one of the most fearsome and persistent solicitors ever to work on Merseyside.

The likes of Anne Robinson, Carla Lane, Freddie Starr, Jimmy Tarbuck and former assistant Merseyside Chief Constable Alison Halford have all had cause to call on Rex at one time or another and, in the process, he has become one of the best-known men on Merseyside.

> "Critics have accused him of being a friend of the underworld due to the numerous cases he has fought and won against Merseyside police, but he prefers to be known as a friend of the underdog"

Born in Birkenhead, his family moved to Liverpool when he was three years old and he has lived in, and been a champion of, the city ever since.

> "Given his high-ranking status in legal circles, it might have been easy for Rex to become a member of the establishment. But he has resisted, preferring to show a healthy suspicion of authority figures due, in his own words, to a hatred of bureaucracy and decisions made by grey, faceless pen-pushers"

True to form, Rex's ECHO column has never pulled any punches. Indeed, the very first one listed 10 well-known people who would "not be missed", starting off with "King Rat Degsie" (Derek Hatton) and "those public servants who exercise their power malignantly on the basis that they are accountable, as a result of which the ordinary citizen is oppressed."

He famously gave a personal gift of £50,000 to the newly-created JMU to set up its E Rex Makin Professorship in Criminal Justice and, among many other donations to city institutions, he made gifts to the National Museums And Galleries On Merseyside.

KITTY WILKINSON

KITTY Wilkinson appreciated that in a life of grime, cleanliness was the key to escaping disease and, in some cases, certain death.

It was her fearless spirit which drove her from the slums to open the first wash house, a Liverpool model that was to be copied in cities across the world.

She was born Catherine Seaward in 1786 in Londonderry. At the age of nine, her family moved across the Irish Sea to start a new life in Liverpool. But the journey was to have tragic consequences as her mother and sister were drowned in a storm.

Kitty was given temporary work with a middle class family who did much for charity. She was to follow their example and became known for her own community work, catering for the sick and teaching young children.

Her marriage to a French seaman ended with his death at sea. Then she married again - this time to a labourer called Thomas Wilkinson.

"In 1823, a cholera epidemic took hold on Liverpool. Many fled but Kitty stayed to comfort , forcing many to flee. Yet Kitty stayed on, comforting the dying"

The Wilkinson kitchen was turned into a large wash house with a continuous supply of hot water.

In one week alone, Kitty washed, dried and returned 34 bedspreads, 158 sheets, 110 blankets, 60 quilts and more than 1,000 garments.

In a 10 year period cholera claimed the lives of more than 1,500 Liverpudlians and infected a further 5,000.

Poor neighbours, with no means of cleaning their own infected clothes and sheets, were invited to make use of her home facilities and by 1846 Kitty and Thomas were appointed superintendents of the new Liverpool Corporation baths in Upper Frederick Street.

Kitty died in 1860, aged 73. Nearly 50 years later, the woman who was known across the city as Saint Kitty was honoured by having her image featured in a stained glass window in Liverpool's Anglican cathedral.

On her tombstone was the following inscription: "Indefatigable, self-denying, she was the widows' friend, the support of the orphan, the fearless and unwearied nurse of the sick and the instigator of public baths and wash houses for the poor"

MARGARET SIMEY

MARGARET Simey was the people's champion who took on Margaret Thatcher, Michael Heseltine and then Merseyside chief constable Kenneth Oxford – and won all the arguments.

Despite being born in Glasgow, educated in London and living in such diverse places as the West Indies and West Kirby, Mrs Simey (she always refused to use her title as Lady Simey) lived most of her 98 years in Liverpool 8 as a city (and later county) councillor representing the people of Granby.

She came to Liverpool at 18, when her father was appointed principal of the old college of commerce.

Liverpool was a different world from her schooldays at the exclusive St Paul's Girls' School in London, where she sat next to Winston Churchill's daughter and her teachers included the composers Gustav Holst and Ralph Vaughan Williams ("When Mr Holst became grumpy with the choir, we always looked forward to the arrival of nice Mr Vaughan Williams.")

She later became Liverpool University's first female graduate in the then new subject of social science, a subject taught by her husband Tom.

Her guiding light in those days was the pioneering feminist Eleanor Rathbone. Later, she was to be associated with the likes of Margaret Beavan and Bessie Braddock.

After taking in Jewish refugees fleeing from the Nazis, she became one of Liverpool's staunchest social reformers, not afraid to take on politicians or the police.

But it was as a councillor for Granby and chairman of the police authority against the background of the 1981 Toxteth riots that Margaret Simey forged her place in Liverpool's history.

She came out as a vociferous supporter of the people of Toxteth, accusing Kenneth Oxford of lack of accountability.

She also vented her wrath about social injustice on Michael Heseltine when he was dispatched to Merseyside as a special minister after the riots.

Her pleasure reading remained the lives of radicals, notably Knox, Marx and Lenin. But in an interview in 1999, she said:

"If I had them in a row on my bookshelf, the Bible, about Jesus, would be in their company.

"Of all the doctrines I have come across, his and John Knox are the ones I like the best. I long to have a political approach to Jesus"

SIR BOB SCOTT

SIR Bob Scott is the legendary "fixer" whose leadership and expertise put together – and won – Liverpool's Capital of Culture prize.

There could be no denying his golden track record, much of it achieved further along the M62 in Manchester.

For here also is the man who brought that city the Commonwealth Games. Before that, he had raised the cash to build the Royal Exchange Theatre, their most important repertory base outside London and Stratford, and transformed the fortunes of the Palace and Opera House Theatres.

Perhaps they were seen as natural missions for the former Merton College undergraduate, who had been president of the Oxford University Dramatic Society, and had played host to Richard Burton and Elizabeth Taylor at the height of their fame during their famous production (with students) of Dr Faustus.

But it was coming to Liverpool to head the Capital of Culture bid that convinced Bob Scott that together, Liverpool and Manchester could form the most formidable UK economic region outside the south east.

He said at the time: "The regional dimension is extremely important. Liverpool and Manchester have to work out a relationship which allows for Liverpool being the tourism and cultural capital."

Born in Minehead, Somerset, Sir Bob has devoted most of his time since preparing and submitting the Liverpool 2008 bid, championing the interests of the city.

His latest role is as an international ambassador heading an exchange programme with other European ports, including Naples, Marseilles and Gdansk.

This "cities on the edge" project pairs places which not only have a nautical history, but, as Sir Bob puts it, "are a little bit awkward and often go against conventions."

Hence future Scott-led initiatives about a whole range of social issues from football to the drug culture.

"Sir Bob's team convinced the UK judges assessing a total of 12 contenders that Liverpool should be the winner of the 2008 prize"

It was largely down to his efforts that the result was positive. He likened the success to Liverpool being given a scholarship more than a one-off prize.

"The real reward of the Scott bid is that it will hopefully provide a legacy for the future and change the lives of Liverpudlians for the better forever"

SCOUSE WIT AND WISDOM

"I always try and have a Scouser in my TV work. They act as a lucky charm. Ricky Tomlinson and John McArdle would agree."

Lynda La Plante
award winning writer, actress and author

Ringo Starr when asked

"Are you a mod or a rocker?"

"I'm a mocker."

"We had this song called Randy Scouse Git we didn't know what it meant. But our drummer Mickey Dolenz did. We couldn't release it in America because it was deemed unsuitable so we gave it the name Alternate Title.

"I now know what a Scouser is now because I've since played The Cavern and met some."

Peter Tork
of the Monkees

"He talks to me as though I were a public meeting."

Queen Victoria on William Gladstone, the first PM with a Scouse accent

"I was given a Liver Bird Trophy for my contribution to music and I picked it up in Liverpool from Radio City's Phil Easton. I am proud to be an adopted Scouser."

Chris De Burgh
singer

"I always said why go to London when everything you need is here."

Scouser **Phil Redmond**
TV guru and film maker

"Liverpool is second in my heart to London."

Charles Dickens
special constable of Liverpool and a frequent speaker in the city

"Liverpool must be the only city with an 'ology."

Terry Wogan
The DJ praising the annual Scouseology Awards for local talent in aid of Children in Need

Brian Burgess of the Adelphi Hotel creating his own catchphrase on BBC TV when he felt challenged by a catering staff member

"Just cook will, yer."

It later became a hit record by the writers of the musical Twopence To Cross the Mersey

The late Wooler's take on how Eppy decided to sign the leather-clad Beatles.

"If B.E. (Brian Epstein) hadn't been feeling that way, that day… no way.

Bob Wooler
Cavern DJ

"The great hope for the city is to develop the immense assets of the South Docks for light industry, housing and tourism."

Arthur Dooley
sculptor interviewed in the ECHO, 1973

"I thought we were Capital of Culture."

Willy Russell on being asked by the Echo about our city's success in becoming Capital of culture in 2008

A bus passenger

"Do you stop at at the Adelphi?"

"What!... On my wages?"

Anonymous Liverpool bus driver

OOLE
UR DOOLE
QUEEN VICTORI
SSELL RINGO STAR
ANTE BRIAN BURGES
TORK CHRIS DE BURG
OND CHARLES DICKEN
WOGAN BOB WOOLE
OLEY QUEEN VICTORI
RUSSELL RINGO STAR
PLANTE BRIAN BURGES
TORK CHRIS DE BURG
OND CHARLES DICKEN
WOGAN BOB WOOLE
LEY QUEEN VICTORI
RUSSELL RINGO STAR
PLANTE BRIAN BURGES
R TORK CHRIS DE BURG
MOND CHARLES DICKEN
RRY WOGAN BOB WOOLE
DOOLEY QUEEN VICTOR
RUSSELL RINGO STAR
PLANTE BRIAN BURGES
TORK CHRIS DE BURG
OND CHARLES DICKEN
OGAN BOB WOOLE
LEY QUEEN VICTOR
RUSSELL RINGO STAR
ANTE BRIAN BURGE

Reflections captured in the Albert Dock at night

Animal magic!

By Natasha Young

What the...?

In 1998 a whole new species of animal appeared in Liverpool.

The aptly named Superlambanana was formed as a commissioned piece by Japanese-based artist Taro Chiezo, as part of Britain's Art Transpennine Exhibition.

The dangers of genetically modified food, as well as the city's history of trading lambs and importing bananas, are said to have been the inspiration behind this unique creation, which moves around the city.

The sculpture has always been intended to change locations while also having changed colour on numerous occasions, altering from a pink period that was sponsored by the Breakthrough charity, to a cow print phase, and then back to its original yellow skin.

Some love it and some loathe it, but nonetheless, Superlambanana has grown to be a popular landmark that also complements Liverpool's thriving art scene.

Souvenir models are a big hit with visitors.

Birds' eye view

The Liver Bird is the symbol of Liverpool, and is therefore used as a signature for a number of the city's institutions, such as within the emblems of Liverpool City Council and Liverpool Football Club.

Probably the most famous presence of the Liver Bird would be on the top of the Royal Liver Building, where two 18ft tall birds are a prominent addition to the city's waterfront.

Local legend has it that if the two birds were to fly away from each other the city would no longer exist, and further myths suggest that one is female and looks out to the sea for seamen to return safely, whilst the other, a male, looks out onto the city to see what time the pubs open.

The birds are the subject of

much speculation, with many having created assumptions about their species and meanings, and nothing actually being set in stone.

Some claim the bird to be a cross between an eagle and a cormorant; the bird of good luck to sailors.

Superlambanana in his yellow coat

Googi's top of the bill

In 1971, 20-year-old Penny Page from Wirral began her rise to fame with puppet Googi the Liverpool duck.

Winning first prize for their ventriloquism act in a talent contest at the London Palladium, Penny and Googi found the break they needed.

Appearing in a 14-week pantomime season at the Palladium alongside entertainers Frankie Howard, Dora Bryan and Alfie Bass, the local double act were tipped to be the next big stars, until Penny decided to quit London and bring Googi back to the North West where they belonged.

As well as performing shows all over the region, Googi and Penny embarked on a music career.

Their biggest hit "Googi The Liverpool Duck", sold over 20,000 copies.

Merseybeat menagerie

The Fab Four and animals go hand-in-paw. The Beatles were first seen on horses for the video for Penny Lane. They filmed it in Hyde Park – if they came back to Liverpool they would have been mobbed.

They frequently mentioned animals in their lyrics. John loved Lewis Carroll and Edward Lear and I Am The Walrus grew out of his passion for the surreal. Previously, on Sgt Pepper, he dedicated a song to his love of circuses in the Benefit of Mr Kite and, of course, Henry the Horse who danced a waltz.

On the White album there was Martha My Dear, about Paul's dog (it later appeared on the cover of Paul is Live on the zebra crossing). Everyone Got Something To Hide Except (for Me and My Monkey) was John's. George's song about Piggies, too was satirical. On Abbey Road, Ringo sang about an Octopuses Garden.

Finally, on an other note, in the film Jungle Book the cartoon vultures were depicted as long-haired Scousers after Beatlemania hit the US.

And did you know that John had a cat called... Elvis.

Vegetarian Paul, who had a solo album called Ram after an animal on his farm, enjoyed success with his Rupert the Bear film and the Frog Chorus. He has also created a cartoon called Wirral The Squirrel.

Pongo and pals monkey about

At one time there was no need to travel to Chester and beyond to catch a glimpse of wild animals in the zoo, for there was one based right in the city.

The Liverpool Inner City Zoological Park & Gardens stood from 1884 to the early 1900s, on the site that is now known as Walton's Cavendish Retail Park.

Large bronze versions of Liverpool's iconic Liver Birds were there to welcome visitors at the gates of the park.

Many enjoyed the zoo's monkey house which was home of Pongo the chimpanzee, who is said to have been the star attraction.

Now all that remains of the zoo is the former ticket booth.

True war hero

During World War II a number of civilian lives were saved, all thanks to a Liverpool dog.

Jet, a rescue dog who was trained at Gloucester's War Dog School from the age of nine months, fulfilled his duty of searching for bodies when there had been a direct bomb hit.

He would go into the targeted buildings pointing out those who had been left inside, signalling whether they were alive or dead.

There was one particular act of bravery amongst all of Jet's hard work that made a news story out of him at the time, and resulted with the reward of a bravery medal.

Emergency services thought they had found everybody that remained in a directly hit hotel.

However Jet's behaviour indicated otherwise, and adamant that there was still somebody alive in the building, the dog remained there for around 11 and a half hours until a woman was taken out of the building alive.

A memorial, arranged by Jet's owner, now stands in Calderstones Park where he is buried as a reminder of the good work that dogs do.

Where the wild things are

Who would have thought that some of the worlds wildest, most endangered animals could be seen in Merseyside?

Knowsley Safari Park provides a safe and natural environment for around 30 species of mammal.

The 200 hectares of Merseyside land are home to jungle royalty such as lions, tigers, rhinos and elephants, right down to smaller creatures including various species of birds and reptiles.

The park has been open since 1971, when the 18th Earl of Derby marked the opening officially. Since then it has become one of the city's major tourist attractions.

We really are good sports. In fact great sports.
It goes without saying – our football legacy is the envy of most cities.
Liverpool and Everton have certainly provided some of the great soccer heroes of all time and our clubs have been managed by the best in the business.
But it's not just on the football pitch where we are winners but on the athletics arenas and the boxing rings and snooker halls.
Scousers are capable of anything when it comes to sport.
And every Scouse school boy and school girl will have a home grown icon to look up to in a particular field.
Scousers strive for success.

JOE MERCER
MARY PETERS
BILL SHANKLY
BETH TWEDDLE
BOB PAISLEY
RED RUM
JOHN CONTEH
BILLY LIDDELL
DIXIE DEAN
STEVEN GERRARD

SPORTS

JOE MERCER

> "Mercer was a bandy-legged wing half with a biting tackle, then became a shrewd manager"

ONE of football's all-time greats, Joe Mercer, spent the best part of 50 years in football – and inspired affection, admiration and respect from fellow professionals and the general public.

A Footballer of the Year honour, a Merit Award from the players' union and OBE for services to the game underlined his popularity.

Mercer was a bandy-legged wing half with a biting tackle, then became a shrewd manager.

In both capacities, he was a winner with a broad smile, collecting his first league championship medal with Everton, along with five England caps, before war broke out.

Although playing in more than 20 unofficial war-time internationals,

he was not capped again, but at club level there was to be more success with Arsenal.

Following a £7,000 move to Highbury in 1946, he won two league titles and an FA Cup win over Liverpool at in 1950.

During this time, he continued to live on Merseyside, training at Anfield. That he was captain of the side that beat Liverpool at Wembley was rather embarrassing; that he should sustain the double fracture of a leg (which ended his playing days) against them four years later was tragic.

As he was carried off, he waved farewell to the crowd. But his football career was still only beginning.

After managing Sheffield United and Aston Villa – winning the first-ever League Cup with Villa in 1961 – Mercer brought the good times to Manchester City in partnership with flamboyant coach Malcolm Allison.

In three seasons, they led City to the League Championship, FA Cup, League Cup and European Cup-Winners' Cup.

Such was his standing, the FA asked him to become caretaker manager of the national side after Don Revie's defection to Saudi Arabia in 1977 and he later became general manager of Coventry.

He continued to live on Merseyside after his retirement and died on his 76th birthday in 1990.

MARY PETERS

"She set 25 British records from 1962 to 1972; at the 1964 Olympics in Tokyo, she just missed out on a medal, finishing fourth in the pentathlon"

MARY Peters was British sport's golden girl in the 1970s. The charismatic athlete was indelibly linked with her beloved Northern Ireland after claiming the gold medal in the pentathlon at the 1972 Olympics.

But if others lost sight of the fact that Mary was born in Higher Road, Halewood, on July 6, 1939, Mary herself never did.

She spent her early years at Kingsthorne junior school, but left for Northern Ireland when her insurance manager father was transferred there just before her 11th birthday.

She regularly returned to visit aunts and uncles in Belle Vale, Cronton and Formby and in her early teens and, during visits to an auntie in Woolton, could be seen at the Liverpool University ground in Allerton practising the shot putt with a 12lb shot made by her father.

Even in her triumph at the Munich Olympics, Liverpool was not far from Mary's mind.

"The crowd was fantastic," she told newsmen afterwards. "It was just like The Kop."

While Munich was the crowning glory of her athletics career, it was not her only achievement.

She set 25 British records from 1962 to 1972; at the 1964 Olympics in Tokyo, she just missed out on a medal, finishing fourth in the pentathlon.

She claimed silver two years later at the Kingston Commonwealth Games, before striking double gold in the pentathlon and shot-putt in Edinburgh four years later.

But it was the world record-breaking gold medal she claimed in Munich in 1972 which captured the hearts of the British public.

Her chief rival was home favourite Heide Rosendahl – and the pentathlon came down to a duel between the two.

Mary was fractionally ahead going into the final event, Rosendahl's strongest, the 200 metres. The German girl won the race, but Mary recorded a personal best time to finish fourth.

She had an agonising wait to find out if she had done enough. But when the points were calculated, Mary knew she had not only won gold, she had shattered the world record and Olympic record in the process.

Mary's gold medal was the only medal for Britain at the Games.

She was made an MBE in 1973, a CBE in 1990 and a Dame of the British Empire in 2000.

BILL SHANKLY

"The fans idolised a man who laid the foundations for a remarkable era in which the Reds completely dominated English football in the 1970s and 80s and conquered Europe"

LIVERPOOL have signed many great stars down the years.

But the club's best "signing" of all was not a player... more a Messiah. Shanks made no secret that one of the reasons which persuaded him to join the Reds as manager from Huddersfield Town in December 1959 was because he felt the Anfield fans "were my kind of people".

It quickly became a two-way rapport. The fans idolised a man who laid the foundations for a remarkable era in which the Reds completely dominated English football in the 1970s and 80s and conquered Europe.

Born in the mining village of Glenbuck, Ayrshire, in 1913, Shankly was one of 10 children.

He always wanted to be a professional footballer – the other option was the pit – and eventually joined Carlisle, before being transferred to Preston, where his greatest moment was helping them to win the FA Cup Final in 1938.

He played for Preston after the war, before becoming manager at Carlisle and subsequently Grimsby, Workington then Huddersfield.

His appointment as Liverpool boss was a masterstroke by then chairman Tom Williams. Shanks, a shrewd Scot with a broad accent, set about fashioning a side that would lift the spirits of the fans, especially those who packed the Kop.

His rebuilt side swept to the Second Division title in 1962 and two years later they were League Champions.

The next year came the trophy Liverpool fans had always yearned for – the FA Cup won against Leeds United. Another title followed in 1966 and in 1973 they completed the double of Championship and UEFA Cup.

The 3-0 demolition of Newcastle in the 1974 FA Cup final was Shankly's swansong, as he shocked the football world by retiring.

He died on September 29, 1981 after a heart attack.

A bronze statue, unveiled in 1998 by his widow Nessie stands behind the Kop, a reminder of a man who lifted the club to greatness.

BETH TWEDDLE

BETH Tweddle made history in 2006, when she became the first British gymnast to win a world championship gold medal.

She honed her world-conquering skills in a training facility in Toxteth. Originally from Bunbury in Cheshire, Tweddle moved to Merseyside as a youngster to train, before becoming a student at Liverpool JMU.

She won her first British National Championships in 2001, an achievement she would repeat every year through to 2004.

She also helped Liverpool win the British Team Championships four consecutive times.

At her World Championships debut in 2001, Tweddle was 24th in the all-around final.

She improved dramatically in 2002, when she won a bronze medal on the uneven bars at the European Championships in Patras, Greece. Her medal was the first for a British gymnast at Europeans.

In the same year, she was a close fourth in the bars final at the World Championships and won three medals at the Commonwealth Games: silver in the team final and all-around and gold on the uneven bars.

In 2003 Beth became the first UK female gymnast to win a medal at the World Championships with a bronze on the bars.

But this was still only a beginning.

The year In 2004 she won silver at the European Championships and the World Cup. She went to the 2004 Olympics in Athens and was considered an excellent prospect for a medal on bars, but missed qualifying for the event final.

At the 2005 World Artistic Gymnastics Championships, she earned her second Worlds medal, a bronze. She was fourth in the all-around at the 2005 Worlds, the highest ever for a UK gymnast.

Injury disrupted her preparations in 2006, forcing her to withdraw from the Commonwealth Games.

But she recuperated in time to compete in the 2006 European Championships, where she captured the uneven bars title with a performance that scored a full point ahead of that of the next competitor.

With her win, Tweddle became the first British gymnast ever to win a gold medal at Europeans.

But the climax to her career was still to come, when she stood supreme as the finest gymnast in her discipline on the planet, striking gold in Denmark.

"Beth helped Liverpool win the British Team Championships four consecutive times"

BOB PAISLEY

BOB Paisley was a reluctant genius. He never wanted to go into management, but having been persuaded to take command of Liverpool Football Club, he surpassed the achievements of every manager in the history of British football.

The humble son of the north east, always more at ease in the wings than on centre stage, amassed an amazing collection of 19 trophies in nine seasons.

His connection with Liverpool stretched back to May 8, 1939, when he signed on as a player for a £10 signing-on fee and weekly wage of £5.

Despite scoring one of the goals which defeated Everton in the semi-final of the 1950 FA Cup, he was left out of the Cup final team by the directors who selected the side.

He overcame that crushing blow to become reserve team trainer and a renowned, self-taught physiotherapist.

He was the natural successor when Bill Shankly delivered his resignation bombshell in 1974, albeit a role he assumed reluctantly.

Liverpool finished championship runners-up in his first season.

"I was like an apprentice that ran wide at the bends," he later declared.

But the following campaign he cleaned up with a League title and UEFA Cup double. It was the forerunner to a season climaxed by Paisley's "perfect day" when his team lifted the European Cup for the first time with a 3-1 defeat of Borussia Moenchengladbach in Rome in May 1977.

The victory installed Paisley as the first English-born manager to lift Europe's greatest prize.

The Roman conquest heralded the end of Kevin Keegan's magnificent Anfield career, but Paisley revealed his command of tactics was matched by his judgement of football talent, snapping up Kenny Dalglish from Celtic for £440,000, £60,000 less than the income from Keegan's transfer.

Dalglish scored the winner when Liverpool retained the European Cup the following season, but Paisley's teams annexed six championships and a hat-trick of League Cup successes – not to mention 23 Bells Manager of the Month awards.

Retiring in 1983, years later he was elected to the board of directors and was an advisor to Kenny Dalglish, Liverpool's first player-manager. Paisley was tragically stricken by Alzheimer's disease and died in February 1996.

RED RUM

"Rummy raced his way into the nation's hearts thanks to series of storming displays at Aintree"

RED RUM is still a household name 12 years after his death and 30 years after his record-breaking hat-trick of Grand Nationals.

But Rummy was more than just a successful racehorse. He was a character, a people's champ, a national treasure.

As winner of the Grand National in 1973, 1974 and 1977 (and second in 1975 and 1976), he became our most beloved four-legged friend, popping up on This Is Your Life, BBC Sports Personality of the Year, Blue Peter, The Generation Game and Record Breakers. He even had his flanks stroked by a leather-clad Sally James on Tiswas.

When Japanese restaurateur Rocky Aoki tried to buy him from owner Noel Le Mare for £500,000 (in the same summer Liverpool paid £440,000 for Kenny Dalglish) as a promotional gimmick, it created a public outcry.

Arriving at trainer Ginger McCain's stables in Southport, Aoki received a sharp crack over the head from a little old lady's umbrella accompanied by the battle cry: "Remember Pearl Harbor."

The deal was promptly scuppered.

Rummy raced his way into the nation's hearts thanks to series of storming displays at Aintree. Red Rum was an Aintree specialist. He lit up when he got there.

His first Grand National victory in 1973 saw him produce perhaps the most exciting finish Aintree has ever seen, as he ate into front runner Crisp's 15-length lead to beat him to the line by three-quarters of a length.

He and trainer Ginger McCain went on to further victories in the 1974 and 1977 Grand Nationals, Red Rum becoming the only horse to win Aintree's famous race three times.

He retired from racing due to a crippling foot disease in 1978. Red Rum came to be recognised as a racing icon by people outside the racing world as much as those within.

Trained on the sands of Southport beach, he lived in modest stables behind Ginger McCain's used car showrooms in Upper Aughton Road, Birkdale.

In retirement Red Rum became a sought-after celebrity as he opened supermarkets, attended charity events and led the parade in many Grand Nationals.

After his death in 1995 Red Rum was buried on the finishing post at Aintree where visitors pay tribute to his memory as the horses thunder past on race days.

JOHN CONTEH

JOHN Conteh is one of Britain's most illustrious boxing champions of all time. In the mid to late 70s he was touted as a possible opponent of the legendary Muhammad Ali.

He enjoyed great fame in Britain and was often on the front as well as the back pages of the leading dailies due to his love of partying and women.

It is accepted, even by the man himself, that this excessive lifestyle brought about a premature decline in his talents.

Born in Toxteth on May 27, 1951, of a father from Sierra Leone and an Irish mother, the family moved to Kirkby soon after, and that is when Conteh stepped into the ring.

He started boxing at 10 at the Kirkby Amateur Boxing Club, and at 19 won the middleweight gold medal at the 1970 Commonwealth Games in Edinburgh.

He turned professional in 1971, scoring a 56-second knockout over Okacha Boubekeur at London's Grosvenor House Hotel. Only 15 fights, and 13 KOs later, Conteh was European champion and on his way to much bigger and more lucrative opportunities. He won the WBC light-heavyweight crown in October 1974 at Wembley, outpointing Argentinean Jorge Ahumada after 15 rounds.

Successful defences came, first against American Lonnie Bennet, and then in Copenhagen against Mexican Yaqui Lopez before Conteh's most memorable performance.

The hugely popular Scouser returned home on March 5, 1977, to halt American Len Hutchings in three rounds at the Liverpool Stadium, on one of the most celebrated nights in the city's illustrious fight history.

His infamous partying finally caught up with him in 1978 however, when he lost a 15-round decision to the Yugoslav fighter Mate Parlov.

He twice failed to win back his old crown in 1979 and then again seven months later in 1980.

He retired from the fight game shortly after. His professional record stood at 34 wins, one draw, four losses with 23 knockouts.

A national celebrity, Conteh also has the distinction of being British Superstars competition champion in 1974, the second year of the televised sporting event.

After an up and down career, which at times reached the very pinnacle of his sport, Conteh settled down later in life and is now a very successful after-dinner speaker all across the country.

"His professional record stood at 34 wins, one draw, four losses with 23 knockouts"

BILLY LIDDELL

"He was club top scorer in eight seasons and, during Liverpool's wilderness years in the Second Division in the 1950s, was particularly prolific"

NO one man is bigger than any football club. But Billy Liddell came close. During his heyday of the 1940s and 1950s, the Liverpool winger became so popular among fans, they rechristened the team "Liddellpool".

An archetypal man for all seasons and all positions, he was included in the Merseyside team of the 20th century voted for by BBC listeners.

One of the all-time greats of British football, he and Sir Stanley Matthews were the only two players to appear twice in UK sides against Europe in 1947 and 1955.

A Scottish international, Liddell's prime position was as a raiding left-winger, but he also excelled on the opposite flank, at centre forward or inside forward.

Such was his versatility that, due to injuries to others, he played in every outfield department and possessed a hammer of a shot in both feet.

Liverpool signed him from Scottish junior club Lochgelly Violet as a 15-year-old amateur in June

1938 and gave an undertaking he could continue his studies to become an accountant.

He remained on the club's payroll until the end of season 1960-61 and his Corinthian attitude meant he was never once booked.

A maker and taker of goals, he starred in Liverpool's 1946-47 Championship season and an early injury to the great Scot at Wembley in the 1950 FA Cup Final against Arsenal reduced his pace as Liverpool slipped to a 2-0 defeat.

He was club top scorer in eight seasons and, during Liverpool's wilderness years in the Second Division in the 1950s, was particularly prolific.

In 1954-55, he struck 30 goals in 40 matches.

On hanging up his boots, he became a bursar at Liverpool University and, on retirement, a Justice of the Peace in 1961.

He suffered Alzheimer's disease during his later years and died in July 2001 at the age of 79.

DIXIE DEAN

ARGUABLY the greatest goalscorer ever to grace English football, undeniably the greatest Everton player was born in 1907.

His memory, however, will live forever.

Scorer of 383 goals in 433 Everton appearances, in the 1930s he captained the Toffees to an unprecedented treble of Second Division, First Division and FA Cup triumphs in successive seasons.

But the achievement for which he is best remembered is the individual goalscoring record of 60 League goals in a season, a record set in 1928 and never likely to be beaten.

His great friend and rival, former Liverpool boss Bill Shankly, delivered a wonderful tribute to Dean at a lunch on the day he died.

"Dixie Dean belongs in the ranks of the supremely great, like Beethoven, Rembrandt or Shakespeare. His goalscoring record is the greatest thing under the sun."

But Dean's story was not exclusively linked to Goodison Park.

He began his football career at Tranmere Rovers before being transferred to Everton for £3,000 in 1925.

During the summer of 1926, however, his football career came under threat after he fractured his skull and jaw in a motorcycle accident.

Thomas Keates's Jubilee History of Everton Football Club recorded: "Doctors were afraid he could not live for many hours. His survival astonished them. When recovery was assured the medical pronouncement was 'This man will never be able to play football again.'"

Play again he did, to such startling affect that romantic tales began to surround his spell in hospital.

Envious contemporaries suggested that surgeons had left a steel plate in his skull.

The stories were nonsensical, but indicated his aura.

With shirt numbering introduced for the first time at the 1933 FA Cup Final at Wembley to aid radio listeners, Dean became the first Everton number nine.

Revered for his sportsmanship as well as his talent, he was never once booked nor dismissed, despite the kind of provocation which once saw him lose a testicle.

For a man whose life was linked so indelibly with Everton Football Club, it was fitting that he died at Goodison Park in March 1980, minutes after the final whistle of a derby.

"But the achievement for which he is best remembered is the individual goalscoring record of 60 League goals in a season, a record set in 1928 and never likely to be beaten"

STEVEN GERRARD

"A product of Liverpool's youth academy, he was spotted playing for local amateur side Whiston Juniors and signed his first professional contract on November 5, 1997"

STEVEN Gerrard is a living Liverpool legend. With his peak years possibly still ahead of him, many Anfield experts rate him as second only to Kenny Dalglish in the club's all-time Hall of Fame of players.

And there are some who will argue his influence on the side has been greater even than King Kenny's.

The only English footballer to have scored in the finals of the Champions League, UEFA Cup, FA Cup and League Cup – his strikes in the two domestic finals were classics.

A product of Liverpool's youth academy, he was spotted playing for local amateur side Whiston Juniors and signed his first professional contract on November 5, 1997.

He made his debut 12 months later and established himself in the Liverpool first team during 1999-2000.

His early years were troubled by injury – growth spurts causing a succession of problems which were eventually cured when his body finally stopped growing.

The 2000-01 campaign brought Gerrard his first trophy successes as he put his injury problems well and truly behind him, making 50 first-team appearances while scoring 10 goals as Liverpool won a trophy treble of League Cup, FA Cup and UEFA.

At the end of that season, Gerrard was named PFA Young Player of the Year.

In October 2003, Gerard Houllier handed Gerrard Liverpool's club captaincy.

Some observers raised eyebrows, citing an indifferent disciplinary record, but in his first season as skipper, Gerrard was booked just twice more.

Approached by Chelsea to sign for them during the summer of 2004, he eventually chose to stay at Liverpool.

It was an inspired decision, Liverpool going on to claim the Champions League trophy in Istanbul in one of the most dramatic matches ever seen in the competition.

Gerrard was the second youngest captain ever to lift the European Cup (Didier Deschamps is the youngest), but the summer proved another troubled one for him as he wrestled once again with overtures from Chelsea.

This time, he seemed to have made up his mind to leave, before making a dramatic about turn... this time for good.

The 2005–06 season was Gerrard's most impressive to date.

He scored 23 goals in 53 games from midfield, was voted PFA Player of the Year by his fellow players and capped the season by captaining Liverpool to victory in the FA Cup – when he scored one of the greatest goals in FA Cup final history.

And the best may be yet to come...

Making TV History
By Barrie Mills

FRED'S weather map; Sandra and Beryl's bedsit; the Boswells' hen; the body under the patio; car Z-Victor One... all part of Liverpool's contribution to British TV history.

It's been an important part, too – some significant shows have been created or set in Liverpool and it's hard to imagine what would be on our screens today if there had been no Z Cars, no Liver Birds, no Black Stuff and no Brookside.

Set your show in Liverpool and you call up a backdrop that is as good as an extra character.

Z Cars, first screened by the BBC in 1962, is often described as the first modern police show, taking the genre away from the homely world of Dixon of Dock Green and bringing it bang up to date.

Modern coppers didn't ride around on pushbikes and help old ladies across roads – they drove after armed robbers in fast patrol cars and smashed crime rings.

Writer Troy Kennedy Martin (who would later write The Italian Job and the TV drama Edge of Darkness) is said to have come up with the idea for Z Cars as he listened to police radio transmissions while recovering in bed from illness.

In a time of social upheaval, Liverpool was the perfect setting for a show that broke with tradition, and Martin's Z Cars (named after the Ford Zephyrs they used) patrolled the fictional areas of Newtown and Seaport – thinly disguised versions of Kirkby and Liverpool itself.

This was a gritty and realistic show which depicted the police as real, fallible people, just as likely to kick the cat as the rest of 1960s society. Without characters like PC 'Fancy' Smith and Charlie Barlow, there would have been no Sweeney (created by Martin's brother Ian)... although the bulky studio cameras of the day meant the Newtown coppers never got to go on car chases.

There would also be no Everton FC theme tune – legend has it that the Z Cars theme, based on a folk tune called Johnny Todd, was played at Goodison Park one Saturday in honour of a group of Z Cars actors in the crowd. With its 'boys in blue' link, the music stuck and has been played as the Everton team takes the pitch ever since.

Z Cars continued to pound the Newtown beat until 1978, having spawned the spin-off Softly Softly for actors Stratford Johns and Frank Windsor. Other well-know names who turned up for duty included Brian Blessed, Colin Welland, Leonard Rossiter, John Thaw and Judi Dench.

Meanwhile, the gentler side of 1960s Liverpool was embodied in the Liver Birds, Carla Lane and Myra Taylor's comedy about two girls sharing a flat in Huskisson Street.

But the warm humour surrounding the efforts of Sandra (Nerys Hughes) and Beryl (Polly James) to find love disguised the fact that this was a piece of television celebrating the new-found independence of women – and once again Liverpool was the perfect setting (although watch an episode today on UK Gold and the first thing that strikes you is how filthy with soot the Liver Building was 35 years ago).

The show ran from 1969 until 1979, with a brief revival in 1996, and regulars included Dawn (played by Pauline Collins for the first five episodes), Carol (played by Elizabeth

SCOUSERS make great TV quiz and game show hosts. Here's a few of the greats
- Tom O'Connor is the king of the buzzer and spent 18 years on Cross Wits. Other game shows included Zodiac and Name That Tune. He is a regular on Countdown.
- Les Dennis spent 15 years on Family Fortunes.
- Paul O'Grady hosted Blankety Blank as his alter ego Lily Savage.
- Anne Robinson is the cruel host of The Weakest Link – an international success.
- Jimmy Tarbuck was an odds on favourite on Winner Takes All. Daughter Lisa also hosts various quizzes and has been presenter on Have I Got News For You.
- Cilla Black gave a lorra lorra ratings to Blind Date.
- The Scaffold – Mike McCartney, Roger McGough and John Gorman in a mould breaking quiz show for kids called Score With The Scaffold.
- Keith Chegwin in Cheggers plays Pop, one of the first TV pop quizzes.

by Peter Grant

THE number of TV shows set in Liverpool grows almost by the week, and performers with Liverpool links are on our screens every day. Here's a list, in no particular order, of some of the most memorable and the year they first appeared: A Family At War (1970), Scully (1984), Waterfront Beat (1991), Mersey Beat (2001), One Summer (1983), Nice Guy Eddie (2001), Liverpool 1 (1998), This Morning (1988), Lilies (2007).

by Peter Grant

SCOUSERS IN SIT COMS
Craig Charles in Red Dwarf (right); Paul O'Grady in Eyes Down; Patricia Routledge (top) and Geoffrey Hughes in Keeping Up Appearances; Paul Barber in Only Fools and Horses and also with Phil Whitchurch in Brothers McGregor; Liza Tarbuck in Watching by the late, great Liverpool writer Jim Hitchmough who also wrote the hit drama The Bullion Boys starring David Jason.

Estensen, who moved in with Sandra after Beryl left), Sandra's mum (Mollie Sugden), Lucien the rabbit enthusiast (Michael Angelis) and Carol's dad Mr Boswell (Ray Dunbobbin) – a name which Carla Lane would later revisit for her second comedy set in the city.

Bread, which ran from 1986-91, charted the lives of the Boswell family and was set amid the terraced streets of south Liverpool.

Although some criticised Bread for portraying Scousers as stereotypical work-shy scroungers, many thought its gentle comedy was never meant to be taken too seriously – and at its peak it was watched by audiences round the 20 million mark.

Characters like battleaxe mother Nellie Boswell (Jean Boht), downtrodden dad Freddie Boswell (Ronald Forfar) and his 'bit on the side' Lilo Lil (Eileen Pollock) became part of British TV culture – and who could forget the extravagantly dressed Aveline (Gilly Coman)?

There has never been a shortage of talented writers in Liverpool and during the 1970s and 1980s people like Alan Bleasdale and Willy Russell were beginning to make their mark.

We have Bleasdale to thank for Boys From The Blackstuff – and the perennial taunt aimed at Merseyside football fans by opposing supporters: 'Gizza Job'.

It may have appeared to set Liverpool in a negative light, but in fact Bleasdale's "absurd, mad, black farce" (as he described it) showed that it was wrong to characterise the unemployed as work-shy scavengers.

The reality of life for many in 1982 was unemployment, poverty and an unending search for work and people like Yosser Hughes (Bernard Hill) were to be found in countless towns across Britain.

But Liverpool added an extra edge to the drama and made sure that Yosser and his mates (an out-of-work tarmac gang, hence the title) would be remembered long after the Thatcher years had passed.

Liverpool has also been a centre of TV production for more than 25 years, with Mersey TV (now Lime Pictures) the most well-known name in the field. Now producing Hollyoaks, the company is best known for the soap opera Brookside, which ran between 1982 and 2003.

When it launched, its only real rivals were Coronation Street and Emmerdale Farm. Three years later, the BBC responded with EastEnders, which owed a huge debt to Brookside for the realism of its treatment of everyday life.

Brookside may be gone, but its characters live on in the memory of its fans: from Bobby and Sheila Grant (Ricky Tomlinson and Sue Johnston, later Jim and Barbara in The Royle Family), to Jimmy, Billy and Lyndsey Corkhill (Dean Sullivan, John McArdle and Claire Sweeney), and from 'Tinhead' (Phil Olivier) to Harry Cross (Bill Dean).

And when writers of current soaps are short of ideas, they can always look at the Brookside back catalogue for inspiration. Were Coronation Street's writers, for example, thinking of the George Jackson Is Innocent campaign from Brookie's early years when they came up with the Free Deirdre Rachid campaign?

TRIVIA
- Scully, written by Alan Bleasdale, featured cameos by Elvis Costello, Kenny Dalglish and Bob Paisley, among other LFC stars.
- Paul and Linda McCartney appeared in an episode of Bread, in which Nellie Boswell failed to recognise them.
- Monty Python star Eric Idle was drafted in as script editor on some early episodes of The Liver Birds.
- Scouse writers Jimmy McGovern (creator of the multi award winning classic Hillsborough, The Lakes and The Street) along with, Frank Cottrrell Boyce, Phil Redmond and Colin McKeown are all passionate about their productions, filming in and around their home city.
- Eddie Braben was the Scouser behind the biggest successes of The Morecambe and Wise TV shows.

Welcome to the House of Scouse

WANT a willing TV guinea pig to subject themselves to 24-hour spy cameras and intimate scrutiny by viewing millions (even in the loo)? Step forward Liverpool, favourite hunting ground of the reality TV maker and particularly those steering the all-seeing eye of Big Brother...

Big Brother 1 (2000): **Craig Phillips** (right), cheeky builder from Seaforth, won the nation's hearts after fronting 'Nasty' Nick Bateman.

Big Brother 4 (2003): **Scott Turner** from Bebington quietly won millions of votes to come third. Sadly he was pipped on the final day by virgin fisherman Cameron from the Orkney Isles.

Big Brother 6 (2005): **Roberto Conte** (left), an Italian-born Liverpool teacher and **Kemal Shahin**, a Turkish transvestite bellydancer and JMU student certainly livened things up.

Big Brother 7 (2006): Aigburth model **Mikey Dalton** (right) didn't win, but he met his fiancee-to-be thanks to BB – dancer and self-confessed Sloane ranger **Grace Adams-Short**.

And then there were the celebs...

Celebrity Big Brother 1 in 2001 gave a post-Brookside leg-up to Liverpool actress **Claire Sweeney**'s career. She went on to star in Chicago and Guys and Dolls in the West End.

CBB2 in 2002 was a rollercoaster for comedian and actor **Les Dennis**. Diary room misery earned him the 'poor Les' label, but his inspired cameo in Ricky Gervais's Extras helped turn his fortunes around.

CBB4 in 2006 became the Rocky Horror Burns Show, as Scouse singer, former Dead or Alive frontman **Pete Burns**, paraded his frocks, gigantic lips and vicious put-downs.

QUEEN WAG: Coleen

Wags to Riches

IT'S not what you know, but who you know... and those girls with footballers on their arms certainly know how to make the most of the limelight.

Ever since they laid siege to the shops while their other halves were slugging it out on the pitch in the 2006 World Cup in Germany, the WAGs (Wives And Girlfriends) have been big business.

Who needs a pay cheque from LFC, when you can score your own lucrative publicity contracts?

In the Premiership of WAGs, there's only one title holder - **Coleen McLoughlin**, Croxteth schoolgirl turned style icon.

With a little help from her Liverpool fashion pals, the 21-year-old fiancee of England striker **Wayne Rooney** has transformed herself from an awkward, puffa coat wearing teen to a confident trend leader. Book deals, magazine columns, fitness videos and a multitude of product endorsements

MINUTES

CELEBRITY is the ultimate dance with the devil: love it while the spotlight's shining on you, but don't be surprised if you get pricked by the horns.

Fickle as a teenage crush, few who make it onto the A-list stay there for long.

Liverpudlians, never known as shrinking violets, have always made excellent celebrities, especially now – thanks to mass market reality TV – it's so much easier to grab those precious 15 minutes of fame.

Some have clutched on by their finely manicured fingertips, reinventing themselves along the way. **Cilla Black** is the survival queen, morphing seamlessly from Cavern coat-check girl to golden-handcuffed doyenne of light entertainment. Others have fared less well.

Kerry Katona, once a chart-topper with Atomic Kitten, admits she feels chewed up and spat out by celebrity. "If you were to ask me now what my job is, I really don't know. I'm too busy being a professionally cocked-up version of Kerry," she's bemoaned.

So, who would really want to swim in shark-infested waters?

An ever-increasing number of wannabes, it seems. Welcome to the brave new world of the famous-for-being-infamous WAGs, reality TV contestants and pop hopefuls ...

RED CARPET STAR: Kim Cattrall

have brought her personal fortune to a reported £10million. Hot on her Christian Louboutin heels is **Steven Gerrard**'s other half **Alex**. In terms of looks, mum-of-two Alex, from Aintree, is the uber-WAG – long blonde hair, fake tan and an extravagant label-packed wardrobe. But Alex is in danger of being out-WAGed by **Peter Crouch**'s model girlfriend **Abigail Clancy**, from Croxteth Park. The statuesque blonde came runner-up in hit show Britain's Next Top Model and is now the star of her own reality series.

WAG CHECK LIST

- [ ] Long straight hair, preferably blonde, possibly extensions
- [ ] Spray tan, the more David Dickinson orange the better
- [ ] French manicure with ultra white tips
- [ ] A 4 x 4 with tinted windows to keep out those prying eyes
- [ ] The very latest Chloe handbag
- [ ] Access to VIP booths in Newz Bar on Water Street
- [ ] The mobile number of your friendly paparazzo on speed-dial
- [ ] Over-sized Tom Ford sunglasses
- [ ] A Roberto Cavalli dress with matching golden jewellery
- [ ] The ability to find Cricket on Mathew Street blindfolded

HALL OF FAME

ALL hail fabulous **Kim Cattrall**, who went from movies Porkies and Mannequin to Emmy nomination and Golden Globe triumph as Sex And The City's chief seducer Samantha. It's a long way from Mossley Hill and the Merseyside Youth Drama Group to the red carpet, but Kim's strolled it.

HALL OF SHAME

WITH bad hair and snow-washed denim, **The Reynolds Girls** must be the one-hit wonders of all time, with 1989 tune I'd Rather Jack (than Fleetwood Mac). At least they're big on YouTube.

I say, I say, I say...

LIVERPOOL and humour are forever linked. A happy reputation to be proud of. Is it something to do with the water?

Or, as many stand-ups have agreed, the natural native wit emerges from the in-built reaction to so many 'downs and disappointments ' that laughter is the best medicine to tackle social and economic ills.

The Liverpool Echo 50 years ago looked at this phenomenon.

It came to a conclusion that said it had nothing to do with the Port or the 'ugly spots' (which need a high degree of humorous fortitude from those who lived in them) nor was it a reaction to the poverty all around.

It was, said the paper confidently, more to do with 'our bracing air - a product of our racial mixture.'

Therefore, it concluded that from the earliest times the would-be comic was sure of an audience because no one appreciated more than a Liverpudlian the quick-witted response and the funny slant on any common place happening.

Our rich heritage welcomed communities from all over the world, from Ireland to Italy, who settled here.

Travellers came and went and left parts of their culture that we as Scousers dip into and out of, and add to.

Humour helps us all cope with tension. From the football terraces to the concert hall hecklers, Liverpudlians like to think of themselves as comedians.

Sometimes, however, we proud Scousers do not find it funny when we are poked fun at by non-Scousers.

The late Bernard Manning said he liked to go to Liverpool to 'visit his hub caps'.

And some wags say that since Liverpool won Capital of Culture status the city has been offering 'night school classes in graffiti'.

They are only jokes, of course, and we can give as good as we get, but these are gags Scousers do not like to hear when people who say them are merely perpetrating the myth about a city full of dubious characters.

This is where the term professional Scouser came from, referring to comedians who have not lived in the city for decades but who earn their living using the accent and creating even more Scouse stereotypes that we have tried to get rid of over the years.

We were given Capital of Culture status because of the people and the humour has and always will play a part in our make up.

It started early on with Liverpool's Professor Codman and his Punch and Judy shows making children and adults alike laugh for decades.

Professor Codman's travelling puppet show got them early. That's the way to do it.

Tommy Handley, kept the country laughing in the 40s with the radio show ITMA – It's That Man Again. Arthur Askey, Ted Ray, Rob Wilton and Billy Matchett were all laughter legends.

On TV, The Army Game had the small screen's first real Scouser in Norman Rossington as Private

Cupcake. There were one-liners delivered by Kenneth Cope's Jed Stone in Coronation Street or Geoffrey Hughes as Eddie Yates. Brookside provided Scouse window cleaner Michael Starke with his shammy scams.

Happily, the city has produced some of the all time comic greats. Ken Dodd, celebrated 55 years in showbusiness in 2007. The star from Knotty Ash (where he still lives) created the Diddymen and the term Mirthyside. A real Scouse ambassdor travelling the country with his surreal take on life.

The list goes on Micky Finn, Jimmy Tarbuck, Norman Vaughan, Tom O'Connor, Freddie Starr, Stan Boardman, John Martin and Pauline Daniels, Faith Brown, Stevie Faye to the late legends Eddie Flanagan, Jackie Hamilton and George Roper.

And there came a new wave of alternative comedy by the likes of Craig Charles and Alexei Sayle.

Our very own home grown Comedy Festival had many spin offs, notably Rawhide with stars of the future such as Chris Cairns, Brendan Riley and Keith Carter. The Rawhide Stand Out scheme now discovers new talent from schools. Veteran Micky Finn says Scouse humour is both conversational and observational. A city, he says, that launched a million quips.

Or Stan Boardman asking if there were any Germans in the audience when he played The Cavern Club.

"Put your hand u... on second thoughts both your hands up... why change a habit of a lifetime?"

Humour has also been a characteristic of our pop stars.

The Beatles won the hearts of the UK with their humour, especially in the United States with their cheeky press conferences.

Beatle producer George Martin said it was their Scouse irreverence that made him want to sign them.

"After a hard day in the studio I asked them if there was anything they weren't happy with. George Harrison looked at me and said, "I don't like your tie for a start."

DJ Pete Price uses humour to diffuse some of the people who phone in to his radio show.

And Billy Butler and Wally Scott made their listeners the real stars of their classic show Hold Your Plums.

"What was Hitler's first name? asked Billy

"Heil." Came the reply

And Les Dennis, host of Family Fortunes for 15 years, said his fellow Scousers made great contestants.

He recalled one incident: "Name an occupation that uses a torch?"

To which a Scouser replied 'Burglar'.

Liverpool humour is evident in literature and the poetry of Roger McGough.

Alan Bleasdale's Boys From the Blackstuff used Scouse humour to great effect notably with downtrodden Yosser Hughes.

The writings of Beryl Bainbridge, Carla Lane and Brian Jacques all reflect our Liverpool language and the Scousisms.

And in Jimmy McGovern's musical King Cotton, God makes a cameo apperance and mentions... Scousers. Now that's universal fame.

Ricky Tomlinson knows exactly what Scouse humour means.

"It separates us from every other city. A trademark; a badge as synonymous with Liverpool as the Liver Bird.

"No matter where you go in the world you will always find a Scouser and laughter is never far behind."

Going to Ma's for dinner

Dockers had a way with words, calling each other by harmless Mersey monikers. Indeed, the Liverpool docker was as articulate as the lorries that trundled down the dock road. Here, Peter Grant – son of a docker, grandson of a docker and one-time writer for Port News – pays tribute to his local heroes, many of whom he met.

Van Gogh: "Let me put you in the picture."

The Sheriff (a foreman): "Where's the hold up?"

Reluctant Plumber: "Won't do a tap."

The Spaceman: "Going to Ma's for dinner."

Wonder Boy: "I wonder what's in this?"

Lino: "He's always on the floor."

The Piano Man: "You're playing on me."

Phil The Cot: "Father of many."

Parish Priest: "Works only Sundays."

The Balloon boss; "Don't let me down, lads."

Bargain Bill: "A forklift driver who'd knock anything down."

The Echo: "It's news to me, la."

The Baker: "Me and me tart went out last night."

Diesel: "Diesel do for the wife and diesel do for the kids."

Gunner: "I was gunner do that."

Batman: "Never leaves a ship without robbin."

Baldy Rabbit: "Lend us a quid... I've lost me fare."

The Surgeon (boss): "Cut it out lads, cut it out."

Dr Jekyll: "I need a change."

The Weight-lifter: "He waits while you lift."

The Martian: "What on earth's all this all about?"

The Novelist: "What the Dickens is going on?"

The Auctioneer: "That's yer lot."

Zookeeper: " I am bit cagey about this lads."

SCOUSE SITES TO BE SEEN

by CATHERINE JONES

Our city's great buildings

LIVERPOOL is England's hidden heritage gem.

While the crescents of Bath, the cloisters of Oxford and even the mills of Manchester have been lauded for their historic and aesthetic value, Liverpool has always hovered under the radar of the average architectural fan.

This is both a blessing and a curse.

A blessing because it has given Liverpool a chance to rescue some of its architectural beauties – thankfully ignored during the modernising blitzkrieg of the 1950s and 60s, give them a fresh lease of life and unleashing their potential on an appreciative Liverpool public.

It is the public that has a deep sense of pride about its surroundings – a pride which has often been dented by the lingering view of the rest of the nation that the city is a giant sink estate, the Mersey lapping against its decaying walls.

But it is also a curse because it is only now Liverpool – complete with its 26 grade I, 85 grade II* and 2,500-odd grade II listed buildings – is getting the recognition is deserves.

For every visitor to Liverpool there is a new convert to its beauties.

I myself was ignorant of the city's charms until I moved here five years ago. Then, I was given the Echo's Stop the Rot campaign to coordinate and, more than that, I opened my eyes and looked properly at my new home.

The icons need no introduction – the Three Graces, two cathedrals, Town Hall, Albert Dock, Bluecoat arts centre, Speke Hall and even the Radio City Tower.

St George's Hall, in particular, sums up Liverpool's history and its civic pride. Created by ambitious merchants, the vision of a young man (Harvey Lonsdale Elmes). But like much of Liverpool it is the hidden or less heralded parts of the grade I listed landmark which are the most interesting. The great hall, with its Minton floor and massive pipe organ, is St George's centrepiece, but the small concert room is the more enchanting.

Behind the gold leaf and pomp, there are gangways and ladders from which you can see how the building was constructed and what makes it both a stunning landmark and a marvellous piece of machinery.

Yet for me, Liverpool's architecture is about more than a few great landmarks.

It's about wandering the old thoroughfares such as Castle Street and Dale Street with eyes tilted upwards to admire the ornate rooftops, about the Everton water tower lit up at night, the 'age of speed' beauty of Rowse's George's Dock ventilation shaft, the bronze doors of Martins Bank, and the turreted 'streaky bacon' Albion building on the Strand.

It's the perfect Georgian architecture of Falkner Square and Percy Street, which can compete with Bath on any day of the week, the faded old dame Gambier Terrace, the ornate decorated barrel roof of the India Building's central arcade, the exquisite interior of Princes Road synagogue, and the stunning art deco doors of the Stanley Buildings in Edmund Street.

Of course, some of the best of Liverpool's architecture can be seen in its pubs, places like the ornate Philharmonic, the Crown and the Vines in Lime Street, the ship-shaped Baltic, tiny White Star, and the Fly in the Loaf.

Stop the Rot, the Echo's longest-running and best known campaign, aims to save the best of the old city.

When you look at the decay of places like the Wellington Rooms, Newsham Park Hospital, St Andrews Church, or the Florence Institute in Dingle – where the community is working hard to regenerate the former boys club – you realise the scale of the challenge.

But even in their ramshackle state, these abandoned edifices have a strange beauty to them, and people who love them enough to want to see them rescued and restored.

It's all down to that Liverpool pride.

From top: The Three Graces, Speke Hall and the interior of St Georges Hall featuring the famous organ

Regeneration

LIVERPOOL'S rush to regenerate is spelled out across its skyline, in the rising towers and Dr Who-like invasion of cranes.

Serious talk about regeneration started in the mid-1990s with plans mooted for developments on the Kings and Princes docks.

In the city centre, Princes Dock was once of the first sites to garner new development with offices populated in 1997 and the Crowne Plaza opening a year later.

But widespread work only began as recently as the start of the new millennium, and has gathered increasing pace ever since.

The largest single scheme has been Grosvenor's £920m-plus Paradise project, but the signs of confidence are everywhere – in the echoing streets of the 'business district', with the arena and associated development at Kings Dock, the somewhat controversial new museum on Mann Island, and start-stop development at the Baltic Triangle.

Each week it seems new schemes are unveiled.

And it is not simply new-build.

Stop the Rot was launched to persuade developers to design sympathetic new uses for the decaying gems they had in their portfolios.

And while there is still some way to go, there have been notable successes, not least St Peter's Church in the Rope Walks which was transformed into the sumptuous Alma de Cuba, and the Old Post Office – once described as a carbuncle on the face of Liverpool – which has metamorphosed into the sleek Met Quarter shopping centre.

Other buildings have been rescued before they get on to the 'rot' list, with warehouses in Rope Walks, the gleaming Tower Building and the Albany in Old Hall Street back in use.

Outside the city centre, regeneration has been slower and more sporadic and there are still plenty of grotty spots in the city for developers to tackle.

In the midst of this race to regenerate, the watchwords must remain quality, harmony and longevity to make sure Liverpool retains its unique charms while showcasing the best of 21st century Britain.

Royalty, public servants and Scousers go back a long way. From 1207 when King John granted our city charter to the time when we saw a Scouse-speaking prime minister at the despatch box.

There was also a war time female Scouse MP taking on Winston Churchill.

There was an adopted Scouser who became a PM filling Huyton with pipe-smoke.

And in the 80s and 90s politicians representing Scousers were taking on the Labour hierarchy.

But there were also public servants – who concentrated on campaigns rather than joining the commons – doing equally great work from law to pensions reform.

"Speakers corner should not be in Hyde Park but Sefton Park. It's ideal for Scousers," said the late, great George Melly.

PUBLIC S

HAROLD WILSON
BESSIE BRADDOCK
KING JOHN
ERIC HEFFER
WILLIAM EWART GLADSTONE
MARGARET BEAVAN
JACK JONES
ELEANOR RATHBONE
HARTLEY WILLIAM SHAWCROSS
SYDNEY SILVERMAN

ERVANTS

HAROLD WILSON

HAROLD Wilson was an adopted Merseysider – even if he never managed to lose his Yorkshire accent.

As MP for Huyton, he became the politician who bestrode the international stage. Yet he was equally at home supporting the Cavern Club, raising money for Liverpool theatres, or even lighting up on behalf of a local pipe-smoking club.

In Huyton, they had known his worldly-wise ultra shrewd manner since they first elected him in 1950.

And he was to continue to serve his constituents for a further 33 years – seven years beyond his shock resignation as prime minister.

Wilson first showed his debating skills as a pupil at Wirral Grammar school.

But he was never an elitist.

His six years in Downing Street saw an economic and technological revolution in the UK. And there was the "pound in your pocket" devaluation crisis.

The founding of the Open University and demise of Empire, with the famous confrontation with rebel Rhodesian prime minister Ian Smith, may have equally characterised the period.

But Harold Wilson could enjoy the ordinary and extraordinary.

He was a fan of The Beatles and appeared with them on television, swapping jokes with John Lennon with as much skill as he had shown facing Tory leader Edward Heath over the dispatch box.

When the Everyman Theatre was rebuilt in the early 1970s, he turned up to support an Adelphi Hotel fund launch.

"Wilson won four general elections and lost only one, in 1970, one of the few miscalculations in an otherwise supersonic career that in 1947 saw him become the youngest cabinet minister since Pitt the Younger"

His resignation as prime minister in 1976 was as spectacular as his entry into parliament in 1945.

One of the great characters of late 20th century politics, he existed somewhere inside a Gannex mac and admitted to a liking for fish and chips. He said the greatest quality needed to be prime minister was "a sense of history".

BESSIE BRADDOCK

BATTLING Bessie Braddock epitomised a revolutionary and socialist chapter in Liverpool's political history quite like no other. In girth and headline count she even managed to out-do her equally famous politician husband Jack.

Bessie, born in Zante Street, Liverpool in 1899, first entered parliament in 1945, when she won the Exchange division for Labour with a majority of just 665. Five years later that had increased to more than 5,000 – and continued to increase.

When elected to Westminster Bessie was a housewife of 46.

But she had already gained a seat on the city council as early as 1930 – a year after her husband Jack – leader of the Labour group – had been similarly elected.

Bessie Braddock claimed she was "born to the Socialist movement". Her father, Hugh Bamber, was an activist based at a Liverpool book shop, while her mother, Mary, was national organiser for the union of distributive and allied workers.

At the age of 21, Bessie was in charge of an unemployment committee in the city. She later became the first woman president of the Liverpool Trades Council and Labour Party, and was a member of Labour's national executive committee.

Bessie once likened the House of Commons, with its doors leading to the division lobby, to a comedy show, and insisted that the "soulless ritual" was in need of reform.

On one occasion Tory Quintin Hogg (later Lord Hailsham) called her his pin-up girl.

The Exchange Labour group sent a letter of protest and a picture of Bessie. Hogg replied that he would have the picture framed. Such was the lighter side of the politics of the day.

But it was the serious dimension which predominated. When criticised for having the Communist hammer and sickle flag on her car, Bessie described herself as "an international socialist" and noted that "the flag means a lot to me."

She remained primarily the carer of her home constituents. She famously described Liverpool slums as: "bug-ridden, lice-ridden, rat-ridden lousy hell holes."

"She was a great champion of women in politics. Speaking in 1968 she deplored the fact that out of 630 MPs, only 26 were women"

However she said that although few in number, they had managed to make their presence felt.

Bessie retired from politics in 1969 and died the following year, seven months after being given the freedom of the city of Liverpool.

KING JOHN

LOVE him or hate him, Liverpool owes its emergence and recognition as a town to King John, not a British monarch to enjoy the best of reputations.

Thirteenth century historians described him as "greedy" and certainly his reputation today has not been helped by a number of films which have painted him as a villain to be mentioned in the same breath as the Sheriff of Nottingham, seen as his henchman in the Robin Hood legends.

> "One nasty rumour – that he lost the Crown Jewels in The Wash, East Anglia, just prior to his death – also appears to be little more than a romantic myth"

So what is known as fact?

He was born at Christmas in 1166, the fifth son of Henry II and Eleanor of Aquitane.

Before his own accession to the throne in 1199, he had already acquired a reputation for treachery against his brothers who included his predecessor Richard The Lionheart.

However, some argue that rather than attempt to overthrow Richard, who was on the Third Crusade to the Holy Land, John did his best to improve a nation ruined by Richard's excessive taxes.

John remained on the throne until 1216 – a year after doing what he is most famous for – signing the Magna Carta, an act forced on him by rebellious barons.

Immediately prior to giving Liverpool its charter, he had a big fall-out with the Pope over the election of the next Archbishop of Canterbury.

Things worsened and John was excommunicated prior to an eventual settlement.

He did live to fight another day, putting down the Welsh Uprising of 1211 before turning his attention back to overseas interests.

It wasn't all bad news. Medieval historian Warren Hollister has called him an "enigmatic figure".

"He was talented in some respects, good at administrative detail... his crisis-prone reign being repeatedly sabotaged."

> "Here we are today – 800 years on – a world class city thanks to the initial grace of one man"

ERIC HEFFER

HE may have been raised in Hertfordshire, but rebellious radical Eric Heffer fell in love with and devoted much of his life to Liverpool.

Born on January 12, 1922, he was the Labour MP for Liverpool Walton from 1964 until his death, aged 69, on May 27, 1991, after an 18-month-long battle against cancer.

The son of a boot-maker, Eric served apprenticeships as an electrician, leatherworker and carpenter.

During World War II, he served in the Royal Air Force in a maintenance unit at Fazakerley. He headed north to Liverpool again in 1945 – to marry Doris Murray, a decision he would forever describe as "the best seven shillings and sixpence I ever spent".

"His love affair with Liverpool eventually led to him being awarded the freedom of the city, which he described as 'the greatest honour in the land'"

Eric, a keen reader and Evertonian, was a Liverpool city councillor from 1960 to 1966 and president of the Liverpool Trades Council and Labour Party in 1959-60 and 1964-65.

During his time as an MP, he was minister for industry from 1974-75, party chairman from 1983-84 and a member of the party's national executive from 1975-86.

In 1989, Eric celebrated 25 years in Parliament and 50 years in politics – and was named Backbencher of The Year in the Spectator magazine awards. The citation highlighted his "subversive spirit of independence".

Independent? This is the man who was expelled from the Communist Party in 1948 for leading an unofficial carpenters' strike against the party's wishes.

And this is the man who left the platform during the Labour Party's 1985 conference, as then leader Neil Kinnock delivered his Militant-bashing speech. Six years on, Eric remained defiant: "I will NEVER forget or forgive him for what he did to Liverpool city council."

Speaking at his funeral, Tony Benn said Eric, whose deep Anglican faith underpinned his socialism, had taken Christ's words "I am my brother's keeper" to heart.

"He added: 'He believed an injury to one is an injury to all, united we stand, divided we fall, and you don't cross a picket line'"

WILLIAM EWART GLADSTONE

LIVERPOOL-BORN William Ewart Gladstone is the only British prime minister to serve four terms in office.

Gladstone, a Liberal, made political history between 1868 and 1894 when he was given the mandate of the British electorate on an unprecedented four occasions.

Born at 62 Rodney Street in 1809, he was the fourth son of the merchant Sir John Gladstone and his second wife, Anne MacKenzie Robertson.

Renowned as a social reformer and Christian moralist, his skill as a politician was shown in changing and even reversing policies to suit the prevailing political and religious climate.

He defended the Anglican faith, then championed civil equality for Roman Catholics.

He attacked British imperial expansion but watched the British infiltrate southern Africa and occupy Egypt.

Gladstone was first elected to Parliament in 1832 as Conservative MP for Newark. Initially he was a disciple of High Toryism, opposing the abolition of slavery and factory legislation. But in 1859 he joined the New Liberal Party under Palmerston and he continued his gradual slide towards the left of British politics.

He became prime minister in 1868 and set upon a course which would lead to domestic social policy and foreign policy becoming much more liberal and progressive than it had been during Benjamin Disreali's term in high office.

Gladstone was famously at odds with Queen Victoria for much of his career. She once complained: "He always addresses me as if I were a public meeting."

But this just endeared Gladstone to his supporters, by whom he was known affectionately as the "Grand Old Man" or "The People's William."

Gladstone died at Hawarden Castle in 1898, at the age of 88, from metastatic cancer that had started behind his cheekbone.

His coffin was transported on the London Underground before he was buried in Westminster Abbey.

"He is still regarded as one of the greatest British prime ministers, with Winston Churchill and others citing Gladstone as their inspiration"

MARGARET BEAVAN

LIVERPOOL'S first female Lord Mayor, Margaret Beavan, campaigned tirelessly on the behalf of the city's children.

Born on August 1, 1877, the eldest of the three children of Liverpool insurance agent Jeffrey Beavan, she attended Belvedere school.

A gifted student, Margaret went on to study maths at Royal Holloway and, on her return to Liverpool from university, she spent a term helping out at a local boys' preparatory school.

She then took a Sunday school class at the Earle Road Mission. With her sister Jessie, she helped out with a church-run girls' club. In 1900, at the age of 23, Margaret began helping as a volunteer with an experimental class for disabled children run by Edith Eskrigge at the Victoria Settlement. She moved to the Invalid Children's Aid and in 1908 when the ICA became independent of the Kyrle Society, Margaret became its honorary secretary. Thereafter her ventures in public life increased.

Margaret went on to develop the idea of post-hospital care for children with the Leasowe Open-Air Hospital for Children, and established the Ellen Gonner Home for Children. In 1918, when her work with children was acknowledged by a cheque for £1,300 from leading citizens of Liverpool. When, in the same year, the Maternity and Child Welfare Act gave each locality the duty of providing for its infant children, she organised the Child Welfare Association.

"Margaret's reputation as a local, and eventually national, expert on child welfare led to her appointment as one of Liverpool's first women magistrates in 1920"

The following year she was elected to represent Princes Park on the city council as a Liberal. The local party leader, Sir Archibald Salvidge, suggested her appointment as Liverpool's first female Lord Mayor in 1928.

By 1924 she had joined the Conservatives and following her triumphant Mayoral year, she agreed to stand as the Conservative candidate for Everton in the May 1929 general election. The campaign was a disaster for her and the party. Her health, which had always been poor, broke down shortly afterwards. She died in February 1931, aged 54, and mourners lined the streets to watch the funeral procession of "the little mother of Liverpool."

JACK JONES

FOR Scousers, there's only one Jack Jones. And it's not the silver-haired balladeer from LA.

"Our Jack", as Liverpool's dock workers called him with pride, retired as Britain's most famous trades union boss way back in 1978. Then he embarked on another career, as the pensioners' champion.

In 1975, Jack beat prime minister Harold Wilson in a Gallup Poll naming the most powerful figure in the country.

"His determination to better the lot of his fellow men was forged in the antiquated docklands, with their sub-standard canteens and vile washrooms"

He had left Banks Road elementary school in his native Garston at 14.

Jack Jones was shot in the shoulder fighting for the anti-Franco forces in the Battle of the Ebro, during the Spanish Civil War in 1938. At the time, he was the youngest member of Liverpool city council, elected only two years earlier.

The Labour Party was in a minority, the town hall controlled by Tories because of the two-vote system (a business and a residential vote).

Following the war Jack returned to Liverpool to organise food ships to Spain.

Later, together with Hugh Scanlon of the engineers' union, and often dubbed his "terrible twin", he was, as general secretary of the Transport and General Workers' Union, to become the most influential union boss, raising TGWU membership to 2.1million, and chairing the economic and policy committee of the overall TUC.

He was the central figure in the "beer and sandwiches" pay talks at 10 Downing Street when he recalled: "They wanted to impose laws which would have made unofficial strikes illegal and would have led to goods being constrained (and a future Tory government did just that). So that's why we tried to talk Wilson and his employment secretary Barbara Castle out of it. I remember Barbara Castle conceding that strikers would not be sent to prison."

Later Jack was to clash with the next Labour prime minister James Callaghan over the abolition of the House of Lords.

And after a lifetime of campaigning to scrap the upper chamber – "a waste of money and a slight on democracy" – Jack Jones, unlike Hugh Scanlon, decided he could not accept a peerage.

ELEANOR RATHBONE

"She was strongly influenced by the dedication of her father to help those less fortunate than herself and her work on behalf of the poor and the disenfranchised marks her out as one of Liverpool's most historically significant daughters"

ELEANOR Rathbone was one of this country's first female MPs and she was also the first woman elected to Liverpool city council.

At a time when the suffragette movement was revolutionising British politics, Rathbone was one of its key campaigners.

The daughter of a Liverpool merchant, Rathbone was born into a family of wealthy social reformers in 1872.

She first made her mark in 1903 when she reported to the poor commission on the results of a special inquiry into the conditions of labour at the Liverpool Docks.

She became Liverpool's first woman councillor in 1909 when she won the Granby Ward as an independent.

During World War I she organised the Soldiers and Sailors Families Association and was responsible for distributing allowances to families who had men in the forces.

When she became Independent MP for the Combined Universities in 1929 she established the perfect platform to pursue her campaigns against poverty.

Her campaign for family allowances came to fruition under the Attlee government of 1945 when the Family Allowance Act was passed.

During the Depression, she campaigned for cheap milk and better benefits for the children of the unemployed and in 1931 she helped to organise the defeat of a proposal to abolish the university seats in the parliament and won re-election in 1935.

Rathbone was one of the first British politicians to recognise the threat of Nazi Germany and in the 1930s joined the British Non-Sectarian Anti-Nazi Council to support human rights.

In 1936 she began to warn about a Nazi threat to Czechoslovakia and she became an outspoken critic of appeasement in Parliament.

Eleanor Rathbone died in January 1946 but her legacy of social justice and equal rights lives on.

HARTLEY WILLIAM SHAWCROSS

"The late Lord Shawcross, Labour MP for St Helens from 1945 to 1958, is regarded as one of the 20th century's most brilliant lawyers"

HARTLEY William Shawcross was a prosecutor at the Nuremberg trials of Nazi war criminals and, as attorney general, helped send infamous acid-bath murderer John George Haigh to the gallows.

In court, it was said his meticulous manner and slow nasal drawl could put defendants off their guard, while his handling of the most complex cases was described as supremely clinical – chilling, even.

As attorney general, he prosecuted in a number of celebrated trials, including that of the traitor William Joyce (Lord Haw-Haw).

Hartley William Shawcross was educated at Dulwich College, where he preached socialism in the debating society (he joined the Labour Party at the age of 16). After taking a short course at the London School of Economics, he studied at the University of Geneva.

On his return to England, he studied for the Bar at Gray's Inn, winning first-class honours in all his examinations.

His first wife Alberta, who suffered from multiple sclerosis, killed herself to spare him the task of looking after her. His second wife Joan, the mother of his three children, died in 1974 after being kicked by a horse.

From April 1951 until Labour went out of office the following autumn, Lord Shawcross was President of the Board of Trade. At the peak of his legal career in the mid-1950s, he was earning up to £60,000 a year at the Bar, an incredible sum in those days (although much of it disappeared in taxation).

In 1957, he announced he was quitting the Bar and the House of Commons after learning that a law was to be passed revoking the right of barristers to collect unpaid fees when they retired.

Shawcross had jobs with Shell and Ford, became chairman of the Press Council and a takeover panel, and sat on the board of the Times.

He died at home in East Sussex on July 10, 2003 at the age of 101, the last surviving member of Clement Attlee's government.

SYDNEY SILVERMAN

LABOUR MP Sydney Silverman was a tireless campaigner against nuclear weapons and the death penalty.

The son of an impoverished draper, he was born in Liverpool on October 8, 1895. Silverman won a scholarship to Liverpool Institute, and then to Liverpool University.

The First World War interrupted his studies, but as a pacifist he refused to join the army. Registered as a conscientious objector, Silverman served several prison sentences for his beliefs. His experiences in Wormwood Scrubs made him a passionate advocate of penal reform.

After the war was over he returned to Liverpool University to complete his studies and qualified as a solicitor in 1927.

"Over the next few years he developed a reputation as a solicitor who was willing to defend the interests of the poor in Liverpool"

This included workmen's compensation claims and landlord-tenant disputes.

A member of the Labour Party, Silverman was elected as a city councillor in 1932. Soon afterwards he was adopted as the parliamentary candidate for Nelson and Colne and entered the House of Commons following the 1935 General Election.

He retained his pacifist views until he discovered what was happening to the Jews in Nazi Germany. He then thereafter gave his full support to Britain's involvement in the Second World War.

Silverman was a strong opponent of capital punishment and in 1948 persuaded the House of Commons to agree to a five-year suspension of executions. However, this clause in the Criminal Justice Bill was defeated in the House of Lords. As a result Silverman founded the Campaign for the Abolition of the Death Penalty. In 1953 he published his book, Hanged And Innocent.

In November 1954 Silverman, Michael Foot and three others were expelled from the Labour Party for opposing its nuclear defence policy. Three years later they formed the Campaign for Nuclear Disarmament (CND).

Silverman continued to campaign against capital punishment and in 1956 he introduced a private member's Bill for abolition. Once again it was defeated in the House of Lords.

After the 1964 General Election the new Labour government agreed to introduce legislation to abandon capital punishment for five years. With overwhelming support in the House of Commons the House of Lords agreed to pass the measure.

Sydney Silverman died in hospital on February 9, 1968.

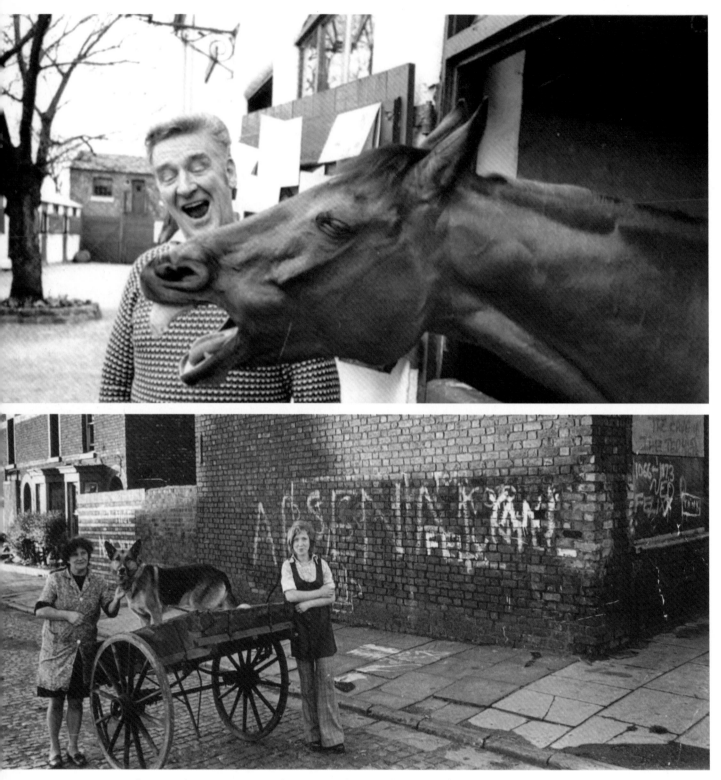

Top   Red Rum and Ginger McCain after winning the Grand National for the third time. "Give him a Polo mint then," said Ginger. I Had come prepared to the Southport stables – Rummy loved mints and he started laughing for the camera. He also loved having his picture taken

Above   Christmas Street, Edge Hill. I found the streets of Liverpool full of characters. This couple were preparing to move out

Top left   After the 60s Cavern days, Mathew Street was alive with Eric's Club and the faces of punk for the 70s

Top right   "You better not take my picture without my teeth in love, you will frighten your readers!" A Scottie Road doorstep
before they pulled the houses down

Above   Ken Dodd backstage – a cuppa before the show at the Philharmonic Hall. Doddy fills the hall every Christmas.
His stamina is amazing. The true Scouser and so proud of Liverpool

Left   Children at Granby Street school, Toxteth, in fancy dress and the clothes of their country.
Headteacher Miss Lopez always welcomed me at this delightful school with so much character – full of lovely faces and warm feeling

Right   Tommy Smith scored in Liverpool's European Cup win in Rome. He ran to trainer Ronnie Moran at the end of the match. "Why?" I asked. "Ronnie was keeping my teeth in his pocket and I didn't want my picture taken without them."
Sorry Tommy!

Top   Shankly wins the championship with his proud Liverpool team at Anfield. First stop – the Kop to thank the fans

Above   It's a treat to be allowed to go where the audience doesn't go – backstage. I love taking pics behind the scenes
          – you see the true picture and often it makes the best photo. This image was taken in the wings at the Empire
          Theatre as the Royal Ballet prepared for curtain up with ballerinas just like butterflies

The Minton tiled floor
inside St George's Hall

by Cheryl Rawlinson

SCOUSE HOUSE OF MYSTERY

THROUGHOUT the beginning of the 20th century, intrigue and gossip surrounded number 166 Upper Parliament St, Liverpool and its occupant.

Reminiscent of that of Miss Havesham in Dickens' Great Expectations, this late 19th century, three-story house in an affluent area of the city, remained largely untouched for over 30 years

Neighbours asked what the Dickens was going on and reported hearing somebody moving about, despite never seeing anybody. Some reported a wedding breakfast lay on the table waiting for a bridegroom that never was, untouched by the heartbroken lady.

Other alleged the house was a wedding gift bought by the lady's brother for her and her bridegroom-to-be, who then died, leaving her broken hearted before the wedding date. There were also those who claim the house was left to the lady by her brother, and that his death devastated her so greatly that she moved out, keeping the house intact as a shrine.

Whatever the truth, the owner was certainly one of means. Despite the dusty blinds and cobwebbed windows the house was maintained.

In 1912 when the chimney blew off, it was repaired within two days. The curious case became known as that of 'the house of mystery'.

THE LIVERPOOL LEPRECHAUN HUNT

'LITTLE green men in white hats throwing stones and tiny clods of earth at one another.'

It may sound like a page from a children's fairytale, but on June 30, 1964, it was this rumour that stirred the city into what would come to be known as the Liverpool Leprechaun Hunt.

Kensington Park saw chaotic scenes as hundreds of people, mostly children, arrived desperate to catch a glimpse of these tiny folk.

As the schools closed for the day the park and bowling green were swamped and police struggled to control the swelling crowds who remained into the night.

The following weeks saw continuing interest, with people scavenging through the shrubbery and ransacking the empty houses in the area.

Mystery shrouded the origins of the rumour, until a confession came 18 years later from Merseysider Brian Jones.

Mr Jones explained that he was mistaken for a leprechaun whilst gardening for his grandfather one summer afternoon. The boys that spotted 'the little feller' were from the local Roman Catholic school and with the strong Irish connection at the time, the sighting spread at an unprecedented speed.

The Liverpool Leprechaun Hunt snowballed at such a pace that, for 18 years, Mr Jones was forced to keep the secret under his hat, and throughout this time you could still find people who would swear they saw a leprechaun on that summer's day.

WHO WANTS TO BE A SCOUSE MILLIONAIRE?

The £7m Giveaway

CHRISTMAS came early for three Merseysiders in November 1971 when a mystery millionaire gave £3,000 to unsuspecting locals.

A flower seller in central station sold a two pence rose for £500. Her daughter walked away with £2,000 to buy a car, and a shop assistant from Seaforth received £500 for offering directions to another store.

An anxious wait followed as the banks were closed for the weekend, but all three were keeping their fingers crossed.

The mysterious man who was described as 'well dressed' and in his 50s, claimed he had £7,500,000 to give away. The money, he said, had brought him nothing but sadness and had supposedly been inherited by marriage.

Whatever the reason, it certainly was welcomed by those who received the surprise windfall and who knows if there were others lucky enough to receive a share?

MONKEY BUSINESS

Taking the Mickey

IN March 1938, a backyard shoot-out spelt the end for four-time zoo escapee Mickey the chimpanzee.

It took 13 shots and marksmen police officers from South Liverpool to bring an end to a chase in which six people, including three children, where injured.

The saga began shortly after 10 o'clock when 14-year-old Mickey smashed through an iron bar on his cage and made a bid for freedom from his home of five years in the Liverpool Zoological Park.

On the rampage, 15 stone Mickey pushed, bit and scratched those who stood in his way. The proprietor of the park, Mr Rogers, pursued Mickey with a rifle as he headed towards Sudley Road Council School. Here, the chimp picked one boy up by the ankle and left another man with a lacerated neck and leg. As his path of destruction spread, a decision was made to shoot and kill Mickey.

Mickey's days ended in a yard in Lugard Road. However in his 14 years, the usually cheeky chimpanzee had made quite a name for himself.

His previous keeper was reported to have laid daffodils on his body, as she remembered fondly the Mickey who, in happier times, kissed a woman who greeted him by name. Others however will

remember him for his temper when he 'went ape'and the stories of his run-ins with the ring master, and also when he wrenched batons from the hands of police officers.

LIP SERVICE

The Kissing Burglar

IN the late 1940s, South Liverpool saw a wave of unusual break-ins by a thief who came to be known as the Kissing Burglar.

Evading police arrest for almost 12 months, this amorous crook stole

jewellery and money before kissing a pretty girl whilst she slept, and escaping down a drain pipe. All his victims were targeted by their open bedroom window and a closely located drainpipe.

His method was so successful he committed in the region of 600 offences, all ended with his trademark Scouse smacker for the robbed girl.

Having served in the army and at one time in the parachute regiment, his agility and athletic skill ensured the police were no match, that was, until a trap was laid.

His spree was finally ended when a male police officer, wearing a wig, was placed as bait in an upstairs bedroom with an open window. Within a matter of weeks the kissing burglar paid the 'sleeping policeman' a visit.

Once caught he was sentenced to three years imprisonment, however, many of the girls were not overjoyed at this, and had in fact been rather charmed by the good looking thief and many had reported being reluctant for him to be caught initially.

One girl who was certainly intrigued by the kissing burglar went on to marry him and they settled down in Canada together. He kissed goodbye to a life of crime.

SCOUSE WHODUNNIT

The Body In The Cylinder

WHO was he? How long had he lain there? How did he get there? These are just a few of the unanswered questions surrounding 'the body in the cylinder'.

World War II saw many bombs both destroying and unearthing long kept secrets. This was no different.

In 1943 a blast uncovered a metal cylinder at the corner of Great Homer Street and Fulford Road. For years it lay there, used as a bench, a plaything and so forth, until one game of hide and seek unearthed a grizzly secret...

The body was found inside the cylinder, and by its attire was clearly Victorian; wearing narrow striped trousers, a morning coat and a bow tie. Police were never able to confirm the identity of the man, however, most speculation suggested the corpse to be Thomas Cregreen Williams, and this was backed up in part by some evidence.

The dead man had in his possession a wad of papers referring to the company T.C. Williams. Furthermore, there were suggestions that the company was facing bankruptcy in the late 19th Century.

Forensic expert Dr Firth concluded that the mystery man died after receipt of a postcard in 1885, and after 1884 no record of T.C Williams can be found in the Liverpool Trade Directory.

Was the cylinder man Thomas Cregreen Williams and if it was, did he enter of his own free will?

From people to institutions, those who represent good work for the community have always been recognised in Liverpool for their total dedication.
There are people who will be forever associated with their achievements for others whether in child care, prison reform or animal rights.
Scousers could – and would – influence and inspire.
Charity and welfare workers, from leading church and religious figures to medical pioneers and those helping the terminally ill, often operated and lived among the poor and the unfortunate.
Here in the role of honour are famous institutions, educational centres of excellence and hospitals, missions and community workplaces.
Pete Wylie sums up this caring side in his song Heart As Big As Liverpool. A true Scouse anthem.

GENERA

JOHN CARMEL HEENAN
ALDER HEY
CHARLES THOMPSON'S MISSION
THOMAS FRANCIS AGNEW
FATHER FRANCIS O'LEARY
WILLIAM HENRY QUILLIAM
FATHER JAMES NUGENT
RSPCA: REVEREND ARTHUR BROOME
DR DUNCAN
LIVERPOOL JOHN MOORES
UNIVERSITY CITIZENSHIP AWARDS

L GOOD

"Heenan received great praise during World War II when he helped rescue injured people from bombed buildings during the blitz"

JOHN CARMEL HEENAN

MORE than 20 years after his death, John Carmel Heenan is still revered among Liverpool's Roman Catholic community as one of the most personable bishops ever to serve in this city.

Born in Essex in 1905, Heenan was the son of a civil servant. His first love was journalism before he was ordained at the age of 25.

He became parish priest at Manor Park in his home county and his pastoral work was so successful that, when the church hierarchy decided to reconstitute the Catholic Missionary Society, Father Heenan was selected as its superior.

In 1951 he was consecrated Bishop of Leeds by the then Archbishop Godfrey, whom Heenan was later to succeed at both Liverpool and Westminster.

Five years later he became Archbishop of Liverpool, a post he held for six years. He would later describe it as his "happiest time as a bishop".

While in Liverpool, Archbishop Heenan decided on the modification of plans for the building of the

Metropolitan Cathedral, originally designed by Edwin Lutyens.

In 1959 he promoted a national competition for a new design, stipulating that the new building was not to exceed £1m and that it should be completed within 10 years.

The competition was won by Sir Frederick Gibberd and Heenan's vision was realised in less than the allotted time. At the consecration he was given the honour of representing the Pope.

A man of ceaseless energy and activity, Heenan received great praise during World War II when he helped rescue injured people from bombed buildings during the blitz.

He sang the first High Mass to be televised in Britain, served on the secretariat for the Unity of Christians and in 1963 he became Archbishop of Westminster.

His greatest love remained Liverpool, of which he once remarked: "I love the place and I love the people, their warmth and their depth of feeling."

ALDER HEY

ALDER Hey, which holds a special place in Merseysiders' hearts, was founded in 1914 and is the largest children's hospital in Western Europe.

To see how much Alder Hey means to the community it serves and how highly people think of it, all you have to do is go to its website and read some of the messages of thanks from former patients and their families.

Or you can simply consider how many different individuals and groups throughout Merseyside are involved, at any given time, in raising funds for the hospital. It is, quite simply, a great source of local pride and a much-cherished and appreciated institution.

The groundbreaking hospital was the birthplace of modern paediatric anaesthesia, with neonatal surgery and children's cardiac surgery pioneered there in the 1940s and 1950s.

One of only a few hospitals to have a University Institute of Child Health, Alder Hey has 20 specialist services, covering bone marrow transplant, burns, cleft lip and palate, cancer, renal replacement and spinal injuries. Other services include cardiology and craniofacial surgery.

The hospital can point to a number of firsts – such as appointing the first paediatric intensive care consultant in the UK and becoming a trust in 1991.

Royal patronage, meanwhile, was granted in 1985 (it's the Royal Liverpool Children's NHS Trust, to give it its full name).

An international centre of excellence, the trust has a first class reputation for saving the lives of sick children and a proud history of medical achievement and clinical innovation.

It treats more than 200,000 children a year from 17 north west health authorities, two health authorities in north Wales and Shropshire and also gives paediatric support to the Isle of Man.

In addition to all the treatment it provides, the trust is a teaching hospital involved in the training of more than 600 medical students.

For the fourth year running, the Royal Liverpool Children's NHS Trust has been rated as "excellent" and received the highest possible score in the national ratings system from the Healthcare Commission, the organisation which inspects NHS trusts to make sure they are working to high standards.

Ask Merseysiders and they will put it in more simple terms – Alder Hey is a big part of Liverpool life and the service it provides is priceless.

> "It treats more than 200,000 children a year"

CHARLES THOMPSON'S MISSION

CHARLES Thompson's Mission has been serving those in need from its landmark building in Hemingford Street, Birkenhead, since Victorian times.

It was opened by grocer Charles Thompson on January 9, 1892, in a former Quaker meeting house, to help alleviate the suffering of poverty-stricken members of the community and, at the same time, spread the Christian message.

Originally calling his centre the Poor Children's Mission, Mr Thompson was supported by people from all over the Wirral, including shopkeepers, business people and individuals, who contributed money, food, clothes and toys.

Mr Thompson died in 1903, but his daughter, Annie Thompson, continued the good work. Like her father, she was much-loved and respected and, in 1953, was awarded an OBE for her services to the people of Birkenhead. She remained mission superintendent until her death in 1963.

The good work continues to this day, under the guidance of the mission's current superintendent, Rob Jeffs. Mr Jeffs, his wife Joyce, daughter Debbie, his assistant Bernie Frost and many an army of volunteers continue to receive into the Mission items of clothing and food.

In addition, from Monday to Friday, the mission – known by many, locally, as "Thommo's" – provides hot food in the mornings, soup and sandwiches in the afternoons and endless cups of tea for the homeless and anyone in need.

And, as in the early days, the organisation takes adults who come to the Mission on free outings and children on free holidays.

It is part of the Liverpool City Mission, which has three Rescue Centres: Charles Thompson's Mission, the Jubilee Chapel Centre in Kensington and the Liverpool City Centre Café Outreach in Mount Pleasant. There are also seven Mission Churches in Liverpool and the Wirral.

Charles Thompson's Mission marked its centenary in January 1992 and, because so many people wanted to share in the celebrations, a second thanksgiving service was held in the May of that year.

Even in this age of relative plenty, there is still a need for places like Charles Thompson's Mission – and its aim remains the same: To help anyone in need and tell them of the love of God.

"Other towns and
cities quickly followed
Liverpool's example"

THOMAS FRANCIS AGNEW

LIVERPOOL businessman and humanitarian Thomas Francis Agnew
changed the face of charity when he set up the first British society for the
prevention of cruelty to children in 1883, the forerunner of the NSPCC.

The idea first came to him on a trip to New York when he saw the work
of the New York Society for the Prevention of Cruelty to Children, the first
of its type in the world.

Inspired, he came back and spoke out at a meeting in Liverpool to
establish a home for dogs, suggesting it should perhaps be turned into a
home for children. That evening, April 19, 1883, the Liverpool Society for
the Prevention of Cruelty to Children was formed.

In an era where cruelty to youngsters was no secret and not even a crime,
inspectors on bicycles would pluck neglected children from the streets and
give them a chance at a better life.

Other towns and cities quickly followed Liverpool's example. London set
up a society a year later, which later became known as the National Society
for the Prevention of Cruelty to Children – the NSPCC as we now know it.

It took several years for the Liverpool SPCC to merge with the NSPCC,
which had branches springing up around the country. From early in the
20th century until 1953, the two societies worked separately but in
co-operation. The NSPCC covered the outlying districts of Liverpool
and the original Society for Prevention of Cruelty to Children covered
the city centre.

Agnew was also instrumental in the formation of the Irish Society for the
Prevention of Cruelty to Children with the Reverend Benjamin Waugh.
In 1889, a branch was opened in Dublin, to be followed in 1891 by others
in Belfast and Cork. The number of branches in Ireland multiplied in
subsequent years and their work continued under the direction of the
NSPCC throughout the Troubles and under the Republic until 1956, when
the Irish Society for the Prevention of Cruelty to Children took over the
assets and responsibilities of the national body south of the border,
whilst the work in the six counties remained an integral part of the NSPCC.

"Father O'Leary looked after the abandoned woman for three weeks, until she eventually died, reportedly kissing a crucifix"

FATHER FRANCIS O'LEARY

CROSBY Priest Father Francis O'Leary set up the globally based charity Jospice International.

Today the organisation has homes in various countries caring for terminally ill people.

Francis O'Leary worked alongside Father Vincent Hughes, a priest working in Edge Hill, Widnes and Southport.

Father Hughes later became located in Peru, while Father O'Leary was based in Merseyside.

Both were former pupils of St Peter and St Paul's School, Crosby.

In 1973, Father O'Leary featured as the subject of television's This Is Your Life, and guests were flown in from the charity's homes in Pakistan.

Francis O'Leary trained at St Peter's College, Freshfield, and was ordained into St Joseph's Missionary Society in London.

His vocation started as a missionary in Rawalpindi, Pakistan, in 1960, where he was faced with finding a home for a desperately poor, paralysed old woman whom no hospital would cater for.

The local overcrowded hospitals needed every bed for younger people with hope of finding a cure for their ailments.

Father O'Leary looked after the abandoned woman for three weeks, until she eventually died, reportedly kissing a crucifix.

His experience gave him the idea of finding special hospitals for such sad cases in future.

In 1982, a celebration of his work was held in Bootle town hall.

By then, more than 20 hospices had sprung up in Pakistan, as well as central and southern America.

But there were also two hospices particularly close to their founder's heart – in Merseyside.

WILLIAM HENRY QUILLIAM

BORN William Henry Quilliam in 1851, Sheikh Quilliam is credited with leading the first British Muslim community here in Liverpool.

The son of a watch manufacturer, he was educated at the Liverpool Institute and went on to become a solicitor in the city.

However, he became particularly interested in Islam after travelling to Morocco in 1882.

Five years later, he formally converted to Islam, taking the Muslim name Sheikh Abdullah Quilliam.

Shortly afterwards, he gave a lecture at the Temperance League, which developed into a weekly Muslim meeting. Sheikh Abdullah's first convert to the faith was a Mrs Fatima Cates, and together they published the monthly Islamic newsletters from 1893, called The Crescent and The Islamic World.

These journals were then distributed to more than 20 countries.

As the group drew in more converts, they moved into their own premises, setting up the Liverpool Muslim Institute at Broughton Terrace at the turn of the 20th century, with more than 150 members. The institute has since been hailed as Britain's oldest mosque.

In 1896, Sheikh Abdullah bought a building in Sheil Road, which he converted into a children's home, called The Medina.

He and many of his fellow English Muslims were persecuted – women leaving the mosque had mud thrown at them, and a prayer caller was once hit with a snowball containing a rock.

But Sheikh Abdullah continued his work undeterred until he left Liverpool for Turkey in 1908.

Meanwhile, Liverpool's Muslim community spread, with many members travelling to Woking to help with the establishment of a Muslim centre there.

Sheikh Abdullah died in London in 1932, leaving three sons and five daughters.

He is buried in Brookfield cemetery in Surrey, close to the Qu'ran translators Yusef Ali and Marmaduke Pickthall.

> "In 1896, Sheikh Abdullah bought a building in Sheil Road, which he converted into a children's home, called The Medina"

"Father Nugent opened a night shelter and refuge for destitute boys in Soho Street and went on to publish the Catholic Times and Catholic Fireside"

FATHER JAMES NUGENT

FATHER James Nugent was a much heralded 19th century social and educational reformer, as well as a prison chaplain, distinguished journalist and parish priest.

He was ordained into the church in 1846, and within months was working with the starving masses who had come to Liverpool to escape the excesses of the Irish potato famine.

He opened the first of what where termed "ragged" schools in Liverpool in 1849.

This was to be the first of many specially set up and dedicated to help the poor.

In 1860 he founded two Roman Catholic newspapers, and two years later he was to become the first catholic chaplain at Walton Prison.

Father Nugent opened a night shelter and refuge for destitute boys in Soho Street and went on to publish the Catholic Times and Catholic Fireside.

In 1869 he opened another boys' refuge in St Anne Street, and a year later took the first party of children on a trip to Canada.

In June 1892, Nugent was made a domestic prelate by Pope Leo XIII while on a visit to Rome.

He opened his last home in the Dingle in 1904 at the grand old age of 82.

The fine principles he stood for, and his general concern for the less fortunate, continues through the Nugent Care Society.

"It costs a staggering £1,000 a day to keep the centre up and running, and all funds are raised locally"

RSPCA: REVEREND ARTHUR BROOME

THE world's first animal welfare charity was set up in Liverpool in 1809. The Society for the Suppression of Wanton Cruelty to Brute Animals was originally created as a sanctuary with the aim of protecting mistreated carters' horses.

From a coffee house in Bold Street, volunteers worked to prevent cruelty to the carrier horses serving the port.

Their cause was taken on by Reverend Arthur Broome in 1822, a man who was determined to change people's attitude to animals. Inspired by the work in Liverpool, he formed the SPCA (the Royal was added later).

For two years Mr Broome struggled to generate interest – and money. By 1824, he was successful, but following a lack of funding he was thrown into prison when the society fell into debt.

His friends hastily collected enough money to pay the debts, and Mr Broome was released.

He continued to work to punish cat skinners, to abolish dog-pits and to alleviate the misery of horses.

The activities of the society became more and more widespread. Not only was it concerned with bringing cruelty cases to court; equally important was its painstaking effort to get new bills on the statute book and its magnificent work in alleviating the cruelty in the slaughter of animals.

In one 10-year period, the RSPCA spent over £250,000 on advocating humane slaughter. It financed mechanical stunning devices and bought the patents of other humane inventions. Men from all walks of life, as diverse as the author John Goldsworthy and Sir Bernard Spilsbury, have become involved on behalf of the RSPCA's demand for slaughterhouse reforms.

Today the shelter at Halewood is the largest RSPCA animal centre anywhere in the country. The team at Halewood take in 4,000 dogs, 2,000 cats and 1,500 smaller animals and birds each year. It costs a staggering £1,000 a day to keep the centre up and running, and all funds are raised locally.

DR DUNCAN

BRITAIN'S first public health inspector, William Henry Duncan, was born in Seel Street in Liverpool city centre in 1805.

Little is known of his early life, but after studying medicine at Edinburgh University, he returned as a GP to Liverpool to find a quarter of the population living in slum conditions.

The city also had an appalling record of death from diseases such as typhus and cholera.

Dr Duncan believed that the high mortality rate in Liverpool was directly connected with the people's living conditions.

Thus, in 1843, he produced a report highlighting the connection between insanitary conditions and poor health. The findings led to the UK's first Public Health Act in 1846.

On January 1 the following year, Duncan was appointed medical officer of health. But by the June, 300,000 Irish immigrants fleeing the potato famine swelled the already overcrowded slums even further.

It was not unusual to find 50 to 60 people living in a house containing only three or four small rooms.

By 1849 Liverpool's death rate was the worst in the country. Deaths from typhus and typhoid fever had risen twentyfold, with hospital ships being set up on the Mersey.

Duncan had noted that people tended to become unwell a matter of hours or a few days before they developed full-blown cholera, and he set up a system of medical visitors to seek out cases and arrange treatment.

As a result of his activities, the impact of cholera was much less when the disease returned in 1854.

Because the germ theory had not been developed, the disease was associated with "bad air".

Ironically, it resulted in the right public health measures – cleaning the streets, improving water supply and building sewers.

Although working to a faulty theory, many of the measures that were taken, such as ventilation and simple disinfection, ended up achieving an overall better result.

Dr Duncan's name is probably best perpetuated today in the name of a popular pub – complete with spectacular ceramic-tiled side bar – near to St George's Hall, the place where the benefits of Duncan's work were first explained to the masses, but also ironically, adjacent to St John's Gardens, the burial site of thousands of the cholera dead.

LIVERPOOL JOHN MOORES UNIVERSITY CITIZENSHIP AWARDS

"It is important that we recognise the young people in our city who are making in a difference"

THE Liverpool John Moores University Citizenship Awards were established to encourage young people to be caring, compassionate and tolerant individuals with a real sense of civic responsibility.

The scheme is now presented in more than 900 schools in Merseyside and the north west, and recognises the often overlooked contributions that young people from different cultures and communities make to society.

The scheme is typified by 10-year-old Lucy Whittaker, a pupil of Bedford primary school, Bootle, who won her award for being a great team player and active participant in all school activities.

Her classmates' nomination spoke of Lucy "being fab in every way."

Local companies have sponsored Good Citizenship Awards in all Liverpool schools and in the boroughs of Knowsley, Wirral, St Helens and Sefton and in the surrounding boroughs of Wigan and Warrington.

Each school chooses a Good Citizen of the Year and a representative from the sponsor company presents the bronze award – made by local sculptor Stephen Broadbent.

More recently the Foundation for Citizenship secured sponsorship from O2 and the Merseyside Colleges Association to fund awards for all the FE Colleges and Sixth Form Colleges.

Lord Alton of Liverpool, director of the Foundation for Citizenship, said: "It is important that we recognise the young people in our city who are making in a difference. We all too often hear about the negative side, but rarely hear about the majority of selfless acts done by our young people."

PADDY'S GREAT PUBS LIVERPOOL

By Paddy Shennan

LIVERPOOL may no longer boast a boozer on every street corner – those must have been the days! – but it can still claim to be the country's capital of pubs. And capital of beer.

Liverpool's pub and real ale scene is not just in a healthy state, it's thriving.

So, to misquote the late, great John Lennon (he loved a pint or two in Ye Cracke in Rice Street), let me take you down, because we're going to... take an all-too-short tour around some of the city's greatest alehouses.

The traditional, no-nonsense pub plays a central role in Liverpool life and is, quite rightly, a much-cherished institution – and three of the judges who decided that Liverpool ought to be awarded European Capital of Culture status for 2008 apparently agree.

Armed with copies of the double-award-winning Liverpool ECHO Pub Guide book (written by yours truly and Mike Chapple, now the Liverpool Daily Post's pub guru), panel chairman Sir Jeremy Isaacs and his colleagues Miranda Sawyer and Peter Stead reportedly enjoyed refreshment stops at two of our finest hostelries – Dr Duncan's and the Philharmonic – during a tour of the city.

How could we not win their all-important votes after that!?

Our historic, flagship brewery, Cains – the Stanhope Street site was acquired by Irish entrepreneur Robert Cain in 1858 – represents the beating heart of the city's pub life. After an uncertain period in the latter part of the 20th century, it was placed firmly back on the map when it was taken over by Ajmail and Sudarghara Dusanj in 2002.

The brothers – who are so far ahead of the game they launched a 2008 ale in 2003 – have been busy spreading the good news about Cains' beers here, there and everywhere since taking over the reins, collecting a staggering array of accolades and awards in the process.

A great starting point for visitors to Liverpool – and a great outing for anyone who appreciates a good pint – is the Cains Brewery Tour, which begins and ends at the brewery's own pub next door. The Brewery Tap, with its full range of Cains ales, its classy wood interior and big, light-inviting windows, is an absolute gem – and, despite being on the edge of town, is well worthy of regular visits.

For similar geographical reasons, the Baltic Fleet on Wapping may not make it into some people's city centre pub crawls – all the more reason to head down to Liverpool's world-famous waterfront to devote an entire evening to the ship-shaped boozer's ample charms, including its mouth-watering selection of Wapping ales, brewed on the premises.

To be honest, it's impossible to devise a single pub crawl which would give a drinker the ultimate Liverpool pub experience. There are so many boozers worthy of our time and attention, including many on the outskirts and in the suburbs, that it could take days – weeks, even – to get around the very best this well-blessed area has to offer.

Take a look at this list for starters...

If you can manage a not-at-all-unlucky 13 city centre pubs in a day, or over a weekend (perhaps a half in each, or the odd soft drink!) I don't think you could go wrong with the following route...

1. **THE LION**, on the corner of Moorfields and Tithebarn Street – exquisitely-crafted features (take a look at the ornate glass dome and all that terrific tiling!) – and exquisitely-pulled pints. The pub's famous cheese board is pretty damn good, too.

2. **THOMAS RIGBY'S**, Dale Street – tasty Okell's ales and tasty food. Go to Rigby's for a mouthwatering (and award-winning) food and drink-matching experience.

3. **THE POSTE HOUSE**, Cumberland Street – this cosy little pub, which oozes history (Adolf Hitler and Prince Philip have drunk here, you know – allegedly) was in danger of being bulldozed in 2001, when developers came a-calling. But the people spoke and the powers-that-be listened. Hurrah!

4. **THE SHIP AND MITRE**, Dale Street – drinkers come from far and wide to sample the impressive, ever-changing selection of beers on offer in this multi-award-winning real ale paradise.

5. **DOCTOR DUNCAN'S**, St John's Lane – the city's first medical officer would have been proud. This Cains house is a real tonic.

6. **THE FAMOUS CARNARVON CASTLE**, Tarleton Street – an oasis in the heart of the city centre. Forget the shopping and spend the day in here instead.

7. **THE GLOBE**, Cases Street, off Ranelagh Street, next to the Clayton Square shopping centre – wonderfully warm and welcoming. Mind the sloping floor – hold onto your pints!

8. **THE ROSCOE HEAD**, Roscoe Street, off Leece Street/Hardman Street – a great 'local' ...in town. Consistency is the key – back in 2003, the Camra Good Beer Guide announced that the Roscoe Head was the only Merseyside pub (and one of only 17 in the UK) to have appeared in all 30 editions of the guide.

9. **THE FLY IN THE LOAF**, Hardman Street – another big and beautiful Okell's pub, like Thomas Rigby's (and, keeping it firmly in the family, landlord Dominic Hornsby is married to Rigby's landlady Fiona Watkin).

10. **THE PHILHARMONIC** in Hope Street – majestic, not least the marvellous marble in the gents' lav.

11. **YE CRACKE** in Rice Street – this fantastic boozer has a scruffy, laid-back charm and is an antidote to all those poncey and pretentous "style" bars.

12. **THE DISPENSARY**, Renshaw Street, at the junction with Oldham Street – extremely effective Cains "medicine" available here.

13. **THE SWAN INN**, Wood Street – a no-nonsense classic. Feed that headbanging jukebox!

But this is only a guide. You could just concentrate on doing two or three of these pubs in one afternoon, evening or day – they are all worthy of as much of your time as possible.

Or you could mix and match with other excellent boozers in the city centre, like, for example, The White Star in Rainford Gardens, The Belvedere in Sugnall Street, the Blackburne Arms Hotel in Catharine Street, Peter Kavanagh's (if you can manage the walk further out into Toxteth, you'll find this famous pub in Egerton Street), The Head of Steam, by Lime Street station, The Crown Hotel in Lime Street, The Everyman Bar and Bistro and the Casa, both in Hope Street, The Excelsior in Dale Street, The Cavern Pub on Mathew Street, The Pilgrim in Pilgrim Street, Ye Hole in Ye Wall in Hackins Hey, off Dale Street, Ma Boyle's Oyster Bar in Tower Gardens, the Augustus John in Peach Street, off Mount Pleasant/Brownlow Hill, the Grapes on Mathew Street, the Cambridge on Mulberry Street, the "Little" Grapes on Roscoe Street, the Railway on Tithebarn Street and, on the edge of town in the Dock Road area, the Bull on Dublin Street and the Farmers Arms on Waterloo Road.

There really are too many to mention, but I hope I've given you at least a few ideas about where to start what, I'm sure, will be a wonderful journey.

more Liverpool Firsts
to be proud of
by Catherine Jones

Arts and entertainment

- On December 21, 1913, the Sunday New York World printed a puzzle called a word-cross, devised by Liverpudlian Arthur Wynne. The puzzle was an instant success and became a world-wide craze in 1924 after a book was published featuring the then re-named ... crossword.

- The Lyceum gentleman's club housed Europe's first lending library, which had been founded in 1757 and moved to the Bold Street building in 1802.

- The Beatles were the first group to have the top five records in the American Billboard charts. They were also the first pop stars to be awarded MBEs.

- The Liverpool Philharmonic Orchestra was the first established symphony orchestra with its own hall.
  It was also the first orchestra to receive Royal assent.
  Another Philharmonic claim to fame is the fact that its musicians were the first to play underwater (in 1994, to mark the 60th anniversary of the Birkenhead Tunnel).

- Liverpool Playhouse was the first repertory theatre in the country with a company which was established in 1911.

- In April 1953 Liverpool singer Lita Rosa became the first British woman to top the UK charts with the song How Much is that Doggy in the Window?

- Sir Oliver Lodge, the first Professor of Physics at University College, sent the first intelligible long-distance radio message in 1897, from the Liverpool University clock tower on Brownlow Hill to his assistant on the roof of Lewis's in the city centre.

Education

- Britain's first School for the Blind.
  The school was founded by anti-slavery campaigner and radical Edward Rushton, who lost his sight at an early age.
  In the late 1780s, Rushton and several friends came up with the idea of raising money to help Liverpool's blind poor.
  The Liverpool School for the Indigent Blind, the first of its kind in the country, opened in 1791 in two houses in Commutation Row at the bottom end of London Road.
  A new school for 70 pupils was built in London Road and opened in 1800.

- Liverpool boasts the first Hebrew day school - now King David primary - set up outside London, in 1841.

Sports

- The first football net.
  Until the 1890s goalposts had no nets. They were invented by Liverpool's City Engineer John Brodie.
  The world's first footballer ever to 'put the ball in back of the net' was Fred Geary of Everton, at a trial game in Nottingham in January 1891.

- Liverpool Rugby club, founded in December 1857, is the oldest open rugby club in the world.

- Liverpool Velocipedes became the country's first cycling club when it was established in 1867.

Business and buildings

- Liverpool was home to the first Woolworth's store in Europe.
  The company's premises at 25 Church Street was opened in 1909.

- Oriel Chambers became what is believed to be the world's first metal-framed glass curtain walled building when it was built in 1864.
  Meanwhile the Royal Liver Building is said to be the first reinforced multi-storey framed building in the world when it was completed in 1911.

- First bank to use a computer.
  In 1960, Martins Bank in Liverpool became the first to use a computer - a Pegasus II - for recording customer current accounts.

- In 1959 the Westminster Bank in Princes Road, Toxteth, became the UK's first drive-thru bank.

- Liverpool boasts the first form of underwriting in the world with the Liverpool Underwriters Association existing from at least 1802.

- St George's Church, Everton Brow, was the first prefabricated, factory-constructed building in the world, made in advance, brought to the site and bolted together.
  That was in 1812.

and those we are not so proud of...

- The first shot in the American Civil War is reputed to have been fired from a gun made by Liverpool firm Fawcett and Preston.
  And the last Confederate ship to surrender at the end of the American Civil War was the Shenandoah, which gave itself up to the Mayor at Liverpool Town Hall in November 1865.

- The first and only British Prime Minister to be assassinated was Spencer Percival who was shot by bankrupt Liverpool merchant John Bellingham.
  Incidentally, John Wilkes Booth, who shot Abraham Lincoln, was the son of a Liverpudlian actor.

- And the redoubtable Bessie Braddock, Liverpool's first woman MP, was also the first woman to be dismissed from the House of Commons for bad language.

Everton

By David Prentice

WHAT does a lifetime of following
Everton Football Club
mean to a man?

There's the obvious answers: worry lines, high blood pressure, sleepless nights – and the occasional dizzying, soaring, giddy highs which make the tribulations seem almost worthwhile.

But me? Following Everton means something just a little different.
I've been fortunate enough to find myself in a privileged position.
As a newspaper man, the Toffees gave me the most entertaining and illuminating decade of my professional life.

In February 1993 I was appointed as a full-time Everton correspondent of the Liverpool Echo. By coincidence it was about the same time that Toffees embarked upon a maelstrom of managerial upheaval. Howard Kendall, Mike Walker, Joe Royle, Howard again, Walter Smith and David Moyes all occupied it in a caretaker capacity during that dramatic decade – and the ownership of the club switched from the Moores family, to Peter Johnson and finally to Bill Kenwright's True Blue holdings.

That was just off the pitch.

On it, Everton twice came as close as they had ever done to the appalling ignominy of relegation from the top flight, they secured a sixth place finish in the Premier League, signed and sold players like Andrei Kanchelskis, Duncan Ferguson and Nick Barmby – oh, and won the FA Cup against Manchester United.
That gave me the opportunity to cover Everton in Europe – and dine out on roast puffin in Reykjavik.

As a sports journalist I wouldn't have missed it for the world.

Actually, in hindsight, I'd have given the puffin a miss. But in addition to a professional impact, the Blues have also had a profound effect on my personal life.

It was as the Echo's Everton correspondent that I was introduced to the beautiful and bewitching grand-daughter of the legendary Dixie Dean.

And in a twist of fate far too long and convoluted for this brief article, she became my wife.

It means I can say without any fear of a sharp back-hander that the woman I share my bed with is openly and unashamedly blue.

And it means that when I start talking about blindside runs which avoid the active area of a deep-lying defence's offside trap, she doesn't glaze over and say "Pardon?"

Not often, anyway.

Melanie and myself go back a long way.

But she was blissfully unaware of the first 10 years or so of our relationship.

You see her mum, now my mother-in-law, was the landlady of the Westminster pub near Goodison Park – and that was my preferred hostelry when I was a match going youth, in the days before journalism got a hold of me.

I would sip my pint of bitter, imagining halcyon moments with my blond haired idol.

Then I'd go to the bar and chat to Melanie about him.

You see, until my mental age reached my shoe size, the only blonds who excited my imagination were footballers.

Andy King, Alan Biley, Mike Walsh (the defender, not the dreadful bubble-permed striker), Adrian Heath and Andy Gray (yes, his hair really was blond until it all fell out) were the heroes of my youth.

But then football makes you do the most ridiculous things.

Blonds weren't the sole objects of my affection. I loved red-heads, too - like Gary Megson and Neil Robinson (I was a little too young to remember Alan Ball), jet black haired full-backs – John Barton special agent, anyone? And, of course, brunettes.

And the most idolised of them all was big, bad, bearded Bob Latchford.

Latchford failed to win a single trophy during his seven years with Everton.

But that didn't mean he was a loser. Far from it.

The late seventies was a time of trial for anybody who viewed their football through Blue tinted spectacles.

While neighbours and rivals Liverpool were conquering all before them at home and abroad (leading to tribes of cheeky young urchins to congregate outside my family home on the night of May 25, 1977 to chant: "Prenny, Prenny show us your scarf!") Everton were left toiling in their slipstream.

But if trophies were out of reach, the least long-suffering fans needed was a folk hero in the true Goodison tradition, a man to lift beleaguered spirits, an incontrovertible source of pride in painful arguments with smug friends.

Bob Latchford was that man, and on April 29, 1978 he gave a 15-year-old Evertonian a glimpse of what it might be like to follow a winning team.

No striker had scored 30 league goals in a single season for six years. The media was so concerned by the demise of the out and out goalscorer that the Daily Express offered a £10,000 cash prize for the first player to reach that mark.

Latchford reached the 30-goal target against Chelsea on a warm and riotously received afternoon at Goodison Park.

A number of fans scaled the perimeter fencing and raced onto the pitch to offer more personal congratulations.

One decided to dig his fingers into the turf and claim the penalty spot.

Well... when in Rome. And after all, I was at an impressionable age.

So I dug up a mound of treasured Goodison turf, placed it carefully in my denim jacket pocket (just below the sew on badge of the Winston Churchill V-sign and the legend "Up The Blues") and took it gingerly home.

It resided in a plastic ice-cream container, next to my bed, until my dad had an environemtally unfriendly moment and ordered me to throw it out.

I decided to replant it in the bare patch under my sister's swing.

So whoever lives at 6 Byland Close, Formby should be aware there's a historic piece of Goodison growing in their back garden.

Ironically April 29 is now my wedding anniversary, but it wasn't chosen because it coincided with Bob Latchford's finest moment – or for the fact that Everton lifted the FA Cup at Wembley Stadium for the first time on that date 45 years earlier.

It was chosen because that was the date the man who lifted the Cup that day, the great Dixie Dean, fathered his only daughter.

Yes, April 29 is my mother-in-law's birthday.

So what does Everton mean to me?

A job, a wife, a myriad of memories – and no reason whatsoever why I should forget my wedding anniversary or my mother-in-law's birthday.

Liverpool is the capital of music, with more number one hits from Scousers than from any other city, a figure recognised by the good people of Guinness.

And Scousers are pure genius when it comes to music. Liverpool is a city that international stars always want to play on tour.

In Mathew Street, a wall of fame highlights the ongoing success of artists who have reached the coveted number one spot.

But Liverpool's musical heritage encompasses every genre from skiffle to folk, rock and roll to pop and classical – orchestral and operatic.

Music is part of the rich Scouse Pie – past, present and future.

Like humour and sport, it is a key ingredient in our global fame and music has helped put us on the map.

THE BEATLES
SIMON RATTLE
GERRY MARSDEN
FRANKIE VAUGHAN
SIR CHARLES GROVES
THE SPINNERS
BILLY FURY
IAN TRACEY
GEORGE MELLY
RITA HUNTER

MUSIC

THE BEATLES

"Imagine the world without them. Impossible"

JOHN Lennon, Paul McCartney, George Harrison and Ringo Starr went on to shake, rattle and roll the world of music, culture and attitude for generations.

Without them, Liverpool would be remembered as a once thriving sea-port with beautiful architecture, a couple of ferries and the added attraction of famous football teams as well as nurturing comedians.

The Beatles stamped their creative talent on music, art, film, literature and fashion. These ordinary long-haired lads managed to lead the way with their outlook.

At the Mathew Street festival each year, 300,000 people mill around the city boosting tourism and the local economy via shops, restaurants, hotels, public houses – everyone having fun under the August Bank holiday skies.

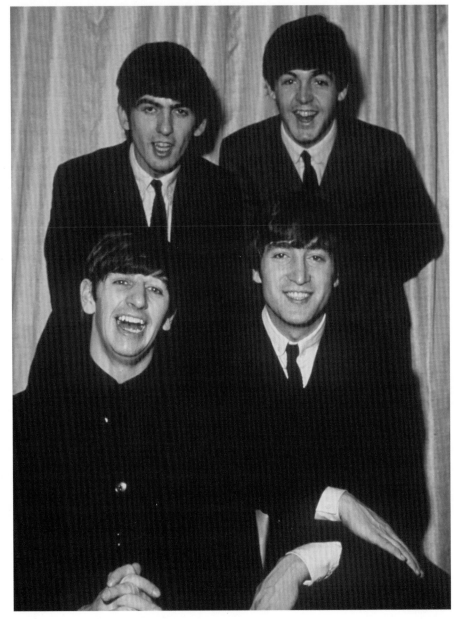

"Without the Beatles, there would still be a Penny Lane and a Strawberry Fields, yes, but minus the special stamp Lennon and McCartney placed on them"

There would be no Eleanor Rigby and Beatles statues, and Mathew Street would probably be just a thoroughfare of drab warehouses; a street with a name, but little else. The Cavern would be just a memory.

Today the work of the Beatles is discussed in schools all over the world; from primary to secondary, from colleges to universities.

More than 400 books have been written about their influence in our society.

Liverpool gave the world many firsts in history – from the School of Tropical Medicine to the invention of football goal nets. But we also gave the world a Fab First. Newspapers and TV programmes use their lyrics in headlines and to illustrate the 60s. Now, hundreds of websites are available in their honour. And the Beatles themselves have their own magical site. Liverpool cannot and will not imagine life – past, present and future – without them.

The Beatles did live and live on. They made their mark here, there and everywhere...

SIR SIMON RATTLE

ALLERTON-raised Sir Simon Rattle is conductor of the world's most famous orchestra – the Berlin Philharmonic.

Sir Simon, 53, took the £1m a year job in 2001, the year he last appeared on home ground to conduct part of the golden jubilee concert of the Liverpool Mozart Orchestra – the first ensemble he conducted, aged just 13.

The former Merseyside (now Philharmonic) Youth Orchestra percussionist has been widely hailed as "the most outstanding living conductor" – and certainly the best Britain has produced – since the days of Sir Thomas Beecham and Sir Adrian Boult.

Sir Simon learned music from scores borrowed from his local library in Liverpool.

A performance of Mahler's Second Symphony (The Resurrection) at Philharmonic Hall convinced him that he should become a conductor.

At the time of playing with the MYO he formed his own ensemble.

He later attended the Royal Academy of Music in London, and won a major conducting competition in Liverpool, going on to conduct the same Mahler symphony to wide acclaim.

In 1974 he was made assistant conductor of the Bournemouth Symphony Orchestra, and in 1977, assistant at the Royal Liverpool Philharmonic.

It was his stint as music director of the City of Birmingham Symphony (from 1980-88) that he fully gained his outstanding reputation.

"The Berlin job is generally regarded as the most prestigious in the entire musical world"

However, the appointment (decided on by a vote of orchestral players) was not without controversy, several members preferring Daniel Barenboim for the post.

However, Rattle won the day – but refused to sign the contract until he had ensured that every member of the Berlin Phil had received a pay review.

GERRY MARSDEN

GERRY Marsden is the man who gave the world famous Kop a distinctive, unique voice.

As the singer who turned Rogers and Hammerstein's You'll Never Walk Alone into the best known football song of all, Marsden has a special place in the history of music.

If this was his only achievement it would be a mighty one, but it is just one on a lengthy list which makes Gerry Marsden a true great of British pop.

Marsden formed Gerry and the Pacemakers in the late 1950s with his brother, Fred, Les Chadwick and Arthur Mack, who was eventually replaced on piano by Les Maguire.

At the outset, little could they have known that they would go on to become one of the torch bearers of a music scene which would become internationally known as Merseybeat.

With their first three singles – How Do You Do It?, I Like It and You'll Never Walk Alone – the group made British music history by becoming the first group to have their first three releases reach No 1 in the charts. Ferry Cross The Mersey

cemented their place in the hearts of British music fans but their success was not only limited to this country as they scored a succession of hits in the USA.

After the group broke up, Dingle-born Gerry maintained a career as a TV personality, and went on to star in the West End musical Charlie Girl.

"With a new set of Pacemakers, he has made more than twice as many albums as he did in the 1960s, including one of Beatles songs"

He also re-recorded two of his most famous hits, You'll Never Walk Alone and Ferry Cross The Mersey, in the 1980s with all money raised going to charities set up in the wake of the Bradford and Hillsborough stadium tragedies.

Gerry still lives on Merseyside and is still a popular performs throughout the UK.

FRANKIE VAUGHAN

LEGENDARY entertainer Frankie Vaughan was that most rare of individuals – a showbusiness superstar AND a man of the people.

Born Frank Ephraim Abelson in Devon Street, off London Road, Liverpool, on February 3, 1928, he loved his home city with a passion.

His widow, Stella, who was married to Frankie for 48 years, told the ECHO:

> "He loved Liverpool so much.
> He always said Liverpool people were so warm,
> but they didn't suffer fools – they could spot a phoney"

His old friend, Liverpool comic Tom O'Connor, said of him: "He was a big star, but he was also modest and a real man of the people – everyone counted with him.

"He certainly taught me a lot about how to behave, both on and off stage – he knocked a lot of the cockiness out of me. Frankie was such a genuine guy and he was really interested in people."

The eldest of four children, Frankie began singing at his Hebrew school, joining the synagogue choir aged 10.

Three years later, with his father serving in the army, Frankie and the rest of his family were evacuated to Endmoor, a village in Westmorland. They later moved to Lancaster, where Frank joined the Lancaster Lads' Club.

And he was to remember these days later in his career, supporting boys' clubs through his tireless charity work.

He adopted his stage name after impressing agent Bernard Delfont at an audition at the Kingston Empire in 1949 – Frankie later explaining: "We came up with Vaughan because my Russian grandmother called me her 'number vorn grandson'."

A star of stage and screen – he famously appeared alongside Marilyn Monroe in Hollywood movie Let's Make Love – Frankie enjoyed 29 hit singles, including number ones Garden Of Eden and Tower Of Strength. He was awarded the OBE and CBE and also made a deputy Lord Lieutenant of Buckinghamshire and vice-president of the National Association of Clubs for Young People.

Frankie said: "My grandmother told me, 'If you make it, you must put something back. If you give, you will never want'. And I've tried to do that."

The father-of-three, who lived with Stella in High Wycombe, died, aged 71, in September 1999.

SIR CHARLES GROVES

SIR Charles Groves – knighted during his 14-year tenure as conductor of the Royal Liverpool Philharmonic Orchestra – was the champion of British classical music.

Among the composers he popularised were Arthur Bliss, George Butterworth, Frank Bridge, Benjamin Britten, Delius, Holst, Walton, Warlock and Tippett.

But his personal favourite was Edward Elgar, and in many ways, Sir Charles' own distinguished appearance brought back memories of those days when British music ruled the waves.

Born in London, he was a chorister at St Paul's Cathedral, and later a student at the Royal College of Music, where he studied piano and organ.

"But in adult life, Charles Groves was to become an adopted Scouser as the longest-serving Phil music director of recent times"

Among the outstanding talents he encouraged in Liverpool were Simon Rattle and Andrew Davis. He recorded with many international labels, who helped to establish his reputation as the foremost interpreter of British music.

During the 1970s, he became a regular conductor of the Last Night of the Proms at the Royal Albert Hall.

He was well-known for encouraging contemporary composers and programming their works.

The Making Music Sir Charles Groves Prize is now a national award given to an individual or organisation making an outstanding contribution to UK music.

THE SPINNERS

AFFECTIONATELY known as "The Other Fab Four", the Spinners changed the face of the folk music scene.

The Merseyside quartet made 37 albums and specialised in atmospheric versions of classic tunes from The Leaving of Liverpool to Maggie May.

The Spinners were born when, in 1958, four musicians with a passion for song and a love of performing met. Hughie Jones, Cliff Hall, Mick Groves and Tony Davis set about producing nearly forty albums.

They made numerous concerts and TV appearances and became immensely popular, reviving some of the greatest folk music and singing new songs in the same vein.

Critics said that their style was musically simple, cosy and sentimental – but this is what appealed to the fans. One of their best known songs was In My Liverpool Home, written by Peter McGovern in 1962. John McCormick was the group's bassist and musical director for the final 17 years.

"After many world tours, countless TV appearances and entertaining sell-out audiences at their spiritual home, the Philharmonic Hall, they split up in 1988 – but the fans stayed loyal"

They met up for a special reunion in 2005.

Cliff said: "We are all older, but when you get up on stage something happens – you are with friends.

"We all have our strengths and styles – Tony has his maritime tales and his sea shanties, I have my calypso music. Hugh has his own distinct folk tradition and Mick has the wonderful Ewan McColl songs. The Spinners are four great friends who on stage try and make the evening entertaining and fun. I think we achieved that."

Summing up the band's success, Tony Davis said: "I think the whole Spinners concept is one of great affection. We loved doing what we did and we had people out there to support it and enjoy it.

"I don't think it can it into words what it feels like playing the Royal Festival Hall, singing on the Clipper Ships, the Albert Hall and the wonderful Christmas shows at the Philharmonic."

BILLY FURY

HE was the city's first rock 'n' roll star – a gentle man with a powerful voice and a powerful stage name.

Billy Fury – born Ronald William Wycherley on April 17, 1940, at Smithdown Road Hospital – overcame his natural shyness to become a much-loved star of stage, screen and studio.

The Sound Of Fury, an early collection of 10 self-penned songs, is still considered one of the best rock 'n' roll albums of all time, but Billy's record label Decca saw him as a "beat-balladeer" and his career direction changed.

His brother Albie said: "If he was alive today, he would be on a par with Frank Sinatra."

But Billy was plagued by ill-health. He suffered from rheumatic fever at the age of six, which led to a weakening of his heart valves and, ultimately, his early death.

He underwent open heart surgery in 1972 and 1976, but he died suddenly, of a heart attack, on January 28, 1983. He was 42.

Billy found fame after meeting impresario Larry Parnes at the Birkenhead Essoldo in October 1958. Parnes pushed him on stage in front of 1,000 people and was so impressed by what he saw that he immediately signed him up.

He may never have had a number one, but Billy enjoyed 19 top 20 hits in the 1960s.

"He had more top 20 hits in the UK than anyone except The Beatles, Cliff Richard and Elvis Presley"

His biggest successes included Jealousy (number two), Like I've Never Been Gone and When Will You Say I Love You? (both number three) – and the song with which he is most closely associated, Halfway To Paradise (number three).

Billy's good looks also made him a natural for TV and film. He made his film debut in 1962 in Play It Cool – director Michael Winner's first major feature – and other films included I've Gotta Horse and That'll Be The Day.

And his memory and music have lived on, thanks to assorted stage musicals – and the tribute concerts staged by Albie, who was also at the forefront of the successful campaign for a statue of Billy, which was unveiled at the Museum of Liverpool Life in 2003.

IAN TRACEY

THEY call him Mr Liverpool Music. Ian Tracey was just 25 when he was appointed Britain's youngest cathedral organist in 1980.

That was the same age at which his teacher and predecessor, Noel Rawsthorne, had taken up the same post back in 1955.

Two years later, Ian had also succeeded the retiring Ronald Woan as master of the choristers at Liverpool Cathedral, which was soon to increase its musical output to include sung services on five days a week.

Even taken alone, this was an exceptional challenge. Directing music in Britain's largest cathedral (and the fourth largest in the world), and presiding at the world's grandest cathedral organ. The instrument has nearly 10,000 pipes and a total volume of 120 decibels – the equivalent of a jet plane taking off. As if that wasn't enough, Ian Tracey was appointed city organist at St George's Hall (another world class instrument, this time with 7,000 pipes); as organist to Liverpool John Moores University (from which he holds a professorship) and also chorus master of the 150-strong Royal Liverpool Philharmonic Choir.

They sing up to 20 major works a season, a workload which could easily increase, given Philharmonic conductor Vasily Petrenko's interest in choral music, including opera.

At both the cathedral and the Philharmonic Hall, as well as at the London Proms, Ian Tracey has been involved in many national and international recordings, broadcasts and television appearances.

At the cathedral he has also provided music for royal visits by the Queen and the late Princess of Wales, as well as for the visit of Pope John Paul.

As a recitalist, Ian Tracey has toured the world, including more than 30 visits to the United States.

He has played at most of the prestige venues in Europe, including two concerts at Notre Dame Cathedral in Paris.

"He is one of only 20 honorary fellows worldwide of the Royal College of Organists, and also has a global recording contract with companies, including EMI and Chandos"

In recent years, he has undertaken more orchestral conducting, having studied with the eminent British music specialist Vernon Handley, himself a pupil of the late Sir Adrian Boult.

One of Handley's gifts to Ian Tracey has been one of Sir Adrian's conducting batons.

Ian Tracey has been awarded a doctorate in music by Liverpool University.

GEORGE MELLY

JAZZ and blues singer, writer, film and television critic, raconteur, university lecturer, sailor, homosexual, heterosexual and bisexual – is there anything George Melly didn't do?

Melly was born in Ullet Road, Aigburth, in 1926 into a comfortably-off middle class family. His father was a leading businessman and his mother was a larger-than-life lady of the Liverpool theatrical scene in the 1930s.

He grew up with live-in servants and nannies and was fascinated by the art of Picasso and Salvador Dali.

At school Melly fell in love with jazz – a passion which remained with him.

But, as for so many from his generation, his passions had to be put to one side during World War II, during which he served in the Royal Navy. He was once asked when asked what prompted him to join the Navy and he quipped "the uniforms were so much nicer."

But once the war had ended he went to work at the London Gallery where he was able to indulge his love for surrealism, before eventually

drifting into the world of jazz, finding work with Mick Mulligan's Magnolia Jazz Band.

Melly took a sabbatical from jazz in the 1960s and became a film critic for the Observer. In 1970 he won the much coveted critic award at the ISB press awards.

He performed his own style of bawdy jazz with the John Chilton's Feetwarmers band for decades and even developed his own show, An Audience With George Melly.

In July 2000 he received an honorary degree from the University of Liverpool.

"At the ceremony he told those gathered:
'Life was always extraordinary in Liverpool – the great comedians, the Beatles and many painters and writers.
'I am proud to be one of them'"

Despite suffering ill health, Melly remained very much active in music, journalism and lecturing on surrealism until his death in 2007, aged 80.

RITA HUNTER

OPERA has had a reputation for championing formidable women. And sometimes bulk has paid dividends.

It certainly did for Merseyside diva Rita Hunter, daughter of a Cammell Lairds boilermaker, who later made his living on the ferries and was producer for the Wallasey Grand Opera.

Rita came up the hard way, singing in the clubs of old Liverpool. She left school at 15 and joined a touring pantomime company, after telling them she was 17 (also in the ranks was Roy Castle).

Then, three years later, an Italian opera troupe visited Liverpool. Young Rita was told she could join them, but only if she paid her own fare to Italy.

That was an impossibility: Her father's weekly wage was just nine pounds.

However, the same audition led to her joining Sadler's Wells Opera. She went on to be the leading soprano at Covent Garden, and bask in the glory of a career that took her to every top opera house in the world.

This included wide fame in America, as well as Australia, where she moved in 1981.

However, the summit of her achievement was singing Brunhilde in the now legendary English National Opera staging of Wagner's Ring Cycle during the 1970s.

It was a magnificently generous – and truly big – performance, luckily to be immortalised on the Chandos Opera in English series.

Rita Hunter would occasionally return to her homeland. Once, in 1993, booked to appear at the Chichester Festival, she was told there was not enough material to make a dress she wanted.

"Rita took the affront in her stride, the spirit summed up in the first line of her autobiography: 'I am proud of my Merseyside heritage. We breed them tough and determined'"

Her final home appearance before her death was for an open-air tall ships gala at the Albert Dock in August 1992, attended by the Spanish king and queen.

Rita Hunter was surrounded by her illustrious counterparts, including Monserrat Caballe, Alfredo Kraus, Dennis O'Neill, Julia Migenes, Justino Diaz, Mario Frangoulis and Dmitri Hvorostovsky – a Who's Who line-up unequalled on an English stage.

Rita was awarded a CBE and a Liverpool University doctorate in music.

One of the clock faces of Mersey landmark
The Liver Building looks over a changing city

Top   West Derby bedtime. Tired of the damp, this family were hoping to be rehoused – a Cinderella family on the
         housing list
Above   An antiques shop on Seel Street. The lady in the leopard skin coat caught my eye. Always keep a film in the
         camera, there's a pic on every corner of a Liverpool street

People stayed on to the last minute, reluctant to give up their homes. Dingle was changing fast and homes standing proudly were replaced by wastelands of bricks and dust – dust that stayed in your nostrils for hours

Top left   Dave Hickson, Goodison legend. A modest, polite footballer – you don't hear that too often today!

Top right   Cathedral stonemasons perched on scaffolding high above the city and kept their caps on as they worked

Above   Sports photography is not just about observing the action on the pitch – watch the crowd and the true story of the game is reflected in their faces. This is Anfield and Liverpool are out of Europe

Left   Faces of Chinatown, young and old, sit on a wall on a summer's evening
Right   Remembrance Sunday and an old contemptible – 90 years of age with shiny black shoes – doffs his cap at the
            cenotaph, St George's Plateau

EST EST EST

Drinks at the Albert Dock

"... I spy with my little eye.....
something beginning with...'L'.."

" ..I think it's time
we changed ends"

Sun sets on a lonely figure from Antony
Gormley's Another Place on Crosby beach

Also available

from Trinity Mirror Books

DISCOVER LIVERPOOL
BOOK & DVD
ISBN: 978-1-905266-35-7

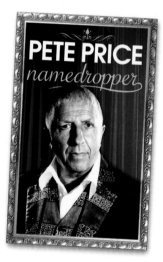

ECHOES OF LIVERPOOL
ISBN: 978-1-905266-34-0

THE JOY OF MURDER
ISBN: 978-1-905266-36-4

PETE PRICE : NAMEDROPPER
ISBN: 978-1-905266-41-8

To place your order please visit www.merseyshop.com
call 0845 143 0001 or write to Trinity Mirror Books, PO Box 48,
Old Hall Street, L69 3EB.

subject to availability

Roger McGough (1937-), poet; Jimmy McGovern (1949-), screenwriter; Pete McGovern (1927-2006), musican; Jimmy McGrail (1936-), boxer; Victor McGuire (1964-), actor; Charles MacIver (1812-85), ship owner; Neil McKechnie (1939-2006), swimmer; Jamie McKeever (1979-), boxer; Grace McKenzie, swimmer; Coleen McLoughlin (1986-), style icon, WAG; Steve McManaman (1972-), footballer; Steve McMahon, footballer; Ian McNabb (1962-), musician; John McNally (1941-), musician; Lee Mack (1967-), comedian; George Mahon, football chairman, founder father Everton; Rex Makin (1925-), lawyer; Beryl Marsden (1947-), singer; Gerry Marsden (1943-), singer; Dr David Marsh, golfer; Alf Matthews (1938-), boxer; Sharon Maughan (1951-), actress; Gary Mavers (1964-), actor; Lee Mavers (1962-), musician and songwriter; James Mawdsley (1973-), campaigner; James Maybrick (1838-89), merchant; Charles Pierre Melly (1829-88), philanthropist; George Melly (1926-2007), musician; Joe Mercer (1914-1990), footballer; Ray Mercer, boxer; John Middleton (1578-1623), Hale giant; Dr Robert Minnitt (1889-1974), medic; Jimmy Molloy (1921-98), boxer; Tommy Molloy (1934-), boxer; Professor Steve Molyneux (1955-), academic; William Philip Molyneux, 2nd Earl of Sefton (1772-1838), peer; Nicholas Monsarrat (1910-79), author; Sir John Moores (1896-1993), retailer and philanthropist; Mark Moraghan (1963-), actor; Robert Morris (1734-1806), financier and revolutionary; David Morrissey (1964-), actor; Johnny Morissey, footballer; Derek Mountfield, footballer; Tony Mulhearn (1938-), politician; Tony Mulholland (1972-), boxer; Jimmy Mulville (1955-), comedian and producer; John Murphy (1965-), composer; Margaret Murphy (1959-), crime writer; Sir Max Muspratt (1872-1934), chemist and politician; Mike Myers (1963-), actor; Shea Neary (1968-), boxer; Ken Nelson (1959-), record producer; Derek Nimmo (1930-99), actor; Steven Norris (1945-), politician; Father James Nugent (1822-1905), philanthropist; Simon O'Brien (1965-), actor and presenter; Tom O'Connor (1939-), comedian; Paul O'Grady (1955-), entertainer; Brian O'Hara (1942-99), musician; Father Francis O'Leary (1932-2000), cleric; Stephen Oliver (1950-92), musician and composer; Phina Oruche (1972-), actress; Jack Parkinson (1883-1942), footballer; John Parrott (1964-), snooker player; Stephen Parry (1977-), swimmer; Brian Patten (1946-), poet; Larry Paul (1952-), boxer; John Peel (1939-2004), DJ; Mike Pender (1942-), musician; Tricia Penrose (1970-), actress; HG Periton (1898-1980), rugby union footballer; Mary Peters (1939-), pentathlete; Sir Charles Petrie (1895-1977), historian; Kostas Petrou (1959-), boxer; Craig Phillips (1971-), presenter; Sir James Picton (1805-89), architect; Albert Pierrepoint (1905-92), hangman; Sir Alistair Pilkington (1920-95), industrialist; John Power (1967-), musician; Edward Carter Preston (1885-1965), sculptor; Jimmy Price (1960-), boxer; Pete Price, broadcaster; Kevin Pritchard (1961-), boxer; Bernard Pugh (1926-96), boxer; Dominic Purcell (1970-), actor; Noel Quarless (1962-), boxer; William Abdulah Quilliam (1851-1932), Islamic scholar; Ray Quinn (1988-), singer; Heidi Range (1983-), singer; Shelagh Ratcliffe, swimmer; Eleanor Rathbone (1872-1946), politician; William Rathbone VI (1819-1902), philanthropist and politician; Sir Simon Rattle (1955-), conductor; Jan Ravens (1958-), impressionist; Austin Rawlinson, swimmer; Ted Ray (1905-77), comedian; Phil Redmond (1949-), TV producer; Nigel Rees (1944-), author and presenter; Peter Reid (1956-), footballer; Robin Reid (1971-), boxer; Alberto Remedios (1935-), opera singer; Dave Rent (1936-2000), boxer; Miranda Richardson (1958-), actress; Kate Robbins (1958-), comedienne and actress; Ted Robbins, comedian; Nicola Roberts (1985-), singer; Anne Robinson (1944-), presenter; Peter Robinson, football administrator; Robert Robinson (1927-), presenter; Ernie Roderick (1914-1986), boxer; Bill Rodgers (1928-), politician; Wayne Rooney (1986-), footballer; William Roscoe (1753-1831), poet, reformer and anti-slavery campaigner; Norman Rossington (1928-99), actor; Leonard Rossiter (1926-84), actor; Alan Rouse (1951-86), mountaineer; Patricia Routledge (1929-), actress; Stan Rowan (1924-97), boxer; Simon 'Sice' Rowbottom (1969-), musician; Herbert J Rowse (1887-1963), architect; Joe Royle (1949-), footballer; Lita Rosa (1926-), singer; Alan Rudkin (1941-), boxer; Robert Runcie (1921-2000), cleric; Edward Rushton (1756-1814), radical anti-slavery campaigner; Willy Russell (1947-), writer; Kym Ryder (1976-), actress and singer; Herbert Louis Samuel (1870-1963), politician; Vernon Sangster (1899-1986), pools promoter; Sara Sankey (nee Halsall), badminton player; Alexei Sayle (1952-), comedian and author; Brian Schumacher (1960-), boxer; Harry Scott, boxer; Tommy Scott (1968-), musician; Wally Scott, broadcaster; Peter Scupham (1933-), poet; Peter Serafinowicz (1972-), actor; Anthony Shaffer (1926-2001), writer; Sir Peter Shaffer (1926-), writer; Lesley Sharp (1964-), actress; Joseph Sharples (1961-), historian; John Shirley-Quirk (1931-), singer; John Sillitoe (1965-), boxer; Sir Sydney Silverman (1895-1968), politician; Mark Simpson (1989-), musician; Joey Singleton (1951-), boxer; Peter Sissons (1942-), broadcaster; Elizabeth Sladen (1948-), actress; Mike Slemen (1951-), rugby union footballer; James Skelly (1980-), musician; Neville Skelly (1975-), singer; Andreas Whittam Smith (1937-), journalist; Herbert Tyson Smith (1883-1972), sculptor; Sir John Smith, football chairman; Steve Smith (1973-), high-jumper; Tommy Smith (1945-), footballer; Tony Smith (1936-), boxer; Sonia (1971-), singer; Jack Southworth (1855-1956), footballer; Maggie Souyave, hockey player; Edward George Geoffrey Smith-Stanley (1799-1869), politician; Frederick Arthur Stanley (1841-1908), politician; Sir Thomas Stanley (1435-1504), noble; Olaf Stapledon (1886-1950), philosopher; Freddie Starr (1943-), comedian; Ringo Starr (1940-), musician; Alison Steadman (1945-), actress; Ralph Steadman (1936-), cartoonist; Allan Gibson Steel (1858-1914), cricketer; Philip Wilson Steer (1860-1942), painter; Thomas Steers (1670-1750), dock engineer; Jimmy Stewart, boxer; Richard Stilgoe (1943-), entertainer; Sir Robert Wright Stopford (1901-76), cleric; Mike Storey (1950-), politician; Rory Storm (1939-72), musician; Gary Stretch (1968-), boxer; Alan Stubbs, footballer; George Stubbs (1724-1806), artist; Dean Sullivan (1955-), actor; Stuart Sutcliffe (1940-62), artist and musician; Claire Sweeney (1972-), actress and singer; Clive Swift (1936-), actor; David Swift (1931-), actor; Terry Sylvester (1947-), musician; Richard Synge (1914-94), scientist; Alan Sytner (1935-2006), businessman; Peter Taaffe (1942-), politician; Jimmy Tarbuck (1940-), comedian; Liza Tarbuck (1964-), actress; Banastre Tarleton (1754-1833), soldier; Nel Tarleton (1906-1956), boxer; AJP Taylor (1906-90), historian; Derek Temple (1938-), footballer; Norman Thelwell (1923-2004), cartoonist; Wally Thom (1926-80), boxer; Phil Thompson (1954-), footballer; Heidi Thomas (1964-), screenwriter; Neil Thomas, gymnast; Walter Aubrey Thomas (1863-), architect; Bill Tidy (1933-), cartoonist; Ricky Tomlinson (1939-), actor; Sir Philip Toosey (1904-75), soldier; Professor Ian Tracey (1955-), musician; Rita Tushingham (1942-), actress; George Turpin (1952-), boxer; Cathy Tyson (1965-), actress; Paul Usher (1961-), actor; Alan Vaughan, boxer; Frankie Vaughan (1928-99), singer; Norman Vaughan (1927-2002), comedian and entertainer; Colin Vearncombe (1962-), musician; Sir William Vestey (1859-1940), shipowner; Dom Volante (1905-82), boxer; Eddie Wainwright (1924-), footballer; Gee Walker, campaigner; Sir Andrew Barclay Walker (1824-93), brewer and philanthropist; Lucy Walker (1836–1916), mountaineer; Keith Wallace (1961-99), boxer; Janet and Graham Walton (1952-), sextuplets parents; Marcus Wareing (1970-), chef; Tom 'Pongo' Waring (1906-80), footballer; Amelia Warner (1982-), actress; Ron Warwick (1941-), sailor; Alfred Waterhouse (1830-1905), architect; Dave Watson (1961-), footballer; Richie Wenton (1967-), boxer; Kitty Wilkinson (1785-1860), health campaigner; Allan Williams (1930-), promoter; Michael Williams (1935-2001), actor; Joseph Williamson (1769-1840), businessman and philanthropist; Kenny Willis, boxer; Tony Willis (1960-), boxer; Alan Wills (1961-), record label owner; Harold Wilson (1916-95), politician; Robb Wilton (1881-1957), comedian; Alan Whittle, footballer; Tony Woodley (1948-), trade unionist; Bob Wooler (1932-2002), DJ and promoter; Lord Woolton (1883-1964), retailer and politician; Carl Wright (1969-), boxer; Tommy Wright (1944-), footballer; Pete Wylie (1958-), musician; Arthur Wynne (1862-1945), crossword inventor; David Yip (1951-), actor; Stephen Yip (1955-), charity director; Mal Young (1957-), TV producer; Anne Ziegler (1910-2003), singer.

This is just the tip of the Scouse iceberg. The list encompasses Scousers, Merseysiders and adopted Scousers. There are many more, not mentioned, who we salute within the Scouse family!